THE COMPLETE
PROBATE GUIDE

THE COMPLETE PROBATE GUIDE

Martin M. Shenkman

John Wiley & Sons, Inc.
New York • Chichester • Weinheim • Brisbane • Singapore • Toronto

This book is printed on acid-free paper. ∞

Published by John Wiley & Sons, Inc.
Published simultaneously in Canada.

This publication is designed to provide accurate and authoritative information in regard to the subject matter covered. It is sold with the understanding that the publisher is not engaged in rendering professional services. If professional advice or other expert assistance is required, the services of a competent professional person should be sought.

Library of Congress Cataloging-in-Publication Data:

Shenkman, Martin M.

    The complete probate guide / Martin M. Shenkman.
      p.   cm.
    Includes index.
    ISBN 0-471-32548-1 (pbk. : alk. paper)
    1. Probate law and practice—United States—Popular works.
  I. Title.
  KF765.Z9S53   1999
  346.7305′2—dc21   98-35651

Printed in the United States of America.

10 9 8 7 6 5 4 3 2 1

PREFACE

The loss of a loved one is one of life's most traumatic experiences. Not only must the bereaved deal with the emotional losses and pain, they must also take care of complex, difficult, and often costly legal, tax, investment, and business issues. Few people have the time, desire, or technical expertise to read a treatise on the probate process. This concise guide explains the process—the steps you should take and what to expect. This will save substantial cost and minimize exacerbating what is undoubtedly already a difficult personal situation.

Probate is simply the process of having the will of someone who dies admitted to the court. Once the will is accepted, the court will provide "letters testamentary"—a formal document authorizing the executor (the person responsible for carrying out the deceased person's final wishes) to do what the will says. The executor has to collect assets, pay bills, interpret the will (almost always with a lawyer's help) and file tax returns. Once this is done, the trustees (if trusts are formed under the will) should manage the trust's money. If there are minors, the guardians assume responsibility for those children. This guide explains in detail the roles of the executor, trustee, and guardian. You will also learn how to begin the probate process, how to hire professionals, which professionals you may need, and what your responsibilities are in the different roles you may serve.

This guide explains in understandable language how every person can deal with the probate process. It describes in simple language the whats and whys of probate. Although the rules differ from state to state, the general concepts are often similar. The book provides practical advice, sample forms, and other materials that you can use in planning. This is the ideal guide for the recently widowed, the heir trying to cope with the myriad problems the death of a loved one brings, those trying to minimize the costs and delays of probate, and those uncertain about the legal process. Just don't be penny-wise and pound foolish. This is not a guide to *avoid* lawyers and other professionals. Almost every estate has some complexity warranting professional help. This guide, if you use it wisely, will help you minimize costs and delays, not avoid them.

Although this book cannot ease the pain of losing a loved one, it should reduce the cost and difficulties of the legal, tax, and other hurdles you will face.

MARTIN M. SHENKMAN

April 1999

CONTENTS

Part One

INTRODUCTION

1 PROBATE IS NOT A FOUR-LETTER WORD

The death of a friend, family member, or other loved one (called the Decedent) raises a host of emotional, personal, business, legal, and other issues. In the vast majority of situations, little advance planning has been done, and what is at best a difficult emotional and personal time is made worse by the need to deal with other nonpersonal issues. This book can help you minimize the business, legal, tax, and other issues so that you can focus your energies on what is most important—comforting the mourners and helping them, and yourself, move on with life.

This book is primarily directed toward the person who manages and handles the Decedent's assets, including legal and tax issues (called the Estate). This person is called an Executor, Personal Representative, or Personal Administrator. However, there is valuable information for anyone dealing with the Decedent's affairs: those receiving money or other assets of the Decedent (called Beneficiaries), those charged with formally managing some or all of the Decedent's assets in trust for longer periods of time for the benefit of Beneficiaries (called Trustees), others concerned with the welfare of the Decedent's family and loved ones, and even many of the professionals involved. Because the Executor is the primary audience, this book is written to the Executor, whether or not the Decedent's assets have to pass through Probate (the courts).

A NOTE ON STYLE

The single most difficult aspect of Probate is wading through the jargon. Lawyers, accountants, insurance agents, and the Internal Revenue Service (IRS) all use technical terminology. If you can understand the buzz words, you will be well along the road of demystifying the Probate process. To help you out, there is a glossary at the end of this book. In addition, words that are capitalized in the text alert you that they are defined in the glossary.

Masculine and feminine terms have been used to make the text readable. There is enough complication in the Probate area without making it worse.

There was no intent to offend any reader, and unless otherwise specified, the information provided applies equally to either sex. Caution must be exercised when using the term *children*. Certain matters (such as state inheritance taxes and the right to inherit under state law if the Decedent died without a Will, for example) are influenced by the fact that the Beneficiary relationship is that of a child. In other situations, it may not matter whether the Beneficiary is a child or friend (e.g., the federal estate tax applies equally to any Beneficiary other than a spouse or charity). The term *spouse* specifically refers to a married person. Most aspects of the estate planning process will not have the same consequences to a married spouse as they will to an unmarried partner. Your sense of loss may be just as great, but the federal tax laws (such as the unlimited marital deduction) and state laws (such as the spousal right of election) apply only to spouses. Thus the term spouse should be understood to have this specific meaning. Do not substitute *partner* when you read *spouse*. If the surviving spouse is not a citizen of the United States, special rules apply so the general discussion of *spouse* cannot always be used.

SHOULD YOU GO IT ALONE OR HIRE A LAWYER?

You should never handle an Estate alone. Although this sounds self-serving from an author who is an attorney, read on (at least finish this paragraph). First, an estate attorney is not the only professional you need to involve. By hiring the right professional for each task, you will be better served and probably save significant costs. Second, the need to hire an attorney and other professionals does not mean you must spend a lot of money. It certainly does not mean that you need to be overcharged or subject to the many problems that are commonly associated with the Probate process. The key is to use professionals wisely. That is what this book will help you do. If the Estate is simple (and the size of the Estate has no bearing on simplicity), you may need no more than a quick one-hour consultation with an estate specialist to make sure that you are not missing anything. It is not worth the risk of not obtaining professional advice. Estate work involves so many nuances and technicalities that even most attorneys do not handle it. How can a nonexpert, possibly in the midst of one of life's most traumatic events, be expected to address all the issues? If you have the time, inclination, and ability to take care of some, or even most, of the Probate and related matters, advise the estate attorney and other professionals of your intent. In many, if not most cases, you can do a significant amount of the work and realize considerable savings (assuming you make sure that the professionals bill the Estate at an hourly rate). The key is to use professional advisers wisely to be sure all issues are raised; then allow them to take care of matters that you cannot, or do not want to handle. Finally, as Executor, you may be held personally responsible if certain transactions are not completed properly. If you distribute property incorrectly or overlook a creditor of the Estate, you can be held personally liable! Never assume, "It's all family," so it is okay. Family relationships have frequently been strained, if not destroyed, over Probate matters. Avoid the personal liability and minimize family friction by getting good advice.

EXAMPLE: A commonly overlooked planning technique is the *Disclaimer* (see Chapter 18). This can be used to save taxes and sometimes to avoid creditors. However, if a Beneficiary takes control over the assets involved, a Disclaimer can no longer be made. During a simple consultation, an estate planner can identify this planning opportunity and inform you of the requirements to qualify.

The moral is do not go it alone, but go it smart. Probate does not have to be expensive, intimidating, or a big deal.

WHAT IS PROBATE?

Probate is simply the process of having the Will of someone who dies admitted to the Court. Once accepted, the Court will provide *Letters Testamentary*—a formal document authorizing the Executor, the person responsible for the Will and carrying out the deceased person's final wishes, to do what the Will says. The *real* process only then begins. The Executor has to collect assets, pay bills, interpret the Will (almost always with a lawyer's help) and file tax returns. This chapter highlights the costs, problems, and time delays Probate can create.

Once you understand generally what Probate and the related matters entail, and get through the jargon, much of what has to be done is common sense. The tax rules are complex (and for them you should rely on professional advisers), and sometimes the legal issues can be difficult. But most of the tax complexities tend to arise when a federal estate tax return has to be filed. For 1999, this requires a minimum Estate of $650,000. This amount increases to $1 million in 2006. The IRS has estimated that only about 1.5 percent of the Estates of people dying file federal estate tax returns. So few people are affected, and they can afford the professional help to address the issues involved. The legal technicalities also do not affect most Estates.

In the typical Estate, the Probate process can basically be summed up as getting the Will admitted to the Surrogate's Court so the Executor can obtain Letters Testamentary. The Executor then uses the authority of the Letters Testamentary to collect all the Decedent's assets, pay the Decedent's expenses, file any state tax returns, and then distribute the remainder as specified in the Decedent's Will (and/or Revocable Living Trust). Although every Estate tends to have some nuances because of the Decedent's unique circumstances or wishes, they do not usually cause serious problems.

Why has Probate received such a bad reputation? For one, it helps sell living trusts and other legal work that may not always be necessary. If the professionals can keep you sufficiently confused through the adroit use of jargon, the mystique of the process can create an undeserved aura of complexity and mystery. This is good for beefing up bills, but is not good for you and the Beneficiaries involved. Do abuses happen? Sure. But they are not nearly as common as the media and hawkers of Probate avoidance gimmicks would have you believe. Amazing as it may seem, most clerks in Surrogate's Court are intelligent, helpful, and caring people. They often cannot do exactly what you want as fast as you want, but that is because they have to follow the laws of your state and the procedures established by the Court. Although the laws and procedures can create additional time delays and costs, that is not the objective. Most of the laws are designed to address the problems created when people don't plan. If you die without a Will (Intestate), state law tries to guess what a typical Decedent would want done. Thus, a bit of planning can avoid most of the problems. If you are already dealing with an actual Probate, it is too late. You will simply have to tough it out. If you are reviewing this book because you were named Executor, encourage the Testator (the person who signed the Will and who is still alive) to organize and plan now. It will make your job much easier.

NOTE: See Martin M. Shenkman, *The Complete Book of Trusts* (New York: John Wiley & Sons, 1997); *Estate Planning After the 1997 Tax Act* (New York: John Wiley & Sons, 1998); *The Beneficiary Workbook* (New York: John Wiley & Sons, 1998) for detailed advice on how to minimize the problems with Probate, Intestacy, and the like.

GETTING PAST BASIC JARGON AND KEY CONCEPTS

The following paragraphs define important words used in the Probate process. You need to understand these terms and the key Probate concepts they represent.

Probate

Avoiding Probate is not the same as avoiding taxes, protecting your assets from creditors, and other important goals. Probate is technically the process of having the Decedent's Will admitted to the Surrogate's Court (although it may be referred to by a different name in your area) and the Court accepting the Will. Once the Will is admitted to Probate, the Court issues a document called Letters Testamentary (although it may have a different name in different Courts) stating your authority as Executor to act on behalf of the Estate. Although the process just described is Probate, in common usage all the work related to settling the Decedent's Estate—paying bills, filing tax returns, distributing assets, selling a business, and so on—is referred to as Probate. Most of the costs and time delays (except when someone challenges the Will) are incurred in the latter definition of Probate, and after the Letters Testamentary are issued.

Probate Estate

The assets distributed by the Decedent's Will, and hence under the jurisdiction of the Court, are referred to as *Probate Assets*, or the *Probate Estate*. This is an important concept for many reasons. First, as Executor, you will only have control over Probate Assets. Assets that are not in the Probate Estate will pass to the designated Beneficiaries without your involvement. These include IRA accounts, which pass to the named Beneficiary on death; life insurance policies, for which the proceeds are payable to a designated Beneficiary on the insured's death; and jointly owned assets (when owned as joint tenants with the right of survivorship), which automatically become the property of the surviving joint owner. These assets are not part of the Probate Estate, but they can affect the Estate. For example, these assets are included in the Decedent's Taxable Estate (see following section). Thus, they can generate federal estate tax, even if they are not part of the Probate Estate. The distinction of Probate Estate and Taxable Estate is widely misunderstood and is the cause of many people neglecting to plan to minimize estate taxes.

Taxable Estate

The Taxable Estate consists of the assets (reduced by expenses and liabilities) that are subject to federal estate tax. One of the most confusing aspects of Probate is the difference between Taxable Estate and Probate Estate. Many people assume that if an asset avoids Probate it avoids taxation. This myth is often fostered by subtle misconceptions on the part of people pushing Revocable Living Trust products. The IRS does not care how the Decedent's assets are transferred. If the Decedent owned a rental property, the fair value of that property (reduced by any mortgage) will be included in the Taxable Estate. Whether the Decedent set up a Revocable Living Trust to own the property, or had the deed retitled to joint ownership with his brother, won't affect the tax consequences. Probate Estate merely refers to the assets passing under the Will. Taxable Estate includes all assets, passing under the Will or otherwise, that are included in the Decedent's Estate for federal estate tax purposes.

Will

A Will (Last Will and Testament) is a legal document signed by a person, called the Testator (or Testatrix for a woman) that specifies how the assets of the Testator should be distributed after death (the Testator then is called the Decedent), who should serve as Executor to oversee the process, who should be responsible for minor children of the Decedent (called Guardians), and so on. The Will is usually prepared by a lawyer and signed in the presence of the lawyer, witnesses, and a notary. When you serve as an Executor, Guardian, or Trustee, the Will serves as your employee manual. You must read and understand it.

Will Substitute

A Will is not the only document or legal mechanism that can be used to transfer the Decedent's assets following death. If the Decedent was married, the home in which the Decedent and spouse resided is almost always owned jointly. On the death of the Decedent, the house automatically (by law and without Probate) becomes the property of the surviving spouse. The legal document that creates this joint ownership for the house is a deed. The deed acts, when it indicates joint ownership, as a Will substitute since no Will is needed to transfer ownership of the house. Similarly, the Decedent's pension plan, IRA, annuity, and insurance policy all have beneficiary designation forms for specifying who should receive that asset on the insured's death. These Beneficiary designation forms serve as Will substitutes. Where assets pass to the intended Beneficiary under a Will substitute, they are not part of the Probate Estate.

Testamentary

Testamentary is anything that occurs at death. If the Testator set up a trust while he was alive, the trust would be called a Living Trust or an Inter Vivos Trust. Trusts are frequently set up under the Decedent's Will. These are called Testamentary Trusts.

How Steps to Avoid Probate Affect the Process

People often take many steps to avoid Probate by using Will substitutes such as Beneficiary designation forms, Revocable Living Trusts, joint ownership of assets, and payable on death accounts. When properly planned and implemented, these steps can save the Estate substantial money and time, and make your job as Executor much easier. Unfortunately, if not properly planned and implemented, these steps can create potentially serious problems that you as Executor may have to address. Too often, steps are taken to avoid the purported evils of Probate with little understanding of the costly consequences these steps create. The cure is often worse then the illness.

NOTE: For a detailed sample Revocable Living Trust with explanations of many of these issues, visit the Web site www.laweasy.com.

EXAMPLE: Sally Senior was getting on in years, and it was increasingly difficult for her to handle bill paying, shopping, and other chores. Sally had three children: Good, Bad, and Worse. Good lived nearby and came over weekly to help out Mom. Bad called to say hello once a week. Worse, a compulsive gambler, sent Mom a homemade birthday and Christmas card each year and no more. Sally Senior attended a number of free estate-planning seminars and bought into the idea of avoiding Probate. Instead of setting up a Revocable Living Trust (which would have worked in this example), she divided all her assets into three joint bank accounts.

One-third of the assets were in a joint account with her son Good. One-third were in a joint account with Bad, and one-third with Worse. Each account was opened with $350,000. You are a long-time family friend. Sally named you Executor because she knew the children would fight about everything. By the time Sally died, the joint account with Good had been reduced to $200,000 because Good used it to pay Mom's bills. The Estate totals $900,000 and a significant Estate tax is due.

This "plan" has created a host of serious problems. There are no assets in the Estate. Each child as a Beneficiary will have to kick in money. How interested will Worse be in doing this? By the time the tax return is prepared, Worse has lost all his inheritance at the Keno tables. What happens? Good, who shouldered all the burdens of Mom's care, not only receives the least, but now has to pay taxes as well! Sally avoided Probate with 100 percent effectiveness. However, the Probate process and the family relationships couldn't be worse. You as Executor will have to deal with the frayed and angry emotions, the obvious unfairness of how much inheritance each child receives (which you can't change), and the problems of finding money to pay Uncle Sam. Incidentally, had a simple Will been used, you could have collected the bank accounts, paid the taxes off the top, and then divided the Estate in three equal shares for each child, which was Sally's initial intent. Probate avoidance can create serious problems and you may have to address them.

A Revocable Living Trust can be used to avoid Probate, according to the simple technical definition of having the Will admitted to the Court and receiving Letters Testamentary. But it avoids none of the other aspects of the Probate process. Typically, when a Revocable Living Trust is used, a *Pour Over Will* is used as well. The Pour-Over Will is a Will that basically says, take all the assets of the Decedent that are subject to Probate and pour them into the Revocable Living Trust which the Decedent established so the Trustee can distribute all the Decedent's assets (both Probate Assets passing under the Will and nonprobate assets which are already in the Revocable Living Trust). As Executor, you may have to concern yourself with reading and understanding two legal documents, the Will and the Trust if you are both Executor and Trustee. You must also figure out any differences between the two documents and what they may require of you. Finally, if the Decedent did not name the same people as Executor under the Will and Trustee under the Revocable Living Trust, you may have to make these decisions in conjunction with others. All these factors create complications and potential traps you may have to address.

Revocable Living Trust

A Revocable Living Trust (sometimes called a Living Trust, Revocable Inter Vivos Trust, or Loving Trust) is one of the most talked about estate planning techniques. Revocable Living Trusts can be used to avoid the expenses, publicity, and delays of Probate. Although they are the most commonly thought of Probate avoidance technique, they are not the most widely used technique. Joint ownership of assets, payable on death bank accounts, and Beneficiary designations on insurance and pension assets are far more common.

A Revocable Living Trust is a Trust that the Decedent set up during his lifetime. On death, the Trust provides for successor Trustees to manage the

Trust assets. The Trust includes provisions that take effect on death that serve the same purpose as a Will to govern the disposition of the Decedent's assets. Thus, other than the technical procedure of an Executor obtaining Letters Testamentary for a Will, the responsibilities and functions of the Trustee under a Revocable Living Trust are quite similar. When the Decedent has Probate Assets under the Pour-Over Will, as well as assets held in a Revocable Living Trust, you may have to reconcile different provisions in each document. For example, each document may provide Specific Bequests (exact dollar amounts to be distributed to different Beneficiaries), contradictory Tax Allocation clauses (which assets are used to pay tax), and even inconsistent directions on how expenses are paid. If these issues arise, get professional help.

HOW TO USE THIS BOOK

Read Chapter 2 to get an overview of the entire Probate process. If you can keep the big picture in mind, the technical minutiae that arise will be much more manageable. Next, read Chapter 3 to understand which professionals you should hire, how to select professionals, how to retain them, and how to minimize their fees. Then hire professionals and organize the Estate's professional team. Set up these appointments as quickly as possible so that you do not fall into any complex technical traps. Meeting with professionals very early on in the process can assure that you get the right start, identify the problems and issues to deal with, and avoid losing out on important tax benefits. Then use the guidance the professionals gave you at the initial meeting as the starting point for reading the rest of this book. Read and review sections applicable to you so that you can best work with the professionals you have hired, keep their costs under control, and understand the process.

WHERE TO GET MORE FORMS FOR FREE

For free sample Probate forms and planning tips, see the Web site www.laweasy.com. New forms and planning tips are added about every three months. Send questions or comments to the e-mail address laweasy@worldnet.att.net.

CONCLUSION

This chapter has given you an overview of the Probate process, defined many of the key terms and concepts so that you can understand what is involved, and offered important advice on hiring professionals and using this book to guide you. The next chapter provides a full overview of the Probate process in the chronological order you will most likely have to address each issue. The rest of the book then addresses those points in detail.

2 THE PROBATE PROCESS STEP BY STEP

The Probate process is often viewed as daunting. Having an overall picture of what the process entails, and how steps fit together, will help everyone involved. However, the Probate of every Estate is unique. Each Decedent has different assets, debts, record-keeping habits, goals, and family. Thus, the following step-by-step description will not precisely match the Probate you are involved in. But your flexibility, while keeping in mind the overall picture, and your careful use of professional advisers will help you complete any tasks you have as Executor more efficiently.

ANATOMICAL GIFTS (ORGAN DONATIONS)

One of the first steps to address is to determine whether the Decedent authorized any organ donations. If organs are not harvested quickly, they will no longer be usable. How do you determine whether the Decedent intended to be an organ donor? This intent could have been communicated in any of several documents:

- *Driver's License.* In many states, the intent to donate organs is indicated on the back of the license.
- *Organ Donor or Anatomical Gift Card.* This should be kept in the Decedent's wallet.
- *Letter of Instruction.* Many people prepare a letter of instruction that addresses many issues, including organ donations.
- *Living Will and/or Health Care Proxy.* A copy is often kept in the Decedent's physician's records or hospital records. The Living Will, which is a statement of a person's health care wishes, may specify the Decedent's intent to be an organ donor. The Health Care Proxy is a legal document in which a person designates an agent to make medical and health care related decisions if the person is unable to do so. The agent under the Health Care Proxy may have authority or instructions to make organ donations.
- *Will.* Although a Will may list the intent to be an organ donor, most Wills are not available quickly. If the decedent's intent cannot be

determined from the other sources indicated, attempt to locate the Will quickly, or at least a copy.

- *Hospital or Doctor Records.*
- *The Family or Estate Attorney.* The Uniform Anatomical Gift Act (or the variation of it adopted in the Decedent's state) may affect what can be done. If legal issues arise, the Estate attorney can assist. Prior to contacting the attorney, the legal advisers for the hospital or hospice where the Decedent died or the legal advisers of the recipient organization which is to receive the organs may be able to assist.
- *The Recipient Organization.* This may be a donor bank, a hospital, or a university. This organization should be contacted to be certain they will accept the organs intended for donation. Oversupply or the Decedent's condition or illnesses may preclude use of the organs.

If the decedent made arrangements to have his body donated for medical research, there should be documents from the hospital or university to which the body is to be donated. Contact the institution involved for assistance.

FUNERAL ARRANGEMENTS

When death occurs, final arrangements—the funeral, ceremony, burial or cremation, and cemetery or other instructions—must be dealt with. Immediate family members generally handle this, but depending on the circumstances, a partner, friends, or others may become involved. The first step is to ascertain the wishes of the Decedent. Most likely, the Decedent has communicated these to you and others. In any event, consider all the sources of information so that you can carry out (or help others to carry out) the Decedent's wishes:

- *Letter of Instruction.* Many people prepare a letter of instruction that addresses many issues, including organ donations, funeral, and burial or cremation requests. Try to locate this letter and review it as quickly as possible.
- *Living Will.* A copy is often kept in the Decedent's physician's records or hospital records. Living Wills often include the Decedent's wishes for final arrangements.
- *Health Care Proxy.* Some people sign only a Living Will, others only a Health Care Proxy, some both. If the Living Will is silent, the Health Care Proxy may include directions as to how to handle funeral and other steps.
- *Deed for a Burial Plot.* Many people purchase plots in advance. Locating this information can resolve the issue in many cases as to where and to some extent how, the Decedent's burial or internment should be handled.

- *Preneed Funeral Trust.* The Decedent may have made arrangements in advance for funeral costs. Review the Decedent's letter of instructions and other important papers for this. Ask close friends and family whether they were aware of such arrangements. Call area funeral homes to find out whether any arrangements were made with them.

- *Will.* While a Will may list the intent to be an organ donor as well as directions for the funeral and other final arrangements, it is often not available quickly enough. If the Decedent's intent cannot be determined from the other sources indicated, attempt to locate the Will quickly, or at least a copy. If the Will is in the Decedent's safe deposit box, expedited procedures are available to get it. Consult with the Estate's attorney.

- *Contact Decedent's Religious Adviser.* If the Decedent had any religious affiliations or beliefs (these are sometimes addressed in the Living Will), request a consultation with the religious adviser concerning the appropriate steps to take for burial, services, mourning, and the like. If the family, friends, and loved ones have any particular religious affiliation, a religious adviser may provide considerable solace for them. A religious adviser can provide you with valuable guidance during the difficult initial phases even if the Decedent's religious connections were limited.

- *Consult Members of the Decedent's Family and Loved Ones.* The Decedent's wishes must be honored, but often requests and feelings of others can also be respected. It can only serve to lessen tension at such a traumatic time.

Because funeral and related immediate costs must be taken care of promptly, they are often paid for by family or others close to the Decedent. The Estate reimburses them later. State law will generally provide that the Estate must reimburse reasonable funeral expenses. Get copies of all bills, receipts, and other documents supporting the expenses you reimburse. If the funeral arrangements were lavish, unusual, or expensive, an issue may arise as to what the Estate can pay for. The Will may provide directions for funeral or other arrangements that could be helpful for you as Executor. If there are any disputes among family or others at a later date concerning these arrangements, the directions in the Will can support your payment of these costs. If the Will is silent and the expenses unusual, consult with an estate attorney before reimbursement to avoid any risk of being personally surcharged.

GRIEVING, MOURNING, AND OTHER EMOTIONAL CONSIDERATIONS

Sensitivity, compassion, caring are the most important characteristics the Executor and all others involved initially need to exhibit. No matter how much notice and preparation preceded the death, the Decedent's family and loved ones will have strong emotions over their loss. They may react with sorrow, hurt, disappointment, or anger. Even the most decisive and organized people can become confused, indecisive, and despondent. It is essential to be attuned to these feelings so that you can respond accordingly. If the Decedent was the primary or sole source of support, the survivors will, along with the many personal feelings, be worried about their future financial stability and security. This is essential for you to address.

A child who was estranged from her now deceased parent may take out her guilt in a host of different ways. The child may fight viciously for every penny of the Estate. A child who did little or nothing to help an elderly parent during the last years may fight the reimbursement of expenses to the sibling who was vigilant in helping. The list is endless. If the problems become severe, consider consulting with a family counselor, social worker, or other mental health professional. Too often, fear or embarrassment prevents people from taking this step. The death of a friend, family member, or other loved one is unquestionably one of life's most stressful situations. Obtain professional help or encourage others affected to do so.

As Executor, to the extent that you can handle the Estate's affairs in an organized and professional manner and address the issues that arise, you can contribute significantly to helping the survivors move forward. Endeavor to keep everyone informed. Uncertainty creates anxiety. Regular communication, by telephone, letters, or meetings, if appropriate, can create a feeling of control.

GET ORGANIZED

The administration of the Estate will be expedited and more efficient if all the required information is collected at an early date in the administration. Take the following four steps:

1. Immediately identify and organize key information. The sample forms on pages 15 and 16 can be helpful.
2. Set up file folders, loose-leaf binders, or some other system to organize Estate information (see Chapter 7).
3. Buy a new calendar and note the key steps and inquiries you make each day. Record the conclusions of any conversations with Beneficiaries, professional advisers, and others.
4. When in doubt, save it and file it, until the Estate's advisers recommend or direct otherwise.

NOTE: For a detailed program on how to organize the voluminous legal, tax, and other paperwork see Martin M. Shenkman, *Beneficiary Workbook* (New York: John Wiley & Sons, 1998).

Basic Background Information on the Decedent

Step to Take	Comment	Person Responsible
Decedent's Name		
Decedent's last Street Address City/State/Zip		
Will Execution Date		
Codicils		
Estate's Employer Identification No.		
Citizenship [Decedent/Spouse]		
Domicile (State)		
Social Security No.		
Birth Date		
Marriage Date		
Driver's License No./State		
Passport No./Exp.		
Death Certificate No./Date/Issuer/Place		
Detail other marriages; residence in community property state; etc.		

Key Estate Professionals

Title/Person Name	Address/Telephone Number	Comment
Executor/		
Co-Executor/		
Trustee/		
Attorney/		
Accountant/		
Family Counselor/		
Insurance Agent/		
Broker/		
Financial Planner/		

Key Estate Deadlines

Deadline/Key Date/Matter	Date of Deadline/Matter	Comment
Date of Death		
Letters [ ] Testamentary [ ] Administration		
Notice to Beneficiaries		
Decedent's Prior Year Income Tax Return, Form 1040 Due		
Decedent's Final Income Tax Return, Form 1040 Due		
Alternate Valuation		
State Tax Payment Due		
State _____ Inheritance Tax Return and Payment Due		
Federal Estate Tax Return and Payment Due		
Inventory to Be Filed with Court		
Final Accounting Due		

ESTABLISH DOMICILE (WHERE THE DECEDENT LIVED)

A Decedent's Domicile will affect which state laws are applied to the Estate. Domicile can affect state inheritance and other taxes. You will likely need a lawyer in the state of the Decedent's Domicile.

Domicile refers to the Decedent's permanent home, where the person ultimately intended to return and reside. Domicile differs from residence, which is where the Decedent merely lived some of the time. Domicile is a stronger concept, and harder to change, than one's residence. This definition includes both the location and intention of the taxpayer. Therefore, both location *and* intention must change to effectively change Domicile. While location is a relatively obvious matter to ascertain, intentions are not.

In most cases, it is obvious where the Decedent lived, what place he or she called home. As society has become more mobile, however, the decision is not always obvious, but the consequences will often be significant. How do you determine the Decedent's Domicile?

The Domicile is based on an analysis of numerous factors, including the following:

1. Where the Decedent voted.
2. Where the Decedent's principal business activity was conducted.
3. The center of the Decedent's social affairs. This can be evidenced by country club, fraternal organization, and other memberships.
4. The location that was referred to as, and treated as, home.
5. The state identified as the Decedent's Domicile in his or her Will.
6. The location where the Decedent lived for the greatest portion of the time.
7. The location of the Decedent's principal possessions.
8. Where the Decedent paid local taxes.
9. Where the Decedent owned burial plots.

The list of items to weigh is large, and will vary depending on each Decedent's situation. The preceding list provides a starting point. If it appears to be a close call, consult a tax or estate specialist who can help you analyze the law of the location involved, as well as the facts.

Once you determine the location of the Decedent's Domicile, that will be the state in which to begin the proceedings if Probate is necessary.

NOTE: In some instances, the Decedent may not have a Domicile in the United States. For example, a foreign citizen may have resided in the United States only occasionally. In such situations, other factors will have to be considered. These include whether the Decedent owned real estate in the jurisdiction in which you wish to have the Will probated. If no real estate is owned anywhere, the decision may turn on the location (situs) of other assets. If these issues arise, consult an estate specialist.

SECURE ESTATE ASSETS

You should immediately take steps to avoid significant loss or problems and to thus protect the Estate. For example, if the Decedent owned a fruit store, someone should sell the fruit or the value of the inventory could evaporate. If the Decedent owned a house and lived alone, take steps to secure and protect the house. It is often prudent to immediately install hard-wired central alarm smoke detectors and burglar protection. An empty house is an inviting target. A published obituary of the homeowner is akin to a neon sign encouraging visits from burglars. Be certain insurance is in force. The steps to take will vary greatly depending on the facts in the particular Estate (see Chapters 10–14).

HIRE PROFESSIONALS

Once you know which states are likely to be involved, consider hiring the appropriate professionals. Hiring an attorney, accountant, financial planner, or other professional does not necessarily mean incurring large costs. But the earlier in the process you seek qualified professional help, the more likely you will be to avoid the many traps and problems the probate process can create. Chapter 3 provides an in-depth analysis of the professionals you are likely to need, and explains how to work with them.

IS PROBATE NECESSARY?

Probate is not always necessary. However, even if it is not required, many or even most of the procedures in this book may still be needed. Once you know the assets involved and the state whose laws will govern, you can determine whether Probate is necessary. Sometimes, even if Probate is necessary, the Court involved may have an expedited Probate procedure for small estates that can save substantial time and money (and may influence how much professional help will really be necessary).

CAUTION: Even if the Estate qualifies for a simplified Probate proceeding, hire an estate attorney. If nothing else, have one meeting with the attorney so that you can be sure you have not missed anything important. If you are the Executor, showing that you took the precaution of retaining a lawyer to review matters can help protect you from personal liability in the event of any later problems.

IS ANCILLARY PROBATE NECESSARY?

If the Decedent owned real property, or tangible personal property (e.g., artwork) located in a state other than where he was domiciled, a second Probate proceeding may be necessary in the other state. This additional Probate proceeding, called Ancillary Probate may be necessary for the Executor to obtain the authority to deal with the property in that state. This will require a Court proceeding in this other state. This, in turn, will require your retaining a lawyer in that state.

Ancillary Probate is not always necessary. For example, if the real estate was owned by a partnership, limited liability company, or corporation that the Decedent owned, ancillary probate may not be necessary. This is because the asset actually owned by the Decedent in the second state was an interest in the entity, not the property (the entity owned the property). Owning an entity which owns property in another state is treated as an intangible property interest. The Executor in the state of Domicile will obtain authority over the entity, which is an intangible asset (and hence the real estate in the other state owned by the entity), through the Probate proceeding in the state where the Decedent was domiciled.

ANALYZE THE WILL OR REVOCABLE LIVING TRUST

Either or both the Decedent's Will and the Revocable Living Trust are the documents that indicate the Decedent's intent, designate the person(s) to manage the Decedent's affairs, and govern how the Decedent's assets should be distributed. One of the first steps to take is to review these documents. See Chapter 4. Steps can be taken, such as a disclaimer, to change the Will.

EXAMPLE: A Disclaimer can be one of the most effective estate planning tools. A Disclaimer, as explained in Chapter 18, requires a Beneficiary to file papers in Court stating that he or she does not want to accept certain assets from the Decedent. The assets will then pass to others under the Will. No matter how persuasive the tax benefits of filing a Disclaimer, if the surviving spouse has just lost her life partner and sole source of support, will she possibly feel emotionally strong enough to disclaim? Often not. All the budget projections aside, it is the uncertainty following the profound loss of a husband, not the financial planner's projections, that governs the decision. To encourage the widow in this example to disclaim will require your sensitivity to her insecurity more than your understanding of the tax law.

COURT PROCEEDINGS

Although the proceedings differ in every state, and even within a state based on the particular county in which you are probating the Decedent's Will, the concept is generally as follows: The Surrogate's Court will require the original of the Will, basic background information about the Decedent and his family, an original death certificate, and so on. These requirements are designed to assure that the Testator has in fact died, that the Will presented is the Testator's last signed Will, and that the Will was properly signed with no inappropriate circumstances. The Court will generally require that you give some type of notice to various people. The people, the relationships, and what they must receive vary in different Courts. Timing is key.

BONDING

The Will or the Court may require you as Executor or Trustee to purchase a Bond from an insurance company or surety to assure your performance and protect the Beneficiaries. If a Bond is required, be cautious about taking actions as an Executor before you purchase it. In fact, the Court may not issue Letters Testamentary until a Bond is secured so you may not be able to act, or if so, only in a limited capacity. Be sure to discuss this with an estate attorney. If you must act prior to the Bond being in place, consult with the attorney you anticipate hiring to represent the Estate.

COLLECT ASSETS

A fundamental job of every Executor is to gain control over the Decedent's assets so that bills and taxes can be paid and the remaining assets distributed as required under the Decedent's Will. The task of collecting assets is not always simple. In addition, steps often should be taken to minimize the likelihood of loss or damage to Estate assets.

INVENTORY

You will have to inventory all the Estate assets and assemble a balance sheet. This is essential for filing any tax returns. This may also be required by the Court where the Probate is being handled. When you resign, or the Estate is closed (or any Trust terminated), an accounting will often be required. A balance sheet, or inventory, as of the dates on which your responsibility began and ended will be the end points of any such accounting.

PAY DEBTS, EXPENSES, AND TAXES

Expenses and debts have to be paid. Finally, the IRS will want its due. Many states also get in on the action and will require the payment of some tax as well.

DETERMINE HEIRS

Construct a detailed family tree. You must understand the names, ages, and relationships of all immediate family members. This is essential to assure that the Will is properly interpreted and assets distributed properly. Even if nonfamily members are Beneficiaries, state law may still require that you give family members a formal indication that the Probate is going to occur. This is called *Notice of Probate*.

OBTAIN RELEASES AND PROVIDE ACCOUNTING

Before you make a distribution to any Beneficiary, you should generally obtain a Release from that Beneficiary. A Release is a legal document in which the Beneficiary (or other party) acknowledges having no future claim against you or your Estate. Some Beneficiaries will require that you provide them with a complete accounting (a comprehensive statement demonstrating all funds that were received by the Estate, what funds were spent, and what is left) before signing a Release. The Court may require an accounting before releasing you as Executor. Often the Release is combined with a Receipt. This is a document in which the Beneficiary acknowledges receiving a specified distribution. This combined document is called a Receipt and Release.

DISTRIBUTE ASSETS

When you have collected all assets and paid debts and expenses, you can distribute the remaining assets to the Beneficiaries and proceed to close the Estate. Distributions can raise a host of issues. How are the assets to be distributed? Who is to receive which assets? What happens if the assets named no longer exist? These and other issues are addressed in the remainder of this book.

WIND UP THE ESTATE

Once all assets have been distributed, you will want to wind up the Estate and be discharged as Executor. The procedures can vary from state to State, and from Court to Court and will also depend on the formality that the Executor and Beneficiaries want to observe. Sometimes, a final accounting is given to the Court prior to the Release. A final tax return may be necessary.

CONCLUSION

This chapter provided a brief overview of the Probate process. The objective is to define many of the key terms and help you understand the typical sequence of steps. At this basic level, most of the steps are logical and tend to follow a rational sequence. The rest of this book expands on each of these categories and provides an in-depth analysis of these essential steps. When reading the detailed discussions in those later chapters, keep in mind the simple overview presented in this chapter.

3 KEY ROLES

A host of key people are involved in every Estate. To best serve as Executor, or to understand your role as Trustee, or your rights as a Beneficiary, you should understand what the technical legal role is for each person involved. This chapter will highlight these roles.

ROLES YOU MAY SERVE

Never assume that, as in the old Westerns, each person wears one hat of one color. Many people can serve in two or more roles in the typical Probate process. You could be the principal partner in the Decedent's business, the Executor, and a Beneficiary under the Decedent's Will; a Co-Trustee under a trust formed under the Decedent's Will; and primary Beneficiary of both. These multiple roles create opportunities and pitfalls.

CAUTION: Any time you serve in multiple roles be careful to observe the formalities of each as if different people were involved. Confirm with the Estate's lawyer any special precautions you should take.

Fiduciary

A Fiduciary is a person serving in a position of trust. This generic term can include an Executor, Trustee, or Guardian. Each of these is described in this chapter. In this book when the term Fiduciary is used, the statements will apply to several or all of an Executor, Trustee, and Guardian.

Executor

The Executor is the person named in the Will to be in charge of the Decedent's Estate. When a female serves in this capacity, the term Executrix is sometimes used. The Executor is also called the Personal Administrator.

Administrator

If the Decedent died without a Will (Intestate), then the Surrogate's Court will appoint a person, based on the provisions in state law, to serve as Administrator. Once appointed, the Administrator will act in a similar manner as the Executor. Most Wills include detailed provisions granting the Executor many powers and rights. These provisions, often looked on as boilerplate in the Will, typically run on for pages. They can be invaluable to the Executor, who must consult the Will before taking any particular action to be certain that he has the requisite power. An Administrator, however, has to look to state law to determine his rights and powers. The state laws (statutes) which you can look up at your local library must be considered, but the many court cases that interpret and analyze the statutes must also be considered. When serving as an Administrator, you should carefully weigh the benefits of consulting with an attorney before you undertake any significant or unusual transactions to be certain that they are within the scope of your permitted actions. Even Executors operating under a Will with detailed provisions should review their rights and obligations with an Estate attorney at the beginning and end of the Probate process, as well as before engaging in any large or unusual transactions, or transactions with themselves or family members.

Trustee

A Trustee is a person designated as having the responsibility and authority to manage the assets of a Trust for the good of the Beneficiary of that Trust. There are many different types of Trusts for which you may be asked to serve as Trustee.

NOTE: For a more detailed analysis of the Trustee's role and the many different types of trusts for which you can be appointed Trustee, see Martin M. Shenkman, *The Complete Book of Trusts* (2nd ed.) (New York: John Wiley & Sons, 1997).

If the Decedent had a Revocable Living Trust, the Trustees of that Trust will be responsible for managing and distributing a portion, perhaps a substantial portion or even all, of the Decedent's assets. Although assets governed by a Revocable Living Trust are non-Probate Assets, many of the steps, tax issues, and other matters discussed in this book (excluding the Probate of the Will if there are no Probate Assets) will apply to the Trustees of the Revocable Living Trust.

Most Wills appoint Trustees for a host of different types of Trusts (called Testamentary Trusts). If the Decedent was married, a Bypass Trust might have been used to preserve the benefit of the Applicable Exclusion Amount ($650,000 in 1999, increasing to $1 million by 2006), and/or a Qualified Terminable Interest Property Trust (QTIP, or marital trust) would have qualified for the unlimited Estate Tax marital deduction. These trusts can be formed under either Decedent's Will or Revocable Living Trust (see Chapter 17). If the Estate is large, the Decedent's Will (or Revocable Living Trust) may provide for a Trust to preserve the benefit of the Generation Skipping Transfer tax exemption (see Chapter 17).

If the Decedent had minor children, the Will probably will have one or more Trusts to hold assets bequeathed to the children. In all these Trusts, the Executor (or Trustees of the Revocable Living Trust) will distribute Estate assets to the Trustee. The Trustee will then hold the assets and invest, manage, and distribute those assets as the Trust provisions contained in the Will require.

Guardian

A Guardian is a Fiduciary charged with the responsibility of a minor child or the property of the minor, or both. A Guardian can also be appointed by the Court if a Beneficiary is incapacitated and thus unable to manage the inheritance.

When the Court has to appoint a Guardian, extensive reporting and oversight provisions are required because of the important and sensitive nature of the responsibilities. The Guardian may have to report on what seems like a far too frequent basis, in considerable detail, to the Court. If the Beneficiary is disabled, the Guardianship process will result in significant restrictions on the person's personal rights and independence. Not only may these limitations attack the dignity of that person, but many family and friends may also be affected by the consequences. Try as Executor to be as compassionate and supportive as possible. Consult with others who have shared similar responsibilities for suggestions.

Guardian of Persons

A Guardian of the person is what most people think of when they hear the word Guardian. A Guardian is the individual, or individuals, designated to take care of a minor child of the Decedent. Usually, the Guardian of any minor is the surviving parent; however, in some instances the Decedent may name a different person. In highly unusual circumstances, the surviving spouse and the court may respect this request. In almost all situations, neither will. Occasionally a Will appoints a husband and wife as joint Guardians. "I appoint my sister Jane and her husband Joe as guardians for my son Tiny Terror." What happens if Jane and Joe are divorced? What if they are in the process of separation? Most likely Jane and Joe would agree that Jane, as sister of the Decedent, would assume the responsibility. However, agreement may not be easy and Court confirmation may be necessary. If thorny issues such as these arise, always consult with the Estate's attorney.

Executors may have responsibility to address financial requirements of the Guardian. Often a Trust is set up for the minors. Once the Trust is formed, the person named as the Trustee to manage assets held for the benefit of the minor will address this need. In these cases, the Trustees can exercise a degree of financial oversight over the Guardian once they are appointed. This is usually by receipt of a document from the Court called Letters of Trusteeship.

Guardian of Property

In too many cases, Wills fail to establish Trusts to protect the interests of a minor child or other minor Beneficiary in the assets bequeathed. In such cases, the Court, state law, or even the Will itself, may establish a Guardianship for the minor's property. Although similar in concept to a Trust, such a Guardianship ends when the minor attains the age of majority under state law (18 to 21 years). The Guardian's job is to manage, invest, and distribute the property.

Guardian ad Litem

If a situation arises when a minor or incompetent person in the view of the Court needs protection, the Court may appoint a special person to protect and represent the minor or incompetent's interest. This person is referred to as a Guardian Ad Litem. For example, your friend is the income beneficiary of a Trust set up under your Will. She is to receive all income of the trust, and on her death the assets of the Trust will be distributed to your niece who is presently age 10. A decision has to be made concerning the trust and how assets will be invested. Because this will affect both Beneficiaries, your friend and niece, both of their interests must be addressed. Since your niece is a minor, the Court may appoint a Guardian Ad Litem to represent her interests.

Beneficiary

The Beneficiary is the person intended to benefit from the assets of the Estate and/or any one or more Trusts. Although the Beneficiary's role is traditionally viewed as a passive one, this is not always appropriate. The Beneficiaries of an Estate may have the right to be informed of the financial transactions of the Estate that affect them, to see the Will or other governing documents, and so forth. Beneficiaries should, to protect their interests, review these documents to be certain that all look reasonable. Beneficiaries of Trusts have an even more active role. Often, the Beneficiaries will have to inform the Trustees of the Beneficiary's financial needs, the Beneficiary's tax bracket, and so on. This information can be essential for the Trustees to best invest trust assets and properly distribute those assets to benefit and protect the Beneficiaries.

Many Wills and Trusts will even provide the Beneficiaries with additional specified powers and rights. For example, the Beneficiaries by a majority or unanimous vote may be empowered to remove or replace a

Trustee. To ascertain what rights and powers they have, Beneficiaries should carefully review the Will and/or Revocable Living Trust (see Chapter 4 for illustrations of some of these rights).

Prior to distributions being made, and certainly prior to final distributions on the winding up of the Estate or Trust, Beneficiaries are requested to sign Receipts and Releases. These are legal agreements in which the Beneficiaries acknowledge receipt of the assets to be distributed to them, and they waive any further claims against the Estate, the Trust, and the Executor and Trustee. Sometimes the document will include a committment by the Beneficiary to return funds to the Estate if needed. Before signing any such document, the Beneficiaries should be certain to review the detailed statements attached (sometimes a full accounting, other times more informal accounting records) before signing. If the Beneficiaries are suspicious that the Executor or Trustee did not have their full interests at heart, or that transactions seem unusual or unclear, or the records provided are inadequate, the Beneficiaries should make further inquiry to protect their interests.

NOTE: Beneficiaries should first consult with the Executor. If they are unclear about some of the matters involved, or unsatisfied with the explanations provided by the Executor, they should request the Executor's permission to consult with the Estate's attorney or accountant for clarification. If the request is denied, or the later explanations are unsatisfactory, the Beneficiary can always retain his own attorney and accountant. However, this should only be done as a last resort. The message that this will send to the Executor, and other Beneficiaries if they are not participating, could be antagonistic.

Co-Fiduciary

In some cases, the Decedent's Will may name more than one person to serve simultaneously; these people will be called Co-Executors. Co-Executors are jointly responsible for all actions affecting the Estate. If you are serving as a Co-Executor, you can be held liable for any acts of the other Co-Executor. Demand that you be copied on all correspondence, receive copies or originals of all bank statements and other reports, and so on. Similarly, you should clear any significant decisions you make with the other Co-Executor in advance. All major decisions should be made by unanimous agreement of all Co-Executors. If the decision is of particular importance, consider having all Co-Executors sign off their agreement in writing. If one of two Co-Executors is unavailable when a particular transaction must occur, the Will or state law may permit the unavailable Co-Executor to delegate the authority to handle the particular transaction to the Co-Executor who will be present. This delegation, however, will not relieve the absent Co-Executor from responsibility for the matters involved. Further, if this arrangement is to be used, the parties to the transaction (e.g., the bank, real estate brokers) should be apprised of this in advance to be certain that they will accept such an arrangement.

Co-Fiduciaries are two or more people who are named to serve as Executors or Trustees at the same time. This is a commonly used planning technique. Having a Co-Executor or Co-Trustee can be advantageous because it gives you someone who can share the burdens of the position. Each of you may have different strengths and areas of expertise. Combining these attributes can assure the Beneficiaries of a better job being done handling the Estate or Trust. If one of you is ill, or on vacation, the other can cover. It is not always so simple, however. If you and your Co-Executor do not get along well, handling the Estate can become difficult and unpleasant. You may not agree on many issues, even important ones. Compromise will be essential to move forward. These difficulties come with a tremendous responsibility. As a Fiduciary, you are held to a high standard of responsibility for actions taken. You cannot avoid responsibility by stating that the Co-Executor was handling that particular matter. You remain in most situations jointly and severally liable. If your Co-Executor makes an investment that was not permitted by the Will and that was inappropriate for a Fiduciary, you can be held liable.

The following sample form illustrates a delegation of power permitted under the Will. Discuss this sample form with the Estate's attorney before completing any transaction:

SAMPLE DURABLE POWER OF ATTORNEY FOR EXECUTOR

KNOW ALL MEN BY THESE PRESENTS, that I, Unavailable Co-Executor, residing at 123 Main Street, Anytown, USA (Grantor), as Co-Executor of the Estate of Decedent's Name (the "Decedent") and Co-Trustee of the Trust under the Last Will and Testament of the Decedent (the "Trust"), do hereby appoint Available Co-Executrix and Co-Trustee, residing at 456 South Street, Big City, USA as my attorney-in-fact (the "Agent"), in my name, place, and stead, in any way which I myself could do if I were personally present, to the extent that I am permitted by law and Decedent's Name Will to act through an agent, in any Estate transactions.

A. SCOPE OF POWER OF ATTORNEY

The scope of this Power of Attorney is set forth in the Last Will and Testament of the Decedent, Article XIV, paragraph AA, which states:

"Any individual Executor or Trustee acting hereunder is authorized at any time and from time to time by revocable power of attorney to delegate to any one or more of his Co-Executors or Co-Trustees any duty or power conferred upon him hereunder and whether any such delegation relates to a discretionary or ministerial power. Any such power of attorney and any revocation of any such power of attorney shall be in writing and delivered to the Co-Executor or Co-Trustee to whom the duty has been delegated."

B. DIRECTIONS TO AGENT

The Agent is hereby authorized and directed to perform all acts reasonable and necessary to carry out and implement the responsibilities of the Executors appointed under Decedent's Name Last Will and Testament.

C. INDEMNIFICATION

To induce any third party to act hereunder, I hereby agree that any third party receiving a duly executed copy or facsimile of this instrument may act hereunder, and that revocation or termination hereof shall be ineffective as to such third party unless and until actual notice or knowledge of such revocation or termination shall have been received by such third party, and I for myself and for my heirs, executors, legal representatives, and assigns, hereby agree to indemnify and hold harmless any such third party from and against any and all claims that may arise against such third party by reason of such third party having relied on the provisions of this instrument.

D. REVOCATION AND SUBSTITUTION

I retain the right to revoke this Power of Attorney. The Agent may also revoke this Power of Attorney. The Agent may also appoint a new Agent to take the Agent's place. I approve and confirm all that the Agent or the Agent's substitute may lawfully do on my behalf.

E. EFFECTIVE DATE

This Power of Attorney is effective upon execution.

F. STATE LAW

This instrument is delivered in the state of State Name, and the laws of State Name shall govern all questions as to the validity of this power and the construction of its provisions.

By signing below, I acknowledge that I have received a copy of this Power of Attorney and that I understand its terms.

Grantor/Principal

_____
Executor's Signature Granting Power

[Witness signature lines and Notary forms not illustrated]

THINGS YOU SHOULD KNOW WHEN SERVING AS EXECUTOR, TRUSTEE, OR GUARDIAN

Your Responsibilities as Fiduciary

Your responsibility as Executor is to carry out the terms of the Will. Your responsibility as a Trustee is to carry out the terms of the Trust. You should carefully review the documents involved to understand what you must do (see Chapter 4). There are, however, a host of general responsibilities with which you must be familiar. The best approach is to address these at an initial meeting with an attorney representing the Estate.

Duties You Owe to the Beneficiaries

You owe a duty of loyalty to the Beneficiaries. You have a generic duty to administer the Estate. This means that you must do what is reasonably necessary for the good of the Estate and those interested in it. The general duty to administer is the source of other duties including the duty of impartiality.

You must act with care and prudence to protect Estate assets, invest assets, and handle Estate matters. You must always maintain accurate records. The suggestions in Chapter 7 will help you meet this requirement. You must act to preserve Estate assets. This can include a host of requirements from making sure there is adequate fire and casualty insurance, to installing a fence around a swimming pool, to being certain that the money managers you have retained follow a reasonable investment policy.

Authority to Retain Agents

You have a duty to the Beneficiaries not to delegate to others acts that you can reasonably be required personally to perform. This does not, however, require you to be an expert in all matters. You can, and often should, hire professionals to perform specialized or expert tasks for which you do not have the training. However, your delegation of a particular act does not absolve you of responsibility to monitor the professionals.

You generally have the power to perform every act that a prudent person would perform for the purposes of fulfilling the directives in the Will or Trust. This includes the power to employ persons, including attorneys, auditors, investment advisers, or agents to advise or assist you in the performance of your administrative duties. How far you will be permitted to act on their recommendations without independent investigation could depend on the facts involved. Therefore, it is always best to have some level of review. This may entail little more than an overview of a periodic report, or it may entail much more. Consult the estate's attorney for guidance.

Avoid Self-Dealing Issues

Fiduciary is defined as a position of trust. You cannot violate that trust by engaging in transactions that a Trustee and independent person would not consider appropriate. You should not loan or borrow money from the Estate. If you must, it should be on an arm's length basis, with written documentation, which is approved in advance by the Beneficiaries and even the Court. Even so, it is always best to avoid any transaction that could be inappropriate or could even appear inappropriate. Self-dealing, such as hiring yourself to perform additional work for additional fees, or buying Estate assets, should usually be avoided. The risk of self-dealing is present anytime you as Executor employ yourself to perform a service that an independent agent (e.g., a realtor, accountant, or attorney) could also perform.

What Can Beneficiaries Consent To?

Consent of all the Beneficiaries, even assuming that they are past the age of majority *(sui juris)*, should not be relied on to justify violation of the duties you owe the Estate and the Beneficiaries as a Fiduciary. If you are going to pursue this approach, such as having the Beneficiaries all agree that you can borrow money from the Estate, consult with the Estate's attorney before acting. Under some states' laws, the Beneficiaries can consent to the termination of a Trust. Perhaps the Beneficiaries may be able to consent to other actions. Even if permitted, formalities will have to be adhered to.

The Beneficiaries may be able to consent to the termination of a Trust, state law may require the written consent of each Beneficiary acknowledged or approved in a manner required by the laws of the state for recording or a conveyance of real property. Signatures of all persons beneficially interested in the Trust, and the creator of the Trust, may be required. Exercise caution. A typical Trust formed under a Will may say that assets are to be held in the Trust for the benefit of the Decedent's children, "per stirpes." Even if all the children are adults so that they can legally sign an agreement, the language *per stirpes* means that if a child dies before the Trust terminates, the children and later descendants of the child would become Beneficiaries. If those children or grandchildren are minors, a Court could require the appointment of a Guardian Ad Litem to represent the interests of those minors. Thus, simply having the adult children, who appear to be the only Beneficiaries, sign off, may be insufficient. Some states may permit the children, through whom later descendants would receive their rights, sign off or consent on behalf of those successors. This procedure, called Virtual Representation, can expedite the process.

Fees

In a typical Probate, two types of fees are involved: Fees to the Executor for managing the Estate, and fees to the Trustees managing the Trust or Trusts formed under the Will or a Revocable Living Trust.

Executor and Trustee fees can be a function of the provisions in the Will or state law, as well as custom in the particular county where the Probate is being handled. Typically, fees are based on state law. State law often provides for a maximum percentage of the assets, decreasing as the Estate increases in size. Trustee fees may be based on the assets in the Trust as well as the income earned by the Trust.

When two or more persons serve as Co-Executors, some type of statutory fee split will typically occur. In some instances, the Co-Executors will simply divide the statutory executor commissions equally. In other instances, each may be entitled to a full commission. In still other situations, Co-Executors may be entitled to split 150 percent of the standard fee. Similar provisions may apply to Co-Trustees.

A corporate or institutional Co-Executor or Co-Trustee (e.g., a bank or trust company) may be entitled to a full commission, whereas the noncorporate Co-Executor may be entitled to only a portion of the fee.

If the Estate is large, it becomes more common to negotiate the Executor commission. Sometimes this may be done in advance by the Decedent and recorded in the Will or in a separate agreement. In some instances, the Beneficiaries may have some latitude to negotiate for themselves. If the attorney who drafted the Will is named Executor, the Court may pay even greater attention to the fee arrangements.

When family advisers, such as a long-time attorney or accountant serve as Fiduciary, often they should be paid only their hourly rate upon presentation of detailed bills.

When the Executors are family members, they often waive any right to Executor or Trustee fees. Several important points should be considered:

- Waiving fees may be preferable to preserve family harmony.

EXAMPLE: Decedent is survived by three children. The eldest two children are named as Co-Executors. The Estate is divided equally among the three children. The Decedent's intent was to divide everything equally. Unless the two children waive their Executor fees, the third child will receive less. Even if the Executor commission is reasonable for the work they will have to do, they may want to waive it if doing so will preserve family peace. Tax planning should be considered.

- Before a family member waives fees, careful consideration should be given to the work involved. Sometimes, a family member waives fees in the interest of family harmony only to find that the duties involved require a considerable effort and time commitment. Also, unpaid Executors often will not expend as much time and effort as paid Executors. This can easily cost the family more money since professional fees will increase as the Estate's attorney and accountant are saddled with work the Executor would have otherwise performed.
- It may be wiser to pay maximum fees to save Estate taxes (see Chapter 18).

In all situations, the fees for Executors and Trustees should be reasonable relative to the services performed. Reasonableness of fees is not necessarily related to the size of the Estate. For example, if an Estate consists of a single brokerage account of $2 million and a $650,000 house, only two transactions may be necessary to complete Probate. Contrast this to a $300,000 Estate that consists of a house valued at $250,000 subject to a $225,000 mortgage, a vacation home worth $150,000 subject to a $100,000 mortgage, $150,000 of securities comprising 15 different U.S. bonds, and various stock and bond certificates all in a one-third interest in a closely held retail store valued at $75,000. Settling this far smaller Estate will require far more work; thus, a reasonable fee for the smaller Estate could easily exceed the reasonable fee for the larger Estate.

The following sample letter illustrates how the attorney for the Estate may calculate Executor fees and inform the Executors and Beneficiaries of the fees involved:

SAMPLE LETTER STATING EXECUTOR'S FEES

SOMEONE, SOMEONE, AND NOBODY, P.C.
JOHN Q. LAWYER, ESQ.
100 MAIN STREET
ANYTOWN, USA

August 14, 1994

Ms. Jane P. Executrix
789 Trusting Way
Small Town, USA

RE: *Executor Fees from the Estate of Decedent's Name.*

Dear Ms. Executrix:

An executor is entitled to a fee of five percent of the corpus received by the fiduciary (i.e., of the probate estate) under the laws of State Name. Probate Code Section XX1. This fee declines as the estate increases, as follows:

First $200,000	5.0%
$200,000 to $1M	3.5%
Over $1M	2.0%

An executor is also entitled to an additional fee of six percent of all income received by the probate estate.

The statute does not authorize a fiduciary to collect compensation in excess of the amounts expressly authorized by the terms of the will or statute. However, under the statute, the courts have discretion to adjust the commissions of fiduciaries to take into account the "actual pain, trouble and risk in settling the estate, rather than in respect to the quantum of the estate." Probate Code Section XX2. The phrase "pain and trouble" is defined as the labor or exertions. State Law Probate Code Practice at § 1532. Risk refers to the hazard of being surcharged and other liability for the assets of the estate. The standards are based on the difficulty of managing the estate's assets.

Except for certain specified instances, commissions are allowable to an executor only on assets that have come into the executor's possession. Except as specified by statute, no compensation can be allowed for his services as a fiduciary in addition to his commissions. The specified instances must arise from the property under the control of the fiduciary and include services rendered in connection with the collection and apportionment of taxes. Outside the exceptions, the statute controls. Compensation for services of a personal nature is not within the scope of the statute.

Under the statute, Jane P. Executrix in her capacity as sole executrix, is entitled to executrix fees of 5 percent of the corpus (principal) of the Probate Estate:

DAN DECEDENT'S ESTATE ASSETS

Cash	$ 12,000
Securities	$ 88,000
House	$ 95,000
Liabilities	none
Total Probate Estate	$195,000
Statutory Commission	× 5%
Executrix Commission	$ 9,750

Jane P. Executrix is also entitled to 6 percent of all income received by the Probate Estate. This amount has been calculated by Susan J. Smith, CPA as $933. Thus, the executor fee on income is $56 [$933 × .06].

Based on the foregoing, you should be entitled to $9,806 [$9,750 + $56].

Sincerely,

Someone, Someone and Nobody, P.C.

_____

John Q. Lawyer, Esq.

enc.
MMS:km
cc: Benny Beneficiary

What happens if unusual circumstances result in your providing far more services than an Executor typically undertakes? The burden of proof is on you to establish the extraordinary services or their value. Although this will not be easy, you can take several simple steps to help support your claim. All Fiduciaries should follow the practice of documenting their efforts in the event anyone should later question their actions. Maintain a calendar in which you list appointments, calls, and the like, as suggested elsewhere in this book. You can use the copies of the sample chart provided here as another method of recording your activities:

Sample Chart for Recording Activities

Services Provided by Fiduciary name for Month of _____ 19 _____

Date	Description of Service	Service Provided To	Hours Spent as Co-Trustee	Hours Spent as Caretaker, etc.	Comment

Fiduciary Liability

Accepting the job of an Executor or Trustee is not without responsibility as discussed earlier. Responsibilities also bring risks and liabilities, none of which should be taken lightly. If you are cavalier about your tasks and a Court finds that you did not act appropriately, you could incur a personal surcharge for expenses or losses. Although the standard of care for a Fiduciary is that of a reasonably prudent person, Beneficiaries and the Court will have the advantages of hindsight in reviewing your actions. What might have seemed reasonable to you at the time may look inappropriate after the fact. Therefore, every Fiduciary should try to minimize the likelihood of being held liable. In addition to the steps discussed throughout this book, consider the following suggestions:

1. If there is any conflict of interest between you and any of the Beneficiaries, be certain to have all the Beneficiaries, and/or the Court approve any actions that could be questioned. Better still, try to find an alternative course of action that does not involve a conflict of interest.

EXAMPLE: The personal property of the Estate is to be distributed as the Executor directs. The Decedent told you how she wanted her jewelry, art, and other personal assets distributed, but there is nothing in writing. You and your three cousins are the Beneficiaries. Any assets you keep for yourself could be questioned by the other heirs. It is best to have everyone agree in writing as to who gets what.

---

2. Do you have sufficient experience to handle the matters you are taking care of? If not, hire professionals when a particular task exceeds your experience. Once you have hired a professional, monitor their performance. Request periodic reports.

3. Be sure to set up a calendar of key deadlines, including deadlines based on the state and court involved (see Chapter 2). State and federal tax deadlines are critical to meet. Do not assume that the professionals will monitor every deadline; you remain responsible to do so as Executor. Many of the legal and tax deadlines involved are discussed in Chapters 6, 17, and 18. If they apply to the Estate you are involved with, watch those dates. Have the Estate's attorney and accountant advise you in advance of deadlines. You should record the dates in the calendar that you maintain for your Fiduciary functions (see earlier suggestions).

4. If you have any significant decisions that affect the Beneficiaries, especially if different Beneficiaries will be affected differently, a written document that explains the options, the decision made, and the consequences should be signed by each Beneficiary affected (a Consent). For example, if your investment mix will be 50 percent income-oriented

and 50 percent growth-oriented, document the specific needs and tax brackets for each Beneficiary.

5. If there is a major issue, particularly a contentious matter, consult the Estate's attorney about obtaining a court order that specifies the action you should take.

6. When a contentious issue is resolved, have all those involved sign a written agreement that states what each person has agreed to and what will happen (a Settlement Agreement).

7. Hire an attorney and accountant who are experienced in Probate matters. Document your discussions with the professionals retained and save a copy of their firm biography in your file to show that you were prudent in hiring them.

8. If you handle certain aspects of the Probate on your own to minimize costs, periodically review the appropriate steps with professionals.

9. Be certain to have any Beneficiary receiving a distribution of Estate assets first sign a Release and Refunding Bond. A Release is a legal document stating that you as Executor, and the Estate, owe the person signing it nothing more. This written acknowledgment that the Beneficiary has no other claims, provided in exchange for a distribution, can provide you with protection if a claim is later asserted. Asking for the Release will also encourage any Beneficiary with a claim to make it before signing (see Chapter 20). A Refunding Bond is a commitment to pay money back to the Estate.

CAUTION: Be certain to consult with a lawyer before sending a release to a Beneficiary to sign. Depending on the Beneficiary's bequest under the Will, the relationship of the Beneficiary to the Decedent, the assets distributed, and other factors, it may be advisable to modify the form of Release used. If the bequest is for a percentage of the Estate, an Accounting of Estate assets may be appropriate to attach.

If You Do Not Want to Serve (Renunciation)

Sometimes it may be advisable to forgo serving as a Fiduciary. If the obligations and potential liability of a Fiduciary seem too overwhelming (you have inadequate background and experience, or your job and other responsibilities are too demanding) or circumstances have changed (you have moved to another state, your relationship with the Beneficiaries has changed), consider declining the appointment as Executor. You do not have to serve.

EXAMPLE: Your two nephews are heirs of your brother's Estate. Your brother named you because at the time he drafted his Will the nephews were minors. He never revised the Will. By the time that your brother passed away, his two children were grown. The rift between them had also grown to the point where the feud between the famed Hatfields and McCoys would have seemed like a mild miscommunication by comparison. Why insert yourself into the midst of the fray? Decline to serve.

People appointed to serve as a Fiduciary often feel guilty about turning down the job. Before refusing the position, consider the trust and reliance that the Decedent had in your capability. Carefully weigh the arguments not to serve against the consequences. Who will serve if you step down? Who are listed as successor Fiduciaries? Are they more or less capable than you? If you are the last Executor on the list, a court proceeding may be necessary to name a successor if you decline. On the other hand, if the Will lists your three younger siblings, each of whom is able and willing to serve, as successor, there may be no detriment to the heirs if you decline. Are your reasons for not serving in the best interest of the heirs (e.g., because of changes in your health since you were named, it would not be possible for you to serve)?

Consider the impact of your resigning on the fees for the Executor. You will forfeit your right to any Executor or Trustee fees if you resign. However, if you are a close friend or family member of the Decedent and you would have waived any fees to preserve all the Estate's assets for the surviving heirs, who will serve if you do not? Will they take fees you would have waived? If you are a Beneficiary and decline to serve, the tax benefits of taking fees versus a larger inheritance will be lost (see Chapter 18).

Alternatively, are the reasons really for your selfish interests and not in the best interest of the heirs (your career is more demanding than when you were named in the Will, but there is no one else who will care for your niece and nephew as well as you). You can decline for any reason, but do you want to?

If you believe that declining is the best option, consider discussing the situation with the Beneficiaries involved to avoid anyone feeling insulted. When Fiduciaries decline an appointment or resign, it is usually for a valid reason and seldom causes offense. Although you do not need the Beneficiaries' consent, your decision will be easier and encourage smoother future relations, if everyone involved understands your reasons.

Once you reach a decision, be certain to inform the lawyer for the Estate. A form will have to be filed with the Surrogate's Court indicating that you are declining to accept the appointment. If you really do not want to serve, it is best to resign the appointment before accepting it. Once you begin to serve, the process of resigning is more complex and risky. If you have served, you will have the legal responsibility for that time period. You may also need to have an Accounting made of all monies you had responsibility for as Fiduciary to prove that everything has been handled properly. If you never accept the appointment, you avoid these issues.

The following forms illustrate the documents that may have to be filed to renounce your appointment as an Executor. The actual forms will differ by state and Court, so consult with the Estate's attorney after organizing the information you may need.

SAMPLE LETTER TO RESIGN APPOINTMENT

SURROGATE'S COURT OF THE STATE OF SOME STATE
COUNTY OF SOMETHING

PROBATE PROCEEDING,
Will of

Dan Decedent

RENUNCIATION OF NOMINATED
EXECUTOR AND/OR TRUSTEE

Deceased.   File No. _____

I, Debby Decliner domiciled at 123 Main Street, Big City, USA, nominated as an Executor and/or Trustee in the (Will) (Codicil) of Dan Decedent dated January 1, 1999, late of Big City in the County of Somewhere, Some State, hereby renounce the appointment and all right and claim to letters testamentary and/or letters of trusteeship of and under the (Will) (Codicil) or to act as Executor and/or Trustee thereof.

I hereby waive the issuance and service or a citation in the above entitled matter, and consent that the Will dated January 1, 1999 (and Codicil dated January 2, 1999), a copy of which has been received by the undersigned, be forthwith admitted to Probate. I hereby consent that Letters
{ X } Testamentary
{ X } Trusteeship

issue to Sammy Successor without the necessity of furnishing a bond. If a bond is furnished, I hereby waive and release all right to make any claim on the bond in any capacity whatsoever.

_____   *Debby Decliner*_____
(Signature)   (Print Name)

Date: _____

[Notary Form and attorney designation omitted].

NOTE: If you never accepted the appointment as Executor, it may be sufficient to file a renunciation with the Court. Since state laws vary, consult with the Estate attorney.

SAMPLE LETTER OF CONSENT AND RELEASE
TO FIDUCIARY RESIGNING

STATE OF SOME STATE
SURROGATE'S COURT, Somewhere

In the matter of the
Estate of

Dan Decedent

CONSENT AND RELEASE

Deceased.

KNOW ALL MEN BY THESE PRESENTS that the undersigned, Betty Beneficiary and Ginny Guardian on behalf of Mindy Minor, a minor, (hereinafter collectively referred to as the

"Beneficiaries") being of full age, do hereby consent and agree to the Renunciation of Debby Decliner, under the Last Will and Testament of Dan Decedent and the Codicil thereto (hereinafter collectively referred to as the "Will") to all right and claim to letters testamentary and letters of trusteeship of and under the Will to act as executor and trustee thereof as the first Executor and Trustee, and do hereby remise, release, and forever discharge Debby Decliner of and from any and every claim, demand, action, and cause of action, account, reckoning, and liability of every kind and nature associated with this Renunciation,

The Beneficiaries herein also consent to the appointment of Sammy Successor as executor and trustee thereunder.

IN WITNESS WHEREOF, this Consent and Release has been signed and sealed by the undersigned on the dates set forth below.

_____   _____
Dated   Betty Beneficiary

_____   _____
Dated   Ginny Guardian, for Mindy Minor

[Notary forms omitted].

NOTE: If you began to serve as Executor, in addition to filing a renunciation and obtaining court approval, you may need the consent of the Beneficiaries. An Accounting and other procedures may also be necessary. Be certain to address the steps in detail with the Estate attorney to minimize your liability.

THINGS YOU SHOULD KNOW ABOUT PROFESSIONALS SERVING THE ESTATE

The following section discusses the use of, and issues concerning, most of the professionals you may hire. The general comments discussed in this section apply to most if not all professionals.

Should You Interview Several Professionals?

If you are the sole heir and you are comfortable with a particular professional, hire him. However, if you are one of several heirs, it's advisable to interview at least two, if not three, professionals before retaining any. Save publicity materials, firm brochures, and meeting notes to demonstrate to the heirs that you made a reasonable effort to hire a qualified professional. Down the road when the Estate is settled and the bills are excessive and the Beneficiaries up in arms, this paperwork may help defuse a crisis and prevent them from trying to hold you personally liable.

Finding the Right Professional

Use common sense. Ask questions. Trust your gut feelings. Professionals are often chosen for the wrong reasons. Understanding these common mistakes will help you understand how to better select professionals to help the Estate:

- Request and keep in your files a resume for the particular professional or a biography of the firm. Read it carefully. Do the materials provided convey confidence and indicate expertise in the matters on which the Estate requires assistance? Inquire about any gaps, unusual items, inconsistencies, or other problems with the information provided, and if the responses are unsatisfactory, do not hire that professional.

- Be certain that the professional has the minimum credentials, or better, for the profession. If you are not familiar with the minimum requirements, you can ask the professional to explain them at your first meeting or during the initial phone call.

- Watch out for the "old boys' club." Professional accreditation and membership in professional organizations can mean that the professional is active as a speaker or participant at professional seminars, thus staying current with new developments and planning ideas. In a few cases, however, it might simply mean that the professional has the right connections or characteristics to join the group. These attributes may, but do not necessarily, have significant relevance when gauging the professional's expertise, integrity, ethics, or other important factors. Always try to find objective information about the professional. An important point to remember is that in some cases you really should hire someone with a particular credential. For example, if the Estate has real estate requiring an appraisal, you might wish to restrict your selection to appraisers holding the MAI designation.

- The professional that represented the Decedent is not necessarily the ideal choice to represent the Estate. The lawyer who wrote the Will is not necessarily the best choice to represent the Estate. Similarly, the accountant who prepared a simple annual income tax return may not have the expertise to prepare a more complex Estate Tax return.

- In all cases, be certain that the professionals you hire have the expertise, experience, professional qualifications, and office facilities to reasonably handle the tasks involved. Retaining professionals used in the past is advantageous when this means that they have records of the Estate and knowledge of the people involved. However, you must evaluate these advantages along with the professional's expertise. Do not continue with a professional solely because of past relationships if the professional's expertise is not suited for handling Estate matters.

- Set up an interview to meet the professional. Whereas some professionals will provide a free initial consultation, many (if not most) do not. You cannot expect a busy professional to provide a free consultation. Remember, a professional who provides free consultations must recover the time lost on unpaid consultations. And it will be the prospects who actually retain the professional who pay that price. Specify the agenda for the first meeting when you make the appointment. The best approach is to pay for a meeting and ask for and insist on, targeted advice relevant to the Estate you are handling. Free meetings often tend to be little more than general explanations and sales pitches, a waste of your valuable time as well. Make certain that the professional understands your objectives. If you are interviewing several professionals, say so. If you are intending to hire the professional you are meeting with if all goes well, say so. The professional may conduct the meeting quite differently for each of the two scenarios. If you are shopping, but paying for the first meeting, the professional should endeavor to highlight specific issues and planning points that pertain to your Estate. Assuming that it is instead an initial meeting for a definite client, the professional may spend far greater time collecting information and reviewing steps for which you must assume responsibility. Although this information is useful, it will be of little benefit if you hire a different professional. Advising the professional of your agenda will help you get the best service to fit your needs.

- Ask other professionals for advice. Uncle Joe may be a great guy and may love his accountant. But does Uncle Joe really have the expertise to know whether his accountant is qualified? Your attorney, banker, or other professionals may be better judges of technical expertise.

Ask Pointed Questions

You have concerns. Ask direct and specific questions about them:

- "I have heard that Estates can go on for years enriching the professionals and impoverishing the heirs. Is this true? Does it happen often? What can be done to prevent it?"
- "How can I monitor your bills so that I know I am being treated fairly?"
- "Isn't Probate a big rip-off designed to enrich professionals?"

If you have a concern, ask. If you cannot feel comfortable asking professionals the worrisome questions before you retain them for the Estate, you will never feel comfortable doing it later. Most important, asking the questions that really worry you gives you a great method for choosing among the professionals you interview. See how they react to and address your concerns.

Fees

Everyone has heard horror stories of Probates going on for years and eating up a shocking percentage of the Estate. In most cases, these horror stories are exceptions and way overblown. There are, however, specific steps you can take to minimize the difficulties with Probate and avoid problems:

- Deal with the emotions. Almost no family is exempt from some interpersonal strife, jealousy, or conflicts. The legal system is not the rational way to deal with these. When siblings or other heirs begin to bicker over personal matters, legal and other professional fees skyrocket.

- Never hire a lawyer, accountant, or other professional without getting a written agreement. Do not wait for surprises later. Always insist on retaining a lawyer on an hourly basis and get a fee schedule for the staff that will be working on your account. Rarely will percentages and other methods of charging give you the best result if the attorney is reasonable, honest, and bills you for the time actually spent. In many cases, a percentage of the Estate can be totally out of proportion to the work that needs to be done.

EXAMPLE: The Decedent owned a house worth $300,000, a $350,000 stock portfolio with a major brokerage firm, and an automobile. There are really only three assets that have to be addressed. The fact that the Estate may be worth nearly $700,000 does not justify a $20,000 or $30,000 legal fee based on a percentage. Most major brokerage firms could be of tremendous help in valuing the securities; closing on a house and a deed may cost a few thousand dollars, often much less. Where there is a surviving spouse, there may be no reason to bother changing the deed on the house. To change the deed, there should be only a nominal charge. One headache is likely to be the car, given the bureaucratic difficulties of dealing with some state departments of motor vehicles. However, this is a matter that you (as an heir) or a family member easily can handle without chalking up big legal fees.

- Never pay any accounting or legal bill, especially for Probate, unless you get an analysis of the work that was actually done. A bill "For Services Rendered" with a big number is not an analysis. You are entitled to know what you are being billed for. In fairness to the attorney though, do not question every single minute of every time charge for every single action that was taken. Some things can be quite efficient, others can take much longer than anticipated. All in all, detailed fair billings can result in substantially lower charges.

- Plan ahead. Consolidate accounts and minimize unnecessary legal paperwork. Although there is little benefit (other than a few free toasters, perhaps) for having dozens of bank accounts, many people still take this route. Also, using a sweep account at any major brokerage firm to hold Estate stocks and bonds, as illustrated in the previous example, can save a tremendous amount of cost and time.

- Move quickly to secure any property before problems develop. If there is a house that is now unoccupied, get an alarm system installed. Often the few thousand dollars spent for a basic alarm system can save substantial amounts of money later. Be certain that water and plumbing are handled properly during the winter months. A little common sense can go a long way in minimizing costs and hassles.

Written Agreements

To protect the Estate from inappropriate fees, lack of experience, and other risks, and to demonstrate that you have made a reasonable effort to retain competent professionals and monitor their services, each professional firm should provide a written agreement summarizing their structure for charges and describing the services they can provide. Many firms use different approaches. If you want additional information or clarification, ask. The following sample letter illustrates some issues that should be addressed:

NAME OF PROFESSIONAL FIRM HIRED
500 EXPENSIVE AVENUE
ANYTOWN, USA

January 1, 1999

Ms. Jane P. Executrix
123 Cautious Street
Anytown, USA

Re: *Retainer Agreement*

Dear Ms. Executrix:

Our sympathies on your recent loss. We will make every effort to assist you with the Probate process of the Estate. If our office can be of any assistance during this difficult time, please do not hesitate to call us.

As the person named to become Executrix under the Will of the late Dan Decedent, you have requested that we assist you in representing the Estate as legal counsel. In this regard, we will rely on you to provide us with all necessary documents and information and will rely on the completeness and accuracy of the information you provide to us in preparing any necessary federal and state estate and inheritance tax returns and Probate filings. We will assist you in preparing the necessary documents to have the Will admitted to Probate once the original Will is provided to us.

You should note that there is a substantial amount of administrative work required in the administration of any Estate, and to the extent that you as Executrix assist in performing any of these functions, it will enable us to minimize the legal fees involved. To the extent that you can gather, organize, and provide us data as to family members, assets, debts, and expenses, you can eliminate a considerable portion of the legal work, and hence fees, involved. We would be pleased to provide you with guidance and direction in this regard. However, we believe that the preparation of the actual documents submitted to the Probate court for filing, and the preparation of the tax returns, are most efficiently handled by our office. If you do not wish to be burdened with any significant administrative work, we would be pleased to handle these matters for you. It is important that you advise us as quickly as possible as to what extent you wish to be involved in the process.

We bill for all services on an hourly basis. As we have previously discussed, my initial retainer is $2,000.00. All work will be billed at standard hourly billing rates. The hourly billing rates are presently: Senior Partner $450, Senior Associate $220, Junior Associate $165, and Paralegal $85. Expenses are billed for reimbursement at our actual cost. They are not marked up. Charges are billed for facsimile, photocopying are billed at $2 per page and 20 cents per page, respectively. While you inquired as to an estimate of the fees involved, it is not possible at this stage to provide a specific estimate. The actual time involved will depend on a host of factors including the administrative tasks you wish to perform, the complexity and organization of the assets involved, whether any Beneficiaries or other persons will challenge the Will or raise other issues, and so forth. To address your concerns, however, we will bill you approximately monthly, with detailed bills reflecting the date and time spent by each professional, as well as itemization of the work performed on each day. This will provide you with a regular and specific report so that you can monitor our work on an ongoing basis. Should you ever have any questions concerning the bill, please call us to discuss them.

Please sign the copy of this letter and the attached statement and return them to me in the enclosed envelope.

I look forward to working with you.

Sincerely yours,

By: _____
    Senior Partner

MMS/sc
enc.

UNDERSTOOD, AGREED AND ACCEPTED:

By: _____
    Jane P. Executrix

Date: _____

Minimize Costs

You should, within reason, endeavor to minimize the costs of professionals retained by the Estate. However, achieving the absolute lowest cost is not always the appropriate goal. Your time and efforts as Executor are valuable. Some tasks, even at a cost that appears significant, can be handled so much more effectively by an experienced professional expert, that the time and effort it would take you to handle the task is not worth the savings. In some instances, you may choose for the sake of family harmony, and your peace of mind, to have professionals handle much of the work. For example, your siblings may be quite jealous, or even angry, over the Executor's commission and fees that you are entitled to. You may choose to avoid any arguments with them by waiving all fees. Keep in mind that you will have to perform the sometimes considerable tasks of an Executor without compensation.

Contrast the preceding scenario with the situation where you are the only heir. In such a situation, the analysis is easy to make. Is each task a professional does worth the cost to you, or would you rather have responsibility of the particular task, and reap the savings in professional fees? If this approach fits your goals, be realistic about both your expertise and available time.

PROFESSIONAL ROLES

The following discussion provides background on most professionals you may need to consider hiring to help with the Estate.

Accountant

Accountants can handle important requirements for Probate. Someone will have to file a final income tax return on behalf of the Decedent. An accountant is often needed to assist with this. The final return has several complications as a result of the taxpayer's/Decedent's death so that an accountant with Probate experience may be a better choice. This is also important because of the interrelationships of the income and estate taxes (see Chapter 17).

Depending on the accountant's expertise, the size and complexity of the business, and other factors, the accountant may be able to provide a valuation report for a closely held business in lieu of an appraiser. For more complex business valuations, the appraiser may benefit from the assistance of the accountant.

If the business is to continue following the business owner's/Decedent's death, the accountant's services may be critical. If the accountant has actively represented the business for many years, the continuity of that relationship may be the key ingredient to the successful continuation of the business in the absence of the principal or founder.

The Estate will generally require an income tax return, as will any Trusts formed under the Estate. Although the Estate's attorney often can handle these filings, a qualified accounting firm will be able to do the work for less cost because it is focused on tax return preparation. Most law firms are not. Thus, accounting firms are familiar with meeting the deadlines, have the tax preparation software, and retain a full range of professional and paraprofessional staff with tax preparation experience. Generally, however, an experienced Probate attorney is the better choice for completing the Estate (not income) tax return. This is because so many components of the return are integrally tied to the Probate and other legal matters the attorney will typically be pursuing for the Estate.

CAUTION: Be certain that the Estate's accountant and attorney are in sync. Each should know who is responsible for what. Failure to coordinate could result in each believing the other firm is handling a matter that then is overlooked. It is also best for the accountant and attorney to work together, perhaps reviewing tax filings and other documentation, because each brings a different perspective and expertise.

How do you select the accountant to assist the Estate? Most Executors continue to retain the accountant who represented the Decedent. The advantages of this arrangement are the familiarity and trust built through years of a relationship. However, the regular accountant should not automatically be retained for Probate matters. You should inquire as to the accounting firm's experience and expertise in handling Probate matters. What are the tasks which the Estate requires the accountant to address? Are these substantially similar to those tasks which the accountant has successfully completed in the past? Do they differ sufficiently to warrant engaging a new accountant for some, or even all, matters?

Appraiser

Appraisers provide important services to many Estates. It is not uncommon for the same Estate to retain several different appraisers. If the Estate has jewelry, art, or other collectibles, they will often have to be appraised. Real estate, whether a personal residence or rental property, may have to be appraised. A closely held business or professional practice may have to be appraised. To understand how best to use appraisers, you must understand the reasons for needing an appraisal. Then some of the different uses of appraisers can be examined.

Appraisals can be necessary for several reasons.

Estate and Inheritance Taxes

If the Estate has to file a federal estate tax return, or a state inheritance (or other) tax return, all assets of the Estate must be valued. In such cases, any significant assets probably should be appraised.

Proving Income Tax Basis

Obtaining an appraisal can be important to document the value of any asset inherited to establish the Tax Basis of that asset for the Beneficiaries receiving it. Tax Basis is the cost of the asset, plus improvements, and less depreciation. Special rules apply when you receive property as an inheritance. On death, the Decedent's Tax Basis for an asset is generally increased (stepped up) to equal its value for federal Estate Tax purposes. This permits heirs to avoid any income tax or capital gain inherent in the assets Decedent owned at death.

EXAMPLE: Dan Decedent purchased stock in a local business in January 1990 worth $10,000. On Dan's death in March 2001, the stock was worth $100,000. If Dan had sold the stock before he died, he would have had a $18,000 capital gains tax [($100,000 − $10,000) × 20%]. If Dan had given his daughter, Harriet Heir the stock before he died, Harriet would have the same tax result if she sold the stock. However, if Harriet inherited the stock from Dan's Estate, the stock would receive a step-up in tax basis to the value at Dan's death, or $100,000. If Harriet later sells the stock for $100,000, she would have no taxable income!

Thus, documenting the Tax Basis of every asset is important. When a closely held business is involved, often the only way to prove the value is through an appraisal.

Distributing Assets as Required in the Will

Sometimes, an appraisal may be essential for you, as Executor, to carry out the instructions in the Will.

SAMPLE CLAUSE:

"I give and bequeath all of my tangible personal property to and among such of my children and the issue of any deceased child of mine, in such proportions or shares and upon such terms and conditions as the children shall agree. I direct that all articles not effectively appointed shall be sold by the Executor and I give and bequeath the net proceeds thereof to and among such of my children and the issue of any deceased child of mine in such proportions and amounts as shall equalize, so far as may be practicable, the value of the articles previously distributed to my children and the issue per stirpes of any deceased child of mine."

The sample provision requires that personal property, such as artwork, jewelry, furniture, and so on, be distributed as your children agree. Any property that they cannot agree to is to be sold. The proceeds should be distributed so that the dollar value given to each child is approximately equal. If all the children cannot agree to a value for each item of personal property that is distributed and not sold, appraisals will be necessary. Without appraisals of all personal property, it will be impossible to determine how to allocate the money received from the sale of the personal property the children did not choose or agree on.

Complying with Business or Other Contracts

Appraisals may be necessary to comply with a shareholders' or other agreement. If the Decedent owned stock in a closely held business, you as Executor may have to negotiate the sale of that stock pursuant to a buyout agreement.

SAMPLE LANGUAGE:

"If the Corporation and the representative of the deceased Shareholders' Estate cannot agree on the fair market value of such Shares, then the Corporation shall, at its sole expense and within six months of the date of the deceased Shareholder's death select an independent appraiser. If the Executor of deceased Shareholder's Estate does not accept such appraised value of the Corporation's interest in the Business according to such appraisal, then such Executor shall, at its sole expense and within the time periods required above, select its own independent appraiser to value the deceased Shareholder's interest in the Corporation. If the appraisers cannot agree on a value for such interest, then the appraisers shall select another independent appraiser, at the joint expense of the Corporation and the Estate, and the appraisal of such appraiser shall control."

To comply with this provision, you as Executor can accept the appraisal of the appraiser hired by the corporation. However, unless every Beneficiary of the Estate is willing to agree in writing to accept the valuation, and especially if the potential value is large and the valuation subject to many assumptions, as Executor it might be best for you to have an appraisal, as permitted under the sample agreement, to protect yourself from later claims that the value the Estate received was inadequate. For example, if you are the Executor and the Beneficiaries include minor children, unless you obtain an appraiser to represent the Estate, how can you demonstrate that the interests of the minor children were protected. The minor children are not able to legally (even if they are intellectually) sign off agreeing to the value of the corporation's appraiser (see Chapter 12).

Attorney

The attorney representing the Estate can be the most important professional in your Estate planning team. The Estate attorney often functions as the team leader for the professionals involved in the Probate process coordinating their respective efforts.

Many concerns arise about hiring an attorney for the Estate. Many people believe, mistakenly, that the attorney named in the Will must be used as the Estate attorney. If the Will does name an attorney, in most states this is deemed only to be a suggestion, not a requirement. If another attorney may be better suited to handle Probate matters, that attorney can be retained. Similarly, many people mistakenly believe that the lawyer who is holding the Decedent's original Will must be used to handle the Probate. The reality is that the attorney holding the original Will is merely that, the person holding the Will. There is no reason to hire that lawyer if he or she is not the best choice.

How should you select an attorney to represent the Estate? Inquire as to the proportion of firm work that is concentrated in Estate and Probate work. Do they have the staff, or relationships with other professionals, to handle unique issues that may arise? If the Estate owns real estate, or is facing litigation, does the firm have the expertise, or relationships with other firms that can provide it? It is not necessary for any firm to have all the expertise, so long as it can coordinate other professionals involved. You are better off with a firm that acknowledges the limitations of its expertise, than with a firm that puffs its capabilities to handle anything. What professional credentials do the attorneys have? Do they lecture, write, or take other steps to keep current?

Does the firm have layers of staff at differing billing rates? This is extremely important because many Probate matters are routine and can be handled by a beginning level associate, or a paraprofessional, or even a skilled secretary, at a fraction of the cost of a senior lawyer. On the other hand, some Probate tax and legal issues are extraordinarily complex and should only be addressed by an experienced attorney. Thus, a broad range of staff is probably in your best interest. There is no reason to pay $350 an hour for a routine matter. On the other hand, if you have a complex business valuation issue for which an IRS audit of lack of marketability discounts is a certainty, you want a senior and experienced estate practitioner to handle that aspect of the Estate.

Are you comfortable with their billing practices? Legal fees can be a significant expense of Probate. Will the firm work with you to minimize fees by involving you in administrative or other work? Or when you inquire, are you put off and left with the feeling that the firm wants to handle all aspects of the Estate?

Financial Professional

Financial professionals are essential in administering any Estate. Unless you are a professional investor, it is always advisable to have a professional manage the Estate's investment assets, or at minimum review periodically the Estate's investments and provide a written report as to the appropriateness of the strategies being pursued. Without a written and factually based plan, which is periodically reviewed and monitored, you could be held personally liable for investment losses the Estate realizes.

If the Estate includes a host of individual stocks, bonds, and other investment assets in the Decedent's safe deposit box or bureau drawer, a financial professional can minimize risk, reduce legal fees, and save substantial time, by taking charge of organizing and retitling the assets to a street name account. The back-office operations of many financial firms can handle the Estate's securities and investments, provide the transfer services to change the assets from the Decedent to the Estate and eventually to the appropriate Trusts or individual Beneficiaries, and provide valuation reports necessary to distribute assets and complete an Estate tax return. This can all be done for what is often little or no cost and can significantly reduce other professional fees.

Insurance Agent

Insurance agents are often an important component of the professional Estate planning team. Often, the insurance agent is one of the first to be contacted to assist the heirs, or you as Executor, in collecting insurance proceeds. Quick settlement of an insurance policy can provide cash to pay funeral expenses, hire other Estate professionals, meet family expenses, and cover other needs. While you can write the insurance companies directly, many heirs prefer the assistance of an agent, especially if there has been a long-term relationship with the family.

Who should be used as an insurance professional? There are several choices. The most common is to use the insurance agent of record on each policy involved. One advantage of this approach is that the agent should have records of the policy and be equipped to help. You can contact the insurance company itself and make arrangements. If a particular insurance agent or financial planner is helping the Estate, that person can assist in the collection process. The Estate attorney can also provide assistance.

Remember, most insurance agents do not bill hourly. The Estate lawyers and accountants will. Thus, any assistance the insurance agent can provide will almost assuredly provide savings. More important, an experienced insurance professional is likely to be the most efficient not only at processing insurance claims, but in helping you evaluate and purchase additional insurance that may be required for the Estate or Beneficiaries.

Real Estate Agent

A real estate agent can assist in several Estate matters. The heirs may have different real estate needs than prior to the Decedent's death. For example, the surviving widow or widower may now prefer the security of a condominium apartment or a smaller home. Skilled real estate professionals can assist in selling the prior home, purchasing a new home, providing appraisals of real estate held by the Estate, and identifying other professionals the Estate can use to help deal with real estate needs. The real estate agent can direct you to insurance agents to review the insurance coverage for real estate held by the Estate. An agent can direct you to a local alarm company to install an alarm to protect vacant property.

Trust Officer

A bank trust officer or an officer of a trust company can be involved with an Estate as a result of the Will appointing the bank or trust company as Executor, Co-Executor, Trustee, or Co-Trustee. When a bank or trust company is named as Fiduciary, it will generally appoint a particular trust officer as primarily responsible for the account. That trust officer will be the main contact for you as a Co-Fiduciary.

In other instances, you may wish to retain the services of an institution such as a bank trust department, or an independent trust company, to assist you. Depending on the particular institution, and the Estate's needs, the level of services can range from merely providing investment counsel, to a complete package of services including handling all expenses, business interests, and so on. If your time constraints, lack of experience, or other factors indicate it is appropriate, hiring an institution can provide a tremendous degree of assistance.

The marketplace for institutional Fiduciaries has become so competitive that the services that can be obtained with an institution serving as an Executor or Trustee, or even merely providing services to the Executor or Trustee for a fee, are often of high quality and priced reasonably. Many of the old worries about institutions serving as Fiduciaries or assisting Estates simply no longer apply, or were unfounded.

CONCLUSION

You and other nonprofessionals can serve many roles. However, there are numerous categories of professionals that you should consider retaining to assist the Estate. Your prudent selection of professionals, efficient management of them once retained, and smooth coordination between the nonprofessionals (whether Beneficiaries or Fiduciaries) and the professionals (attorneys, accountants, etc.) will help assure a cost- and time-effective settlement of the Estate.

Part Two

LEGAL MATTERS AND COURT PROCEEDINGS

4 HOW TO READ THE WILL

Reading and understanding the Will is an essential step for every Fiduciary (Executor, Trustee, and Guardian) and even for any Beneficiary who wants to be sure that he or she received everything provided. If the Decedent signed a Revocable Living Trust to address many or all of the issues covered in a Will, then the Trust will have to be read as well as the Will.

Just as importantly, this discussion of the provisions in a comprehensive Will provides an excellent overview of many aspects of the Probate process. Many Will provisions highlight decisions, steps, or issues you may face as an Executor, Trustee, Guardian, or Beneficiary. Thus, even if the estate you are handling is an Intestate Estate (i.e., the Decedent died without a Will) reading through the explanatory notes in the illustrative Will can provide useful information and planning points.

This chapter provides a detailed discussion of a hypothetical Will. You should not consider this Will to be a model because it includes inconsistent provisions for illustrative purposes. Many boilerplate provisions that are unlikely to have much relevance to readers have simply been omitted. Also, the comments are directed to the decisions you will face as an Executor after the death of the Testator who signed the Will. The decisions that the Testator should make before signing a Will are quite different.

NOTE: For a comprehensive sample Will, see Martin M. Shenkman, *The Complete Book of Trusts* (2d ed.) (New York: John Wiley & Sons, 1998), Professional Edition. Also see the Web site: www.laweasy.com.

The actual Will you are working with for a particular Probate will undoubtedly differ significantly from the Will illustrated. Every attorney has his or her own style, every Estate its own nuances. If the attorney was not an Estate specialist, the Will is likely to be much shorter and will not address many of the provisions discussed in the illustrative Will. If the Estate is complex, the Will undoubtedly contains lengthy provisions that are not addressed here. However, the illustrative Will includes many instructive sample clauses and explanations of planning points that can still be of help.

An understanding of the provisions of the Will alone is not enough. In many cases, the customs and practices of the local Surrogate's Court where you take the Will for Probate are important. You can get this information from telephone conferences with the clerks in the Court and from the local professionals you hire.

CAUTION: The sample Will in this chapter is not intended to illustrate an actual Will. It is not a complete Will. Key provisions have been left out. It also includes some contradictory provisions. The purpose is to provide a sample of many of the important Will provisions you will have to deal with, to help you understand how to read a Will, and to then use it as the road map for the Probate of the Decedent's Estate. Although the Decedent's actual Will differs, it should have many provisions similar to those shown here. Thus, even if a provision is not a perfect match, the comments will still provide relevant guidance. As with any legal document, confirm your understandings with the Estate attorney.

LAST WILL OF DAN DECEDENT

NOTE: Verify early on whether the Decedent, and the surviving spouse, if any, are United States citizens. This can have important income and Estate tax consequences. If either is not a citizen, be sure to obtain help from an Estate attorney or tax accountant. Also, most Wills state where the Decedent was resident or domiciled in the first paragraph. This can be important for determining the state and county in which you will have the Will admitted to Probate. However, if the Decedent moved after signing the Will, a different county or state may be appropriate.

NOTE: Although most every Will states that prior Wills are revoked, do not discard any old Wills. In the event of a Will challenge by a disgruntled heir, they might be extremely useful to show the progression of the Decedent's intent, from Will to Will over time (see Chapter 6).

I, Dan Decedent, a Citizen and Resident of the United States, residing at 123 Main Street, Anytown, USA, make, publish and declare this my Last Will and Testament (my "Will") and revoke all Wills heretofore made by me.

B. *Burial Instructions*

NOTE: Burial instructions are often included in a Will. However, the Decedent may have provided direction in his Living Will or may have prepared a Letter of Last Instructions to address funeral and burial instructions. A copy of this letter might be in the Decedent's safe deposit box. Be sure to check all these documents. However, it can be advantageous to include such information in the Will as well if any significant costs are to be incurred. The inclusion in the Will can enable the Executor to have authority to incur the required expenditures.

I direct that I be cremated and my ashes spread from a hot air balloon over the ocean while my favorite tune is played on the radio.

C. *Debts and Administrative Expenses of the Estate*

NOTE: This provision is almost always included in the Will as a directive to the Executor since expenses must be paid or the Executor may be held personally liable. It provides generally for the prompt payment of final expenses and debts of the Decedent. The purpose of the debts clause may be to state the source from which certain debts are to be paid (this is important because you do not want debts to reduce the marital deduction property) and to establish as debts items that might not otherwise be considered the Decedent's obligations. If there are any significant or unusual financial arrangements, the Decedent may address them in this type of clause. Also, consider the provision, "Foregiveness of Debt or Mortgage," concerning relief of indebtedness of certain parties.

Be very careful to diligently identify all debts that you are required to pay. Many states permit the publication of a notice in an official newspaper to limit the time period in which creditors of the Estate can present their claims. If you distribute Estate assets before claims are satisfied, you could be held personally liable. Also, some claims against the Decedent may not have to be paid. Consult with the Estate attorney for clarification. Be sure all debts are properly reflected on the Estate tax return.

I direct that any expenses of my last illness and funeral, any administrative or similar expenses incurred as a result of my death and the administration of my Estate, as well as any of my debts, be paid as soon after my death as would be advantageous to the administration of my estate. These debts shall not include:

NOTE: You may choose to prepay real estate mortgages only where the rates have come down significantly. If rates have risen, leave the mortgages intact. This should all be coordinated with the Estate's liquidity needs (see Chapter 8).

---

1. Obligations secured by mortgages on real estate or cooperative apartments, which debts I direct the Executor to pay in such Executor's discretion; or

2. Debts owing insurance companies secured by insurance policies, which debts I intend should be first satisfied out of the proceeds of the policies securing them.

3. This provision shall not serve to revive any of my debts barred by the statute of limitations or limit the payment by the Executor of periodic obligations as due.

4. I direct that all Estate management expenses, but transmission expenses, be allocated and paid from the Q-TIP or other marital deduction, if any, if they will not result in a reduction of the marital deduction.

D. *Estate, Inheritance, and Other Death Taxes*

NOTE: The provisions of a Will setting forth how taxes shall be paid, and from what assets of the Estate, are vitally important to understand. For any Estate that has a tax obligation, these provisions can be critically important to determining what each Beneficiary under the Will ultimately inherits. Applying the tax allocation provisions, and understanding the tax consequences, as well as state law implications, for any Will using more than the most basic approach, is extremely complex. Never attempt to address this without professional tax advice. These more complex situations are discussed in Chapter 18. The following illustrative provision is similar to that used in a basic Will.

NOTE: The following provision merely provides that as Executor you will pay the Estate taxes "off the top." After taxes are paid, you will then follow through sequentially the other distribution provisions of the Will. There can be exceptions, so if the Estate is large or there are unequal distributions to different persons, consult with your probate attorney or tax accountant before proceeding. If there is also a Revocable Living Trust, and the Estate taxes are significant, consult an Estate tax specialist as to how the tax costs should be allocated.

All estate, inheritance, legacy, succession, transfer or other death taxes (and any interest and penalties on such taxes) imposed by any domestic or foreign taxing authority with respect to all property taxable by reason of my death, whether or not such property passes under this Will and whether such taxes otherwise would be payable by my estate or by any recipient of and such property, shall be paid out of my estate as an administration expense without apportionment within or outside my residuary estate and with no right of reimbursement from any recipient of any such property (including reimbursement under Section 2207(B).

NOTE: The following sections begin to address distribution of the Decedent's assets. A number of general considerations concerning such distributions should be addressed. Carefully identify and document the decisions as to who is to receive what assets. If a Beneficiary named has died, the next successor Beneficiary will share in the Bequest. If there are no successors named, Wills typically have the personal property distributed under the general "Residuary" clause (the provisions saying where everything else goes). If the Will left assets to the Decedent's two children by name then gave birth to additional children after signing the Will, do those additional children receive a bequest? The answer can depend on the wording of the Will and state law. Consult with an Estate attorney. If the Decedent named a class or group of people (e.g., "all my first cousins"), make sure it is absolutely clear who is included and not included in that group and document your conclusions.

E. *Specific Bequest of Tangible Personal Property*

I give and bequeath my collection of fishing rods to Jay Apple. If such beneficiary does not survive me, then all property appointed under this provision shall be disposed of as provided in the General Bequest of Tangible Personal Property provision, below.

NOTE: Many Wills list specific personal property: pleasure boats; pictures; books; linen; china; livestock; household furniture; automobiles. Be certain that you have identified all property listed. If specific property is named ("My diamond ring to my daughter Jane") and that property is not owned by the Decedent at death, consult with the Estate attorney. You may want to take precautions to satisfy the IRS and Jane that the ring was previously disposed of. They may both be concerned that someone took the ring following death.

Review any Letter of Instructions to address how personal property such as jewelry should be distributed if the Will is vague or silent. Depending on the language of the Will, the Letter of Instructions, and state law, the terms of the Letter of Instructions may or may not be binding. If there is any disagreement between the Beneficiaries listed, consult the Estate attorney. Be certain to have all the Beneficiaries named sign off in writing agreeing to the allocation of personal property.

Personal property will often have to be appraised. Insurance may be necessary. You may also have to take steps to safeguard the assets pending their appraisal and distribution. Quick action, especially with expensive and small objects such as jewelry, is important.

F. *General Bequest of Tangible Personal Property*

NOTE: If the Decedent divorced or legally separated (and signed a separation agreement), be certain to review the applicability of any provisions providing bequests to the Decedent's spouse. They may, or may not, still apply.

---

1. *Distribution of Tangible Property Generally*

I give and bequeath all of my tangible personal property, not disposed of in prior provision of this Will, wherever located, to my spouse, Susan Spouse (herein "spouse"), or if my spouse should not survive me, I give and bequeath such articles of my tangible personal property to and among such of my children and the issue of any deceased child of mine, in such proportions or shares and upon such terms and conditions as the Executor may direct and appoint by a written instrument delivered to each appointee with respect to the specific article or articles so appointed. The receipt of the appointee if adult, or if a minor of his or her parent or the person with whom he or she resides, shall be a full and sufficient discharge to the Fiduciary from all liabilities with respect to the specific article or articles so appointed. I direct that all articles not effectively appointed shall be sold by the Executor and I give and bequeath the net proceeds thereof to and among such of my children and the issue of any deceased child of mine in such proportions and amounts as shall equalize, so far as may be practicable, the value of the articles previously appointed to or for the benefit of each of my children and the issue per stirpes of any deceased child of mine.

NOTE: Even if the Will does not address the following issues, you will have to address the disposition of personal property when a minor is the Beneficiary. (Can you just give it to the minor's Guardian?) Storage, shipping, selling expenses, insurance, and other practical issues will have to be addressed even if the Will is silent. If this is the case, you should check with the Estate's attorney as to the responsibility for any significant costs. For example, assume the Decedent lived in New York City, and one Beneficiary lived in New York City and the second in San Francisco. The Decedent bequeathed his valuable antique furniture collection equally to each child. The child in New York will have little shipping costs to claim her share. The costs to ship the furniture to San Francisco could be substantial. Who pays? The Estate? The Beneficiary? Clarify the answer before committing to the costs.

---

2. *Property of Minor May Be Stored*

My Fiduciary may store any tangible personal property (other than cash) hereby given to any minor until such minor shall attain majority and charge the expenses of such storage to such minor and/or sell such property, for such price and upon such terms as my Fiduciary shall determine, and dispose of the net proceeds of such sale as if such net proceeds had been given to such minor by the provisions hereof.

3. *Shipping and Related Costs*

All costs, if any, of shipping, packing, and insuring any of my personal property transferred under any provision of this Will shall be paid by my Estate. In addition, any insurance policy covering personal property, shall, to the extent advantageous to the administration of my Estate, be transferred with the property insured.

4. *Disposition of Proceeds from Sale of Tangible Property* ·

In the event any items of tangible personal property are sold, if the proceeds of such sale are material in amount, as determined in the discretion of the Executor, then my Fiduciary may direct that such proceeds be given to any of my minor children, or minor issue of any deceased child of mine in trust in accordance with the applicable trust provisions below.

G. *Distribution of Real Estate*

NOTE: Consider the address where the real property is located. If the address is outside the state of Domicile for the Decedent inquire as to facts relating to residency and Domicile. Be certain to pin down the proper state for the Probate proceeding. Tax and other considerations can be substantial. Many people want to see a clause in their Will assuring that their spouse obtains the marital residence on death. In other situations, the following type of clause could be extremely detrimental to the intended tax plan. If the estate exceeds $650,000 (1999) and the Decedent could benefit from using a Bypass Trust to protect this exemption amount, the house may be one asset intended to be used (or essential to be used) to fund the Trust. Be certain to review the issues of funding the Bypass Trust in the context of the balance sheet of Estate assets you assemble, the provisions of the Will, and the title to the assets involved before making any major distributions. A Disclaimer may be used to remedy the situation.

I give, devise, and bequeath (i) all real property and interests therein, wherever situated, and (ii) all stock in any co-operative apartment corporation, together with the appurtenant proprietary lease covering any apartment, which I may own at the time of my death and which property my spouse and I shall be occupying as a place of residence, whether permanent, temporary, or seasonal, to my spouse, if my spouse shall survive me.

H. *Forgiveness of Debt or Mortgage*

NOTE: Confirm the details of any actual note or loan arrangement. Is the Estate entitled to interest that has not been paid? For tax planning purposes, some taxpayers include a provision that cancels the note on their death. This is called a "Self-Canceling Installment Note." It is sometimes referred to by the acronym "SCIN." The use of a SCIN raises complex issues that should be addressed with the Estate's tax adviser.

If I am a mortgagee on any mortgage on the real property located at 123 Main Street, Anytown, USA, and Mary Mortgagor has an equity interests in such property, then an amount equal to the value outstanding balance due to me or my estate from such person under such mortgage shall be transferred to such person for repayment of said mortgage and such mortgage shall be canceled.

I. *Specific Pecuniary (Dollar) Bequests*

CAUTION: If the Will provides that payment should, for example, only be made on the death of the last of the husband and wife, if they died in close time to each other, you should have the Estate attorney carefully review the "Simultaneous Death" provision in the Will and what the state law provides. You may have to be careful to interpret the Will properly in light of which of the two is deemed to have died first.

The following sample clauses illustrate another potential problem. If the dollar bequest is limited to a percentage of the Estate, you may not be able to distribute it until the entire Probate is concluded in order to be sure that the limitation does not apply.

When analyzing pecuniary bequest provisions, determine whether interest has to be paid on the bequest. Some Wills specifically state that no interest should be paid. If the Will is silent, you must analyze state law. The Surrogate's Court may also be able to provide guidance.

You should also carefully read the "Tax Allocation" provisions of the Will. If any tax is due (even if no federal estate tax is due, there could be a state inheritance or estate tax) are the persons receiving the specific dollar bequests to bear any share of it?

Finally, it is often wise to obtain a signed and notarized "Receipt and Release" from each Beneficiary wherein the Beneficiary acknowledges that they have received the bequest under the Will in full and that they have no further claims against the Estate.

---

1. On the death of the last of myself and my spouse, I give and bequeath the following legacies to such of the persons hereinafter named as shall survive me and to such of the organizations hereinafter named as shall at the time of my death be in existence, for their general purposes:

a. $10,000 to Larry Lucky, or such beneficiary's issue, per stirpes, if such beneficiary is deceased. However, in no event shall this bequest exceed 1 percent of my gross estate.

b. $95,000 to John Smith, or such beneficiary's issue, per stirpes, if such beneficiary is deceased. However, in no event shall this bequest exceed 3.5 percent of my gross estate.

2. No interest shall be payable on the above legacies by reason of nonpayment prior to the final determination of the federal estate tax.

J. *Charitable Bequest*

NOTE: Charitable bequests may require additional reporting requirements. Check with the Estate's attorney. Before making charitable distributions, request a copy of the charities' tax exempt ruling from the IRS so that you will have a record in your files demonstrating that the bequest is deductible for federal estate tax purposes.

I give the sum of $15,000.00 to Caring Charity. I direct my Fiduciary to distribute outright to the charitable organizations named such bequest. If the institution named does not exist at the time of my death, or is for any reason unable or unwilling to accept the bequests under the terms and conditions of this provision, if any, then the bequest and devise to such charitable organization shall be disposed of as part of my residuary estate. If the organization is subject of a mere change in name, or merger into a successor organization serving substantially the same purposes, such organization shall be considered to exist and the gift and bequest below shall not lapse. Where any such charitable organization shall not be qualified as a tax-exempt organization under the Internal Revenue Code as an organization to which testamentary gifts are deductible for federal estate tax purposes, then the bequest to such organization shall lapse.

K. *Generation-Skipping Transfer Tax (GST) $1 Million Trust*

NOTE: If the Estate is sufficiently large, a Generation-Skipping Transfer (GST) Tax Trust for grandchildren and other heirs may have been established under the Will. Be certain to review the required election provisions on the federal estate tax return with the Estate's attorney to assure that the election is properly made to achieve the desired estate and GST result. If a GST trust is established, the "Bypass Trust" illustrated in the following provision would likely be omitted. If there is no specific GST bequest in the Will, don't assume that GST is not relevant. It may be advisable to allocate the GST exemption amount to the Bypass Trust illustrated in the next provision. The exemption amount was indexed in the 1997 Tax Act so the actual bequest can exceed $1 million unless the Will is written capping the amount at $1 million, as in this sample Will.

---

1. Determination of GST Trust Amount

I give, devise, and bequeath, an amount not in excess of my remaining GST exemption (within the meaning of Code Section 2631) that has not been allocated to any other property during my lifetime or after my death. I direct that this GST-Exempt Trust shall be funded with an amount such that it shall have an applicable fraction of One (1) and an inclusion rate of Zero (-0-) (within the meaning of Code Section 2642) for all property comprised in this GST-Exempt Trust. No descendant of mine who is an executor shall participate in the allocation of my GST exemption for purposes of this provision.

2. GST Pot Trust for Grandchildren

The Trustee shall hold the amount determined in the preceding paragraph, in trust, for the use and benefit of my Grandchildren, to be held in a single trust of all of my Grandchildren then surviving. The Trustee is hereby directed to manage, invest and reinvest the same, to collect the income thereof, and to pay over the net income to or for the benefit of such one or more of my Grandchildren living from time to time, to such extent, in such amount and proportions and at such time or times as the Trustee shall determine appropriate for the health, education, maintenance and support of such Grandchildren. Any net income not so paid over or applied shall be accumulated, and added to the Trust Estate at least annually and thereafter shall be held, administrated, and disposed of as a part of the Trust Estate of this GST-Exempt Trust. Upon the youngest of my Grandchildren living upon my death reaching the age of Thirty Five (35) years, or upon the death of my youngest Grandchild living at any time if my other Grandchildren living shall all have then reached the age of Thirty Five (35) years, or upon the death of the last to die of all my Grandchildren if none of them shall reach the age of Thirty Five (35) years, whichever event is the first to occur, the GST-Exempt Trust provided for under this provision shall terminate and the Trustee shall transfer, convey, and pay over the principal of the trust to my then living issue per stirpes.

L. *Preresiduary Bypass Sprinkle Trust to Use the Applicable Exclusion Amount*

NOTE: For 1999 and later, the "applicable exclusion amount" permits taxpayers to give away up to $650,000 in assets without incurring any gift or estate tax. This amount has been increased, in periodic increments, to eventually reach $1 million. This benchmark is extremely important. If the value of the Estate is under the exclusion amount, or exemption at it is sometimes called, no federal estate tax return has to be filed.

---

1. Determining Amount of Bypass Trust

NOTE: The following provision is a pecuniary Bypass Trust. Any appreciation or income earned during the settlement of the Estate will inure to the benefit of the residuary Beneficiary and not to the Bypass Trust. To have appreciation and income inure to the benefit of the Bypass Trust, the Will would have had to use a pecuniary bequest for the marital bequest and the residuary clause for the Bypass Trust. Alternatively, a fractional share approach could be used so that the gains and losses are shared proportionately between the Bypass Trust, and the marital residuary. These complex tax and legal drafting concepts are important since they should be considered in determining what property to use to fund the different trusts. They will also affect the income tax consequences of the funding. If you fund a pecuniary Bypass Trust with assets that have appreciated since the Decedent's death, a taxable gain may be realized. If you are not clear on the best approaches to address the facts for the Trust you are funding, then these issues should be discussed with the Estate attorney or accountant (see Chapter 17).

---

a. If my spouse survives me, I give to the Trustee, in trust, a pecuniary sum equal to the largest amount which will not result in any federal estate tax payable after giving effect to the unified credit to which I am entitled, as well as the state death tax credit and other credits applicable to my estate. This amount shall be determined without regard to this provision of my Will. The trust formed, if any, under this provision, shall be known as the "Bypass Trust."

b. In determining the credits applicable, state death tax credit shall only be considered to the extent that it will not increase the state death tax liability.

NOTE: The following paragraph indicates why the Bypass Trust cannot simply be funded with the maximum exemption amount ($650,000 in 1999). Other distributions or gifts may apply to reduce the exemption still available. This is why the proper valuation of any previous distributions the Will provides (other than to charities or for a surviving spouse) is so important. It is also essential for you to confirm whether any taxable gifts had been made by the Decedent before death.

---

c. The amount so calculated shall be reduced by the following: (i) The value of property transferred under previous provisions of this Will which do not qualify for the marital deduction (or for which no marital deduction is claimed); (ii) Property passing outside this Will which is included in my gross estate and does not qualify for the marital deduction (or for which no marital deduction is claimed); (iii) Administration expenses and principal payments on debts that are not allowed as deductions for my federal estate tax; and (iv) the amount of any adjusted taxable gifts as defined under Code Section 2001, which were made by me after December 31, 1976.

d. For the purpose of establishing the amount disposed of by this provision the values finally fixed in the federal estate tax proceeding relating to my estate shall be used. I understand that no sum may be disposed of by this provision and that the sum so disposed of may be affected by the action of the Trustee in exercising certain tax elections.

NOTE: Your decision as Executor to elect, or not to elect, to qualify certain distributions in Trust for the surviving spouse for the Estate tax marital deduction may affect the amount of the Bypass Trust.

---

e. I recognize that no amount may be disposed of under this provision of my Will, or that if any amount is disposed of under this provision, that such amount may be affected by the actions taken, or not taken, by my Executor.

2. *Sprinkle Bypass*

NOTE: The Bypass Trust can be drafted to permit income and principal to be sprinkled to named Beneficiaries or solely for the spouse. It is important for the Trustee of the Bypass Trust to follow these guidelines. Also, carefully identifying the Beneficiaries of the Bypass Trust may help you make a better GST planning decision for the Estate. If the Bypass Trust includes language such as "to my spouse and my descendants" then distributions may be made in the future to grandchildren. It may then be advisable to allocate GST exemption to the Bypass Trust so that future distributions to grandchildren will be exempt from GST.

---

a. The Trustee shall hold, manage, and invest the amounts held in this Trust. The Trustee shall collect and receive any income, and shall pay over or apply any portion or all of the net income or principal, or both, whether equal or unequal, at such times as the Trustee shall determine, to or for the benefit of such one or more members of a class consisting of my spouse, my children, and other descendants living from time to time (collectively, the "Recipients"), as the Trustee shall determine necessary or advisable for the health, support, and maintenance of the Recipients. Any net income not so paid over or applied for the benefit of the persons named in this provision, shall be accumulated and added to the principal of the Trust Estate, at least annually, and thereafter shall be held, administered and disposed of as a part of the Trust Estate of this Bypass Trust.

      b. Any determinations as to distributions shall only be made by the Trustee then serving, or next appointed, other than my spouse.

      c. These payments and applications may be made irrespective of the fact that such payments may exhaust the principal of the trust being held for the benefit of any persons. The determinations of the Trustee as to the amount of principal payments or applications under this provision shall be final and conclusive on all persons with any interest in this Trust. Upon the making of any payments or applications under this provision, my Trustee shall be fully released and discharged from any further liability or accountability.

      3. *Termination of Bypass Trust*

NOTE: The Trustee must understand when any particular Trust is to end. At that point an accounting should be made, the remainder (final) Beneficiaries sign Receipts and Releases, and distributions are made (see Chapter 20).

This Trust shall terminate upon the death of my spouse whereupon the fiduciary shall transfer and pay over the Trust Estate to my then living descendants, per stirpes.

      M. *Lapsed Bequests and Devises Disposed of as Part of Residuary*

NOTE: Any Probate assets not distributed under the prior provisions (or whatever specific provisions the Will you are working with provides) are then distributed under the final provisions of the Will. These remaining Probate Assets—what is left—are referred to as the Residuary, or the Residuary Estate. One common implication to this is that many Wills provided in the Tax Allocation Clause that all taxes are allocated or paid from the Residuary Estate. When this occurs, the preceding provisions (e.g., distribution of specific dollar bequests, distribution of personal property) are made free of any need for those Beneficiaries to pay taxes on their inheritances. Taxes are then paid from the residuary, after which remaining assets are distributed as provided in the Residuary Will provisions.

In the event that any Beneficiary or recipient to whom any prior provision of my Will gave, devised, or bequeathed property did not survive me (as determined in accordance with the Simultaneous Death provision below, and applicable law) and no alternative disposition was specifically provided for such property, than such gift, devise, and bequest, shall lapse and such property shall be disposed of in accordance with the provisions below disposing of my Residuary Estate.

      N. *Residuary Estate*

NOTE: When determining the specific people to receive assets under the Decedent's Will's Residuary clauses, be careful with your interpretations of the wording used. If two children are named in the Will, what if there are children who were born after the Will was signed, are they to be included? While fairness obviously dictates so, consider whether the omission was accidental or intentional.

What does state law provide for? Should adopted children be treated the same as the Decedent's natural children? Anytime these types of issue arise, you should consult with a Probate attorney for guidance. Also, if there is any uncertainty, it may be advisable to have everyone involved agree in writing to the decisions made. If a minor is involved, it may be necessary (and even if not required, it may still be advisable) to have a Court confirm the decisions.

All the rest, residue, and remainder of my property, wherever situated, and all property that I shall be entitled to dispose of at my death after deducting all my debts, funeral expenses, and any expenses of the administration of my Estate (my "Residuary Estate") shall be disposed of as follows:

  1. *Disclaimer to Use Lower Progressive Tax Rates*

NOTE: The federal estate tax rates are progressive. This means that the larger the Taxable Estate, the higher the percentage tax rate that applies. In some situations, it may be advisable on the death of the first spouse to intentionally cause some tax to be paid at the lower estate tax rates (see Chapter 18).

Should my spouse renounce any portion or all of this distribution, and such renunciation is effective for purposes of federal income tax and applicable state law, such distribution shall instead be distributed as provided in the following paragraphs:

a. The portion of such assets renounced which equal the maximum dollar amount that would be taxed for federal estate tax purposes at marginal federal estate tax rates which are less than the then highest marginal federal estate tax rate shall be distributed to, and become part of, the Bypass Trust, established herein. The purpose and intent of this provision is to permit my surviving spouse to take advantage of the graduated federal estate tax rates in my estate where I predecease my spouse.

b. Any assets renounced by my spouse above the amount provided for in the preceding paragraph shall be distributed in accordance with the provision "Distribution to Multiple Children's Trusts," below. I suggest, but do not require, that my spouse not consider renouncing assets greater than those set forth in the preceding paragraph.

  2. *Disclaimer Bypass Trust*

NOTE: If the estate may not exceed the applicable exclusion amount ($650,000 in 1999), in lieu of an automatic Bypass Trust the following Disclaimer approach, as illustrated, may be used. When this is done, it is essential that you and the tax advisers to the Estate prepare a family balance sheet to determine whether the combined estate is likely to exceed the exclusion amount. If it will, consideration should be given to encouraging the surviving spouse to Disclaim assets into a Bypass Trust assuming the Will permits this. If the Will does not have such an arrangement, a Disclaimer could still be used but then the surviving spouse will not have any access to the assets (see Chapter 18).

---

a. I give, devise, and bequeath my net residuary estate to my spouse, if my spouse should survive me for Sixty (60) days.

b. If my spouse shall Disclaim and Renounce any portion or all of the preceding bequest, then such disclaimed and renounced portion, but not in excess of the amount specified in the following provision, I give, devise, and bequeath to the Bypass Trust provided in the following provision.

NOTE: If the surviving spouse Disclaims Probate Assets to fund a Bypass Trust (or disclaims non-Probate Assets, such as certain joint assets or assets on which the surviving spouse is named Beneficiary), these assets can be used to fund the Bypass Trust. These provisions are similar to those in the Bypass Trust illustrated earlier and hence are not repeated here.

3. QTIP Trust for Surviving Spouse

NOTE: A common planning technique, especially for second marriages is to leave all assets in a trust. This permits the Decedent's Estate to qualify for the unlimited estate tax marital deduction while still controlling who the ultimate Beneficiaries and Trustees are. The following paragraphs can be used to establish a Trust that can qualify for the unlimited Estate Tax marital deduction to hold the surviving spouse's share (i.e., the balance of the Estate after the Bypass Trust bequest) in a marital trust. A host of points should be considered. Consider the investment provisions in the Will and the requirement under the federal tax laws that the surviving spouse must receive income annually from this QTIP trust. If trust assets are invested to minimize income, a substantial tax benefit could be jeopardized. The Tax Allocation Clause should not allocate taxes against the marital deduction distributions. If it does, there will be a "spoiler" effect—additional taxes will be triggered as the marital deduction is reduced. What powers have the surviving spouse and Trustees been given over the QTIP trust? The Trustees or spouse may have various degrees of power to invade the principal of the QTIP trust. Be certain that they are aware of the rights they have. Finally, you will have to make an election on the Estate Tax Return to qualify the QTIP trust for the marital deduction. Be certain to review this with the Estate's attorney preparing the forms.

a. QTIP: Bequest to Spouse in Trust

If my spouse shall survive me, I give, devise, and bequeath my net residuary estate to the Trustee of the Trust created hereunder, in Trust, to pay or apply the net income thereof to or for the benefit of my spouse in annual or more frequent installments. I intend by this bequest to secure for my Estate the benefit of the marital deduction provided in Code Section 2056 and, in particular, to create in my spouse a qualifying income interest for life in my net Residuary Estate. The Trustee shall, in the Trustee's discretion, determine whether to elect under the Code to qualify all, or any part, of this trust for the marital deduction. I would anticipate, however, that the Trustee would elect to minimize the federal estate tax payable by my Estate. If required by applicable tax law or regulation to qualify this trust for the unlimited marital deduction, I direct my Trustee to distribute any income earned by such Trust, through and including the date of death of my surviving spouse, to the estate of my spouse in the year of the death of my spouse.

b. Right to Spouse to Compel Investment in Productive Assets

I direct that my spouse shall have the right and power to compel my Trustee of the Trust formed under this provision to convert any nonproductive property held in this trust into income-producing property and that any provision of this Will which would prevent the allowance of the marital deduction for federal estate tax purposes shall not apply to this Trust.

c. Limited Power of Appointment over QTIP Trust

NOTE: If you serve as Trustee of any Trust under the Decedent's Will, you have to be alert to the presence of a Power of Appointment granted to anyone. The following paragraph gives the Decedent's surviving spouse the right or power to designate persons to receive distributions from the QTIP Trust. If someone has such a power, you should be certain that they are aware of their rights. If the person given the power wants to use it, be certain that the use conforms strictly with the requirements under the Will (or Trust). Be certain to save a copy of the document (e.g., Will) used to exercise the power in the permanent records of the Estate or Trust.

During the life of my spouse, and thereafter, the Trustee shall distribute such amounts from the principal of the QTIP Trust, to such one or more of my issue, in such proportion and manner, in Trust or otherwise, as my spouse shall appoint by a written instrument signed, acknowledged, and delivered to my Trustee, during my spouse's lifetime, or as my spouse may appoint by my spouse's Last Will and Testament or any codicil thereto. However, no property shall be appointed in discharge of any legal obligations of my spouse, and no appointment shall be effective absent a specific reference to this provision.

   d. *Disposition of Trust Estate on Death of Spouse*

On the death of my spouse, the Trustee shall transfer and pay over the Trust Estate per stirpes to such of my issue as shall then be living.

   4. *Pour Over Residuary into Revocable Living Trust of Testator*

NOTE: When the Decedent had a Revocable Living Trust a "Pour Over" Will is generally (but not always) used to transfer, or "pour" Probate Assets into the Trust for distribution from the Trust. What happens if the Revocable Living Trust was not properly formed, or is found for some reason to be invalid? Be certain to confirm the status with the Estate attorney before completing any transfers. Watch out for any inconsistencies between the two documents that may affect taxes or distributions.

---

   a. I give, devise, and bequeath my net residuary estate to the Fiduciary in office at the time of my death under a certain Trust Agreement entitled Dan Decedent Revocable Living Trust made January 1, 1999, between myself and Tommy Trustworthy as Co-Trustee, to be held, administered, and disposed of by my Co-Trustees in accordance with the provisions of said Trust Agreement.

   b. In the event that for any reason the above named trust is held or found to be invalid, or if for any other reason the assets of my estate cannot be properly transferred to such trust, then, in such event, all the rest of my residuary estate shall be disposed of in accordance with the following provisions of my Will.

   5. *Residuary to Children*

NOTE: The Trustees must understand the termination dates or triggers for each Trust, and the distribution provisions thereafter. Also, they should be alert to necessary changes in investment strategies as Trusts are changed. There may also be changes in the persons serving as Trustees of the various Trusts.

---

   a. On the death of my spouse, if my spouse survived me, the principal and any undistributed income not then added to principal of any QTIP Trust or other Trust designated as terminating on the death of my spouse; or if my spouse did not survive me, on my death, my net Residuary Estate shall be divided into a sufficient number of shares so that there shall be set aside one such share for each child of mine, Per Stirpes, to be disposed of as follows:

      (1) If any child of mine has previously died, the share, if any, set aside for his or her then living descendants shall be transferred, and I give, devise, and bequeath the same to

such descendants, shares per stirpes. These transfers shall be either in trust, or free from trust, in accordance with the principles set forth in the following provisions.

(2) If any child of mine shall have then reached the age of Thirty-Five (35) years, the share set aside for such child shall be transferred, conveyed, and paid over, and I give, devise, and bequeath the same to such child.

(3) If any child of mine shall not then have reached the age of Thirty-Five (35) years, the share set aside for such child shall be held in Trust by, and I give, devise, and bequeath the same to, the Trustee hereinafter named, in Trust, for the following uses and purposes (the "Distribution by Age"):

NOTE: Be sure to obtain proof of every Beneficiary's birthdate and calendar required distribution dates. Watch income distribution requirements. They can vary significantly between Wills, and even for different Trusts in the same Will.

(a) To manage and invest the assets of each Trust, to collect the income from the Trust, and if the child is under the age of Thirty-Five (35) years at the time his or her share is set aside, to apply so much of the net income and the principal as determined by my Trustee in such Trustee's discretion, for such child's support, maintenance, health, or education to such extent and at such time and in such manner as the Fiduciary shall determine, without court order and without regard to the duty of any person to support such child. Any net income not so applied shall be added to the principal of the Trust and thereafter shall be held, administrated, and disposed of as a part thereof. Until the termination of the Trust, the Trustee shall pay over to the child, or apply for the benefit of the child, when the child has reached the age of Eighteen (18) years all of the net income of such part, at convenient intervals but not less often than quarter annually. These payments of income shall be made without court order.

(4) When such child reaches the age of Twenty-Five (25) years the Trustee shall transfer, convey, and pay over to such child One-Third (1/3) of the principal of the trust, as it shall then be constituted. When such child reaches the age of Thirty (30) years, my Trustee shall transfer, convey, and pay over to such child One-Half (1/2) of the principal balance of the trust, as it shall than be constituted. When such child reaches the age of Thirty-Five (35), my Trustee shall transfer, convey, and pay over to such child the entire remaining balance of the trust, as it shall then be constituted.

(5) If the child shall have reached age Twenty-Five (25) but not the age of Thirty (30) at the creation of the trust, the Trustee shall pay to the child, One-Third (1/3) of the principal of the trust at the creation of the trust, and shall hold the balance in accordance with the terms of this provision. If the child shall have reached the age of Thirty (30) but not the age of Thirty-Five (35) at the creation of the trust, the Trustee shall pay to the child, Two-Thirds (2/3) of the principal of the Trust at the creation of the trust, and shall hold the balance in accordance with the terms of this provision. If the child shall have reached the age of Thirty-Five (35) prior to the creation of this Trust, then no Trust shall be set up hereunder and instead such assets shall be distributed to such child outright and free of any trust.

b. On the death of such child before reaching the age of Thirty-Five (35) years:

NOTE: If the assets of the Trust are not distributed automatically to the child's estate at death, and if the child did not die with the right to appoint assets to his creditors or Estate (called a General Power of Appointment), tax consequences may be important to address. Consulte a tax specialist regarding GST.

---

(1) My Trustee shall transfer the principal of the Trust to such persons other than the child, his or her estate, his or her creditors, or the creditors of his or her estate, to such extent, in such amounts or proportions, and in such lawful interests or estates, whether absolute or

in trust, as such child may by his or her last will and testament appoint by a specific reference to this power.

(2) If the Power of Appointment is for any reason not validly exercised in whole or in part by such child, the principal of the trust, to the extent not validly appointed by such child, shall, on his or her death, be transferred to such child's then living descendants, shares per stirpes, or, if no such descendant is then living, then the principal of the trust, shall upon his or her death, be transferred to such child's siblings then living in shares, or the issue of any deceased sibling, per stirpes.

NOTE: Are later adopted children included? Always assemble basic family data. As discussed previously, exercise caution in interpreting provisions like the one following. When in doubt, consult a professional.

---

c. My children shall include: Larry, Moe, and Curly and any laterborn or adopted children.

7. *Bequests and Devises to Persons under Age 25*

a. If any person under the age of Twenty-Five (25) years ("Minor-Beneficiary") becomes entitled to any property from my Estate upon my death, and such person's share is not subject to the provision of any other Trust provided for under this Will (such as any children to whom bequests shall be governed by the preceding provision "Residual to Children") or any property from any trust created hereunder upon the termination thereof, the share set aside for such Minor-Beneficiary shall be held further in Trust, and I give, devise, and bequeath the same to my Trustee, in trust, if such is not prohibited by the application of the applicable Rule Against Perpetuities, if any, to my Trustee, for the following uses and purposes: to manage, invest, and reinvest the same, to collect the income thereof and, to distribute such principal and interest in accordance with the provisions set forth below.

b. If any Minor-Beneficiary under this Will shall not then have reached the age of Twenty-Five (25) years, the share set aside for such Minor-Beneficiary shall be held in Trust by, and I give, devise, and bequeath the same to, my Trustee hereinafter named, in trust, for the following uses and purposes. To manage and invest the assets of each trust, to collect the income from the trust, and if the Minor-Beneficiary is under the age of Twenty-Five (25) years at the time his or her share is set aside, to apply so much of the net income and the principal as determined by my Trustee in such Trustee's discretion, for such Minor-Beneficiary's support, maintenance, health, or education, to such extent and at such time and in such manner as my Trustee shall determine, without court order and without regard to the duty of any person to support such Minor-Beneficiary. Any net income not so applied shall be added to the principal of the trust and thereafter shall be held, administered, and disposed of as a part thereof. When such Minor-Beneficiary reaches the age of Twenty-Five (25) years, my Trustee shall transfer, convey, and pay over to such Minor-Beneficiary the entire remaining balance of the Trust, as it shall then be constituted.

c. On the death of such Minor-Beneficiary before reaching the age of Twenty-Five (25) years:

(1) My Trustee shall transfer the principal of the trust to such persons including the Minor-Beneficiary, his or her estate, his or her creditors and the creditors of his or her estate, to such extent, in such amounts or proportions, and in such lawful interests or estates, whether absolute or in Trust, as such Minor-Beneficiary may by his or her Last Will and Testament appoint by a specific reference to this power.

(2) If the power of appointment is for any reason not validly exercised in whole or in part by such Minor-Beneficiary, the principal of the trust, to the extent not validly appointed by such Minor-Beneficiary, shall, upon his or her death, be transferred to such Minor-Beneficiary's then living descendants, per stirpes, or, if no such descendant is then living, then the principal of the trust, shall upon his or her death, be transferred to such Minor-Beneficiary's siblings then living in shares, or the issue of any deceased sibling, per stirpes.

d. Such shares to be disposed of as provided for in this provision. Any beneficiary of such amounts under the age of Twenty-Five (25) shall have such amounts held in Trust as provided above, unless the application of the provision concerning the Rule of Perpetuities would require otherwise.

e. If any tangible personal property shall at any time be held as part of such Minor-Beneficiary's Trust, my Trustee shall have no duty to convert the same into productive property and the expenses of the safekeeping thereof, including insurance, shall be a proper charge against the assets of the Trust.

NOTE: The following type of discretion is common. When the child or other Beneficiary is mature and there are no imminent risks and/or the amount to be held in Trust is small, consider the advantages of not funding the Trust if the Will permits and rather distributing the money to the Beneficiary or a custodial account for the Beneficiary. If the Will does not provide for this flexibility, a Court hearing may be necessary.

---

f. If my Trustee shall determine at any time not to transfer in Trust or not to continue to hold in trust any part or all of such property, the Trustee shall have full power and authority to transfer and pay over such property, or any part thereof, without bond, to such Minor-Beneficiary, if an adult under the law of the state of his or her domicile at the time of such payment, or to his or her parent, the guardian of his or her person or property, or to a custodian for such individual under any Uniform Gifts to Minors Act or Uniform Transfers to Minors Act, pursuant to which a custodian is acting or may be appointed, or to the person with whom such individual resides.

NOTE: Prior to making any distribution to a minor or incapacitated person, inquire of the Estate attorney as to what responsibility you may have to see to the proper use of those funds.

---

g. The receipt of such individual, if an adult, or the parent, Guardian or custodian or any other person to whom any principal or income is transferred and paid over pursuant to any of the above provisions shall be a full discharge to my Fiduciary from all liability with respect to such transfer.

7. Residuary Gift over Provision

NOTE: If all the people under prior provisions of the Will are not living, a final distribution provision is often provided to a charity or the heirs at law. If "heirs at law" applies, confirm with the Estate attorney how this is defined. Obtain and document a complete family history. Consider whether an investigation firm specializing in identifying heirs should be retained.

I dispose of any remainder interest in any Trust, or otherwise, which was not distributed pursuant to any prior provision of my Will, or a power of appointment granted with respect to such property, if any to my heirs at law, under the laws of descent and distribution of the State, as if I had died intestate at that time.

O. Trust Distribution Standards

NOTE: The following sections provide limitations on distributions to be made under various Trusts formed under the Will. You as Executor, and each Trustee, must be certain to understand the criteria for making decisions on distributions. There are so many different variations that you should never assume any particular approach applies without first analyzing the Will, the Trust and any relevant provisions of state law. If you are ever sued for violating any of the distribution criteria, the claimant suing you will have the benefit of hindsight—what really happened. Keep this in mind when making decisions. While it might seem perfectly reasonable that a particular Beneficiary needs a distribution to pay for college, what does the Trust say? Are you required to consider the Beneficiary's other sources of cash to pay for school? If so, are there other Trusts for the same Beneficiary? Does the Beneficiary qualify for any types of financial aid or scholarships? Document your decision and save any documents you rely on in the permanent files you maintain for the Trust. In this way, if a question is raised later as to the rationale for your decision, you will have the ability to address it and protect yourself.

Where any trust is formed under this Will, the following provisions shall provide general rules as to the distributions to be made from such trust, unless specifically provided to the contrary ("Standard for Payment").

    1. *Ascertainable Standard for Payment of Income and Principal*

The Trustees of any trust created under this Trust Agreement are authorized, at any time, with respect to any beneficiary of any trust formed under this Trust Agreement then eligible to receive the net income from such trust, to pay to, or apply for the benefit of such persons such sums out of the principal of such trust (including the entire principal amount), as the Trustee considers advisable to provide for such beneficiary in accordance with the broadest definition of an "ascertainable standard" as such term is defined by Code Section 2041(b)(1)(A), the regulations under Section 20.2041–1.

    2. *Fiduciary Required to Consider Beneficiary's Other Income*

NOTE: Some Wills and Trusts explicitly require the Fiduciary to consider the Beneficiary's other sources of cash when determining whether to make a distribution. Others state that it is not necessary. Many are silent. Consider periodically soliciting information from the Beneficiary as to his or her cash needs, sources of cash, and other assets. Save these records in the permanent trust records. Even if the Will or Trust says you are not required to consider other sources, documenting some information will help you demonstrate at a later date some rational basis for the distributions made. You could send a fill-in-the-blank questionnaire to the Beneficiary, request that the Beneficiary provide you with a periodic balance sheet and a copy of his or her personal income tax return, and so on. If you have informal telephone conversations with the Beneficiaries, maintain records of the calls. A simple way to do this is to have a separate calendar for the Trust in which you record any actions you take as Trustee.

In determining the amounts of income and principal, if any, which shall be paid or disbursed pursuant to any discretionary powers given herein, my Fiduciary shall be required to take into consideration any assets owned by or other sources of income of the person for whose benefit such power might be exercised, unless specifically provided to the contrary.

    3. *Spendthrift Clause*

NOTE: The spendthrift clause makes it harder for a creditor or other claimant of a Beneficiary to break into Trust funds. The IRS and any creditor who provided things to the trust Beneficiary that are considered "necessaries" (e.g., housing, food, car) can often reach Trust assets. Most others would probably have a harder time. When serving as a Trustee, if any creditor or other third party requests funds from the Trust (or if the Beneficiary requests that you pay a bill due to a third party), confirm whether the Trust has a spendthrift clause. If it does, consider having an attorney advise you as to whether you have the authority to make the distribution requested. Even if you have the authority, are you required to? Also, review the general distribution standards for the Trust. Is the payment requested appropriate within those guidelines?

NOTE: If the Trust does contain spendthrift language, Courts will be reluctant to terminate the Trust before the Will provides for it because doing so would violate the Decedent's intent in setting up the Trust.

Except as specifically provided otherwise in my Will, no transfer disposition, charge, or encumbrance on the income or principal of any trust, by any beneficiary under my Will by way of anticipation shall be valid or in any way binding on my Fiduciary. The right of any beneficiary to any payment of income or principal is subject to any charge or deduction that my Executor or Trustee may make against it under the authority granted to them by any statute, law, or by any provision of my Will. No beneficiary shall have the right to transfer, dispose of, assign, or encumber such income or principal until the assets shall be paid to that beneficiary by my Fiduciary. No income or principal shall be liable to any claim of any creditor of any such beneficiary.

4. *Discretionary Authority Where Executor or Trustee Is Also a Beneficiary*

NOTE: To avoid tax and possibly other problems, if you are a parent of a Beneficiary or the Beneficiary yourself, you may not want to make decisions on distributions to your child or yourself. The Will or Trust may in fact prohibit you from doing so. The following provisions accomplish this objective. Thus, if you are the Trustee, think twice before signing a check to yourself or paying for any expense for which you may have a personal legal obligation. In many instances, all that will be required is to have the other person serving as Co-Trustee with you instead make the decision as to the distribution, and then distribute funds. If there is no Co-Trustee ask the Estate attorney how to address this issue.

Notwithstanding anything herein to the contrary, no Fiduciary shall have any power or discretion to, or be deemed to be a Fiduciary with respect to:

a. Payments, applications, or allotments of income or principal to or for the use or benefit of himself or herself as a Beneficiary of any Trust under my Will or for his or her benefit, where such payments or application would cause the inclusion of the assets from which such payments are made in the Trustee's personal estate.

b. Payment or application of income or principal to or for the benefit of any person whom such Fiduciary, in his or her individual capacity, is legally obligated to support, if such payment or application would constitute the discharge of any part of such Fiduciary's support obligation.

c. This provision, however, shall not limit a Executor's right as Executor, to determine the distribution of personal property if such power is specifically granted above.

d. Where a Fiduciary is prohibited from taking an action as a result of this provision, then the other serving Fiduciary who is permitted after the application of this provision to serve, shall then serve alone with respect to such action (the "Independent Fiduciary"). If no Fiduciary is then qualified to serve as an Independent Fiduciary, the person listed herein as the next successor Fiduciary shall be appointed as Co-Fiduciary.

P.   *Authority to Terminate or Not Fund Trust*

NOTE: If any Trust formed under the Will becomes so small that the minimum costs of maintaining the Trust are unreasonably large, consideration should be given to terminating it. If the Will is silent, and even in some cases where the Will permits this, a Court proceeding will be necessary. Great care must be exercised to be certain that if a Trust is terminated all Beneficiaries, including potential contingent Beneficiaries, are properly considered.

Notwithstanding anything to the contrary contained in this Will, if the Fiduciary of any Trust created hereunder (or, if any such Trust shall not have been funded, the Fiduciary of this Will) shall determine that the aggregate value or the character of the assets of such Trust (or the Estate Assets available to fund such Trust) makes it inadvisable, inconvenient, or uneconomical to continue the administration of (or to fund) such Trust, then my Fiduciary may transfer and pay over the Trust Estate (or the Estate Assets available to fund such Trust), equally or unequally, to one or more persons then eligible to receive the net income from such Trust; provided, however, that if the Fiduciary of this Will shall determine not to fund such Trust and the Fiduciary of this Will and the Fiduciary of such Trust should not be the same, the Fiduciary of this Will shall obtain the consent of the Fiduciary of such Trust before distributing the estate assets otherwise available for funding such Trust.

Q.   *Exculpatory Provisions for Fiduciary*

1. The exercise by any Fiduciary of the discretionary powers herein granted with respect to any property given hereunder or the payment, application, or accumulation of income or the payment or application of principal of any Trust created hereunder shall be final and conclusive upon all persons interested hereunder and shall not be subject to any review whatsoever.

2. It is my intention that each Fiduciary (unless specifically provided to the contrary herein) shall have the greatest latitude in exercising such discretionary powers, and that the person or persons entitled to receive the principal of any Trust created hereunder shall upon the termination of such Trust be entitled only to such principal, if any, as may remain after the last exercise of such continuing discretionary powers.

3. Notwithstanding anything in this Will to the contrary, under no circumstances shall any person who is then eligible to receive any property given hereunder or the principal or income of any Trust created hereunder who may be acting as an Fiduciary participate in the exercise of any discretionary power granted hereunder with respect to such property or the principal or income of such Trust.

R.   *Appointment of Fiduciaries*

NOTE: The roles of Executor and Trustee are primarily financial in nature. They have to marshal assets, make investments, make distributions and payments, and provide record keeping. Resignations, incapacity, or death can alter the persons serving.

---

1. *Appointment of Executor*

I appoint Elliott Executor, as Executor of this Will. If Elliott Executor is unable or unwilling to act as Executor, then I appoint Sammy Successor, as Executor. If Sammy Successor is unable or unwilling to act as Executor, then I appoint Tommy Trustworthy, as Executor.

2. *Appointment of Trustee*

I appoint as Co-Trustees the first Two (2) persons named and appointed in the preceding provision appointing my Executor to serve as Co-Trustees.

3. *Replacement of Institutional Trustee*

NOTE: If an institutional Trustee is not performing in the manner desired, the first action should be to communicate, in writing, the concerns. If the Will gives a power to the noninstitutional Trustee or the Beneficiaries to change the institutional Trustee, exercising this right might be the best course of action for serious concerns that are not being addressed. Most Wills do not provide such rights. If the Will is silent, a Court proceeding will probably be necessary. The likelihood of success will depend on the terms of the Will, the extent of the institutional Trustee's poor performance, and other factors.

By unanimous vote of all current income Beneficiaries of a Trust formed under my Will, it shall be permissible to remove an institutional Trustee, if one should then be serving. Notice of the removal and replacement of an institutional Trustee shall only be given once in any twenty-four (24) month period by the current income Beneficiary or Beneficiaries of any trust formed hereunder. In the event that any aspect of this provision could result in the inclusion of any portion of the Trust Estate in my Estate, then the Trustee shall have the express authority to modify and limit this provision to prevent such inclusion. Notice of any replacement of an institutional Trustee shall be given to the then serving Trustee, the next successor Trustee named hereunder, and the current income Beneficiaries.

4. *Appointment of Guardians*

NOTE: If a couple is named, which of the two persons should be guardian if the couple divorces? If this situation arises, consult with the Estate attorney.

If my spouse should predecease me and if any child of mine shall not have attained his or her majority at the time of my death, I appoint Gerry Guardian as Guardian of the person and property of any such minor. If Gerry Guardian is unable or unwilling to serve, I appoint Wally Watcher as Guardian of the person and property of any such minor.

S. *Administrative Provisions Affecting Fiduciary—Bond, Inventory, Service*

1. *Fiduciary Compensation*

NOTE: Be certain to review the Will provisions before paying any Fiduciary compensation. Many Wills include restrictions or other provisions governing compensation. Have the Estate attorney advise you what is permissible and required. Depending on the relationship of the persons serving, the Courts may scrutinize the fees carefully.

---

a. Each Fiduciary acting hereunder shall be entitled to withdraw from the estate, or the trust estate of the Trust hereunder for which such Fiduciary is then serving, without obtaining court or other approval, the compensation which is allowed to a executor or trustee, as the case may be, under the laws of the State which govern compensation to an executor and trustee, computed in the manner and at the rates in effect at the time the compensation is payable.

b. Where an institutional Trustee is serving hereunder, such institutional Trustee shall be entitled to the compensation set forth in such institutional Trustee's regularly issued fee and compensation schedule which is applicable to such institutional Trustee's trust customers at the time the services are rendered, or as otherwise agreed in writing.

c. The commissions and fees payable from income for any given tax year may be paid from either the trust income of that year or from the Trust income of any other tax year. However, the preceding sentence shall not be applied in the case of any Trust hereunder for which a marital deduction is sought. In such instances, compensation and fees shall be payable from principal or income or partly to each in the discretion of the Trustee.

2. *No Bond Required of Any Fiduciary*

NOTE: Fiduciaries may be required to post a bond to secure their performance. Ask the Estate attorney what must be done. In some instances, even if the Will indicates that a bond is not required, it may be necessary, or simply prudent, to have one.

I direct that no bond or security of any kind shall be required in any jurisdiction of any Fiduciary acting hereunder. If any bond is required by law, statute, or rule of court, no sureties shall be required thereon.

3. *No Inventory Required to Be Filed by Any Fiduciary*

NOTE: State law may require filing a listing of assets (inventory) even if your Will says it is not necessary.

I direct that no fiduciary acting hereunder shall be required to file any inventory of my estate, or of any trust formed hereunder.

4. *Service of Person under Disability*

NOTE: If any Beneficiary or other person potentially interested in the Estate (e.g., someone who would inherit if there was no Will, but whom the Will excludes) is under a disability, discuss with the Estate attorney what steps must be taken. The Court may require that a Guardian ad Litem be appointed to represent that disabled person's interests. This may be required even if the Will says otherwise.

In any judicial proceeding relating to my Will, my Estate and/or any Trust or other fund created hereunder, where a party to the proceeding has the same interest as a person under a disability, it shall not be necessary to serve the person under a disability.

5. *Resignation of Fiduciary*

Note: If you do not feel capable of serving, do not have the time, or circumstances have changed from when you were appointed, consider resigning. If the Will has a provision telling you how to do this, you should review the provision with the Estate attorney and resign. Inquire as to whether you need Court approval, are entitled to a fee on terminating your serving as a Fiduciary, and whether it is advisable to have a full accounting rendered for the time period you served.

Any individual Fiduciary may resign at any time by an acknowledged instrument filed in the court in which this Will is admitted to Probate. The resignation shall take effect upon the filing whether or not a successor Fiduciary has been appointed.

T.   *Investment Goals for Estate and Trusts*

NOTE: Review the investment provisions of the Will carefully. Whatever the Will says, if you do not have professional investment expertise, hire a financial professional to advise you (see Chapter 9).

---

1. *Investment Goals for QTIP, QDOT, or Other Trust or Bequest Intended to Qualify for Marital Deduction*

Any Trust formed hereunder which is intended to qualify for the estate tax marital deduction, notwithstanding any investment directives herein to the contrary, shall not be invested in a manner which would disqualify such Trust from the estate tax marital deduction.

2. *General Investment Preference/Philosophy Statement*

NOTE: The following provision may not obviate the need for the Trustee to consider asset allocation concepts and diversification of investments.

Assets may consist of securities of one issuer, or securities of a few issuers, or a diversified portfolio of various types and issuers of securities. The Fiduciary is not directed to distribute or dispose of any particular securities or other assets which may come into the Fiduciary's possession, where such distribution or disposition is primarily for the purpose of diversification of investment holdings. The Fiduciary is not required to liquidate or adjust holdings solely because such holdings have a limited market. The Fiduciary is not obligated to diversify the investment holdings and is hereby indemnified and held harmless from any such failure to diversify.

In addition to the investment powers and the discretion conferred on the Fiduciary under this Will or any Trust formed hereunder, the Fiduciary is authorized (but is not directed) to acquire and retain investments not regarded as traditional or prudent for trusts, allocations of investments within the Trust's portfolio which would not be deemed prudent or advisable, including but not limited to investments and/or investment strategies that would be forbidden by the prudent investor standard applicable at such time. The Fiduciary may therefore invest, any portion or even all of the Trust Estate, or my net residuary estate, in any manner in the Trustee's discretion, including in any type of security, option, improved or unimproved real property, tangible or intangible property, direct or indirect interests, joint ventures, limited liability companies, general partnerships, limited partnerships, mutual funds, corporations, foreign or domestic investments, closely held business investments, and so forth. This authorization, however, shall not be given, and shall not be executed to such extent that, where such investment must be made in a particular manner to avoid an adverse tax result, by way of example and not limitation the disqualification of a trust for the marital deduction where such deduction would be advisable or intended.

3. *Investments in Closely Held Business*

NOTE: If the Will does not authorize you to retain family or other closely held business or investment interests, discuss this matter with the Estate's attorney. You may at minimum have all Beneficiaries agree in writing that you can or should retain these special assets. Be certain to understand what state law requires.

In formulating any investment policy or making any decision with respect to any assets, and assets relating to mine, or my family's closely held Widget manufacturing and related business and investment interests, it is my direction and intent that such interests be held so long as it is reasonable for the purpose of providing long-term financial security to my family, an opportunity for employment for my family (including my spouse and my children, and if practicable, my grandchildren as well). I further state that as a result of my family's long involvement with such Widget manufacturing business and investment interests I have an emotional attachment to such interests and I therefore direct the Executor and Trustee to consider this in making any determination to sell, liquidate, or restructure said business interests. However, I do not intend this statement to be interpreted as an absolute prohibition on the Executor or Trustee from mortgaging, selling, leasing (even long term), liquidating, or restructuring any portion or all of such interests if the circumstances demand it. By way of example and not limitation, if the physical or geographical surroundings of any particular property (or property owned by an entity in which my estate or a Trust hereunder owns an interest) has so deteriorated, or in the judgment of the Fiduciary is likely to so deteriorate in the foreseeable future, that a sale or other transaction is advisable to avoid economic loss, then such transaction should not be prohibited. Further, by way of example and not limitation, if none of my family members is able or willing, and in the reasonable judgment of the Fiduciary is unlikely to be able or willing in the foreseeable future, to assist in the management of, or be gainfully employed (full or part-time) by, any property or entity constituting part of such interests, then sale or another transaction should not be prohibited.

U. *Fiduciary Powers*

NOTE: The goal of the following paragraphs is to supplement the powers state laws give Executors and Trustees so that they will have the flexibility and authority to deal with whatever situations arise. Also, by reviewing the detailed listing of these provisions, you may find the answers you need. Because these powers can be quite lengthy, and the listing will differ in every document, they have been omitted here. You should never take any action as a Fiduciary unless you are certain that you have the power and authority to do so. If not, you could be held personally liable for exceeding the scope of your power.

V. *Special Powers and Discretionary Authority of Fiduciary*

Without limiting in any way the generality of any powers hereinbefore granted or those conferred by law, I specifically give and grant to the Fiduciary the following additional powers:

1. *Administration of Trust Assets in Aggregate or Individually*

NOTE: If the Decedent's child or other Beneficiary already has a Trust, this provision may enable the various Trusts to be consolidated to save legal, accounting, and other costs.

For convenience in administration, the Fiduciary may administer in aggregate (i) the assets of any Trust created hereunder, and (ii) any property held pursuant to the provisions of any provision of my Will. It is my intention, however, that a separate record shall be kept of the transactions for each separate trust created hereunder or for the property held pursuant to the different provisions of my Will. Except as otherwise provided in this Will, in any case in which my Fiduciary is required or permitted to divide my estate or any part thereof into trusts, funds, or shares, they shall not be required physically to divide any of the investments or other property held hereunder, but may assign undivided interests therein to the various trusts, funds, and shares, provided that no such undivided holding shall be deemed to defer or postpone the vesting or distribution in accordance with the terms of my Will of any property so held in Trust.

2. *Generation-Skipping Transfer Tax (GST) Powers*

NOTE: These powers can be exercised to split Trusts into separate Trusts to maximize the GST tax benefits. See Martin M. Shenkman, *The Complete Book of Trusts* (2d ed.) (New York: John Wiley & Sons, 1997) for details. Because GST is so complex, it is essential to retain both an experienced CPA and Estate attorney.

With respect to the tax on generation-skipping transfers set forth in Chapter 13 of the Code, the Generation Skipping Transfer Tax (the "GST"), my Fiduciary shall have the following additional powers:

    a. The power to allocate any portion of my GST exemption, as set forth in Code Section 2631(a), as amended, or any successor statute, not allocated during my lifetime, to any property with respect to which I am treated as the transferor for purposes of Chapter 13 of the Code, including, but not limited to, any property transferred by me during my lifetime, at such time and in such manner as set forth in Code Section 2632 or any successor statute and the regulations promulgated thereunder.

    b. The power to divide property or part thereof with an inclusion ratio, as defined in Code Section 2642(a)(1), of neither One (1) nor Zero (0) into Two (2) or more separate Trusts representing fractional shares of the property being divided, with One (1) or more of said shares having an inclusion ratio of Zero (0) and the other share or shares having an inclusion ratio of One (1).

    c. With respect to all, or any part, of the principal of any Trust or part thereof being held under any Trust formed under my Will which may be subject to the GST, by a written instrument filed with the records of my Estate or Trust, with copies to any interested beneficiaries:

    d. The power to create in a beneficiary, other than my spouse, Susan Spouse, a general power of appointment within the meaning of Code Section 2041, as amended, that may dispose of the property on the death of that Beneficiary. However, the exercise of such power shall require the consent of my Fiduciary, other than the beneficiary, if such consent requirement shall not prevent the power from being treated as a general power of appointment as defined in Code Section 2041.

    e. The power to eliminate such a general power of appointment for all or any part of the principal as to which such power was previously created.

    f. The power to irrevocably release the right to create or eliminate such power.

    g. The power to divide the Trust Estate of any Trust formed under the provisions of my Will, into Two (2) fractional shares based on the then portion of the Trust Estate that would be included in the gross Estate of the Beneficiary holding such power if he or she died immediately before such division (in which case the power shall be over the entire principal of One (1) share and over no part of the other share) and each such share shall be administered as a separate Trust. However, my Fiduciary, other than any beneficiary, shall in his or her discretion have the right to thereafter combine such separate Trusts into a single Trust. In authorizing such action, I hope, but do not require, that a general power will be kept in effect when my Fiduciary, other than any Beneficiary, believes the inclusion of the property affected by such general power of appointment in the Beneficiary's gross estate, may achieve a significant savings in transfer taxes by having an estate tax rather than a GST imposed on the property subject to the general power of appointment, which may also permit a greater use of the GST exemption under Code Section 2631(a) of any Beneficiary, or spouse of any Beneficiary.

    h. The power to exercise the special election provided by Code Section 2652(a)(3) of the Code as to any Trust created for the benefit of my spouse which qualifies for the marital deduction. If my Fiduciary shall so elect and an allocation of GST exemption is made to the Trust, my Fiduciary may, in my Fiduciary's discretion, set apart a fractional share of the such Trust in a separate trust to cause its inclusion ratio to be zero.

3. *Allocation of Receipts*

NOTE: Allocating receipts between income and principal is not a matter to be taken lightly. Assume that a Trust under the Will provides that "My Uncle Joe shall receive all income from the trust until his death. Upon his death the trust assets shall be distributed my nephew Tommy." To the extent that you allocate a receipt to income, Joe will receive the money. If you allocate the receipt to principal Tommy will eventually receive more. For any unusual transactions, be sure to consult with the Estate accountant or attorney. If the transaction is significant and the different Beneficiaries have different interests consider the advisability of having them sign off in writing as to the treatment you chose.

In the administration of my Estate, other than the portion of my Estate given to my spouse, and in the administration of each Trust, other than any trust which qualifies for the marital deduction, my Fiduciary shall allocate between income and principal of my Estate or of such Trust in such manner as my Fiduciary shall determine any receipt or expense which could be deemed to be or charge to either income or principal, including any dividend in the stock or other securities of the distributing corporation, any cumulative dividend and any accrued interest.

4. *Beneficiary under Disability*

NOTE: If a person who is to receive a distribution under the Will (or under a Trust formed under the Will) has developed an emotional, drug, or other serious problem, the following paragraphs may provide you or the Trustees the flexibility to withhold distributions until the problems are resolved. If they are not provided, Court approval may be necessary.

---

a. Whenever pursuant to the provisions of this Will, any donee property shall become distributable to a person under a disability, title thereto shall vest in such person but the payment thereof may be deferred until such disability ceases and, if so deferred, such donee property shall be held by the Fiduciary, who shall apply the principal and income thereof, or so much of such principal and income as the Fiduciary may determine (without regard to the income or other resources of such person under a disability or of his or her parents or spouse), for the health, education, support, and maintenance of such person under a disability, and when such disability ceases, the Fiduciary shall deliver to such person formerly under a disability the then remaining donee property, together with the accumulations, if any, of income therefrom, or if such person should die, the Fiduciary shall deliver the donee property and any accumulations of income to the legal representatives of the estate of such person. Income accumulations hereunder, if any, shall be added to and accounted for as part of principal by the Fiduciary. Notwithstanding the foregoing provisions of this Article, the Fiduciary may, at any time and from time to time deliver all or a portion of the donee property which shall then remain, together with the accumulations, if any, of the income therefrom, to a parent, a guardian, a custodian under the Uniform Gifts to Minors Act of the state of my Domicile, a committee, a conservator of the property, or an individual with whom such person under a disability resides, and the receipt of such parent, guardian, custodian, committee or conservator or of such individual with whom such person under a disability resides shall constitute a full and sufficient discharge to the Fiduciary for such payment or delivery.

b. Each Fiduciary acting hereunder shall be entitled to withdraw from the donee property held hereunder, without obtaining judicial authorization therefor, such full compensation as would be allowed to a sole Trustee under the laws of the state of my Domicile governing compensation to the Trustee of a testamentary trust, computed in the manner and at the rates in effect at the time such compensation shall be payable.

W. *In Terrorem*

NOTE: This provision provides that anyone challenging the Will should not be entitled to any inheritance under the Will. If a Will challenge occurs, be certain that the Estate attorney has estate litigation expertise; if not, hire another specialist. This provision may not be upheld in Court.

If any beneficiary under my Will in any manner, directly or indirectly, contests this Will or any of its provisions, any share or interest in my Estate given to the contesting beneficiary under my Will is revoked and shall be disposed of in the same manner provided herein as if the contesting beneficiary and his or her issue had predeceased me.

X. *Attestation Clause*

NOTE: The format used for the signing of the will must conform with the minimum state law requirements. If it does not, additional Probate steps (e.g., witness affidavits) may be necessary.

IN WITNESS WHEREOF, I, the said Decedent's Name, sign, seal, publish, and declare this as my Will, in the presence of the persons witnessing it at my request, this January 1, 1999.

_____ (L.S.)
Decedent's Name

CONCLUSION

The Will (and/or Revocable Living Trust) is your primary source document, instruction guide, and road map all-in-one for serving as Executor. Read it. Discuss it with the Estate attorney. Make notes and comments all over a copy of the document so that you can look up, read, and understand any provision and what it means to the Probate.

5 PROBATE PROCESS AND THE COURTS

Relax. Most of what you have heard about the horrors of Probate Court proceedings just isn't so. And even when delays, costs, or frustrations are involved, they are rarely the stuff the folks hyping Revocable Living Trusts and other Probate avoidance techniques would have you believe. In the majority of Probate situations, the Court's involvement is limited. You (or the Estate attorney) will contact the Probate Court for the appropriate papers, which you will complete, sign, and file along with the original Will, an original death certificate, and the appropriate fee (be sure to retain copies of anything you file). The Court clerks will typically review the documents, accept them with minor changes or clarifications that they will request, and then issue Letters Testamentary authorizing you as Executor to transact business for the Estate. If the Will includes one or more Trusts, Letters Trusteeship will be issued authorizing you as Trustee to transact business for each Trust.

Remember, the Court's involvement is to assure that minor children are protected, taxes due are paid, and the Decedent's wishes concerning his property are carried out—goals you would agree with. Protecting these various interests requires some formality. For most Estates with no problems, no inappropriate actions, and no mistrust, the procedures create paperwork and costs that might seem unnecessary. Most clerks are quite compassionate and helpful. You will get the most help if you similarly try to be reasonable and understanding of the difficulties clerks in many Courts face. Compared with the typical law office, clerks are overworked and have inadequate support staff, facilities, and equipment. Most significantly, Court clerks are prohibited from giving legal advice. It may sound like only a simple question to you: "What goes on line 3(b)?" but to the clerk, it may require the rendering of legal advice. No clerk, however, helpful and considerate, can be expected to risk his job to help.

Court involvement in Probate, however, can range from a nominal amount of time and money, to the major focus of the process. The degree of involvement will depend on many factors:

- *The size of the Estate.* Very small Estates will generally qualify for simplified and expedited Probate proceedings, larger Estates will not.

- *The state and Surrogate's Court involved.* The rules, procedures, and customs vary considerably in different Courts. In some, the Court clerks prepare most or all papers and the process is quick and inexpensive. In other Courts, attorneys will generally prepare more extensive documentation, more people will have to receive notice, and the procedures are more formal. These factors create greater time delays and costs. The philosophies of different Courts' approaches to Probate is part of the reason. In some Courts, the presumption is that the Executor can, unless indicated otherwise, be trusted to fairly deal with the process. In other jurisdictions, the view is that all persons who would inherit the Decedent's assets if there were no Will must be notified of the proceeding. This can create some additional paperwork and cost. However, the idea behind such notices is to protect the potential heirs of every Estate.

- *How well the Beneficiaries get along.* If everyone is amicable and agreeable, everything tends to go smoother, hence less time delays and less costs. If Beneficiaries become suspicious, or worse, antagonistic, expect the costs and expenses to increase. In a friendly situation, Beneficiaries may agree on less formal ways of dealing with things. For example, if a Decedent's jewelry is to be divided among three siblings who get along, the three might sit around a table with the Executor and go through the jewelry and simply agree on values and who should get what. If the three siblings do not get along, the Executor is more likely to have each piece of jewelry formally appraised and to use a more formal procedure for distributing the jewelry. Prior to distribution, the Executor will probably insist on all three siblings signing a written statement agreeing to the values and distribution of the jewelry. The second situation will create more cost, expense, and time delays.

- *Whether litigation is involved.* If someone challenges the Will, the Court costs, legal fees, and time period required to resolve the Probate will increase significantly.

- *If there are minor orphaned children.* The Court will have greater involvement to assure that a Guardian is appointed and the children's financial interests are addressed. You would not want it any other way.

- *Whether a federal or state Estate Tax return has to be filed.* Although tax filings have little to do with the courts, they do affect the cost and complexity of the process. A federal Estate Tax return is the most complex and lengthy tax return and requires more detailed exhibits and attachments than any other return. Formal appraisals are necessary for many assets. Many complex tax Elections must be considered. The Will, financial statements for business interests, and appraisals for real estate properties may all have to be attached. Expenses are often estimated because they may not be known exactly when the filing occurs. Certain expenses have to be allocated between the Decedent's income tax return and the estate tax return, and so forth. This process is expensive and requires some time. Also, many Estate attorneys prefer to complete the final tax return near the filing deadline for the Estate Tax return. This is because small assets or expenses tend to be found by Executors or family and any change will require a change in many of the interrelated tax schedules on the federal Estate Tax return. Thus, when a federal Estate Tax return is due, the Estate is unlikely to be concluded in its entirety prior to the nine-month deadline.

The rest of this chapter will provide an overview of many of the common Court proceedings. The forms, terminology, and practices differ in every court. One of the first things you should do is contact the appropriate Surrogate's Court (it may go under a different name in your area, Orphans' Court, Probate Court) and request a copy of the current forms necessary to probate a Will (or to handle an Intestacy if the Decedent did not sign a Will). The clerks may also be able to provide you with other information on the procedures and fees. Also, as cautioned throughout this book, hire an attorney. If the Estate is truly simple, you may be able to handle most of the administrative matters, and even some or all of the Court matters, on your own.

WHO CAN START THE PROBATE PROCEEDING AND IN WHICH COURT?

Probate proceedings, whether Affidavit Probate, Summary Probate, or formal Probate (all described in this chapter), must be brought in the correct Court. In most cases, the appropriate Court is obvious: the Court having responsibility for Wills and Probate in the county where the Decedent lived. In some situations, however, the decision is not as apparent. Two issues are involved. First, you must determine the appropriate county in which the courts will have the right to handle the Probate (Venue). This is based on where the Decedent had his permanent residence and ultimately intended to return (Domicile). Domicile was explained in Chapter 2. Once you have determined the county where the courts can handle the matter, you must determine the specific Court within that county that handles Probate matters. Most counties have many different courts. One will handle traffic tickets and other minor matters. Another may handle small claims. One will handle matters relating to Wills, Probate, and related issues. While this Court has been referred to as "Surrogate's Court," or simply Court in this book, it may go under a different name in the county involved. Look up the court telephone numbers in the local telephone book, or call a main telephone number for the court system. It should be relatively easy to find the appropriate court.

The decision as to which state the Decedent was domiciled in is extremely important. The laws concerning inheritance taxes, spousal right of election (Chapter 6), and other important matters vary considerably from state to state. In fact, a state seeking to collect taxes from the Estate may contest a Domicile decision and claim the Decedent permanently resided in its state.

Who formally begins the Probate proceeding? In almost all cases, it is the person named in the Will as the Executor. If there is no Will, generally the person that the state law would appoint as the Administrator of the Estate. The Administrator is analogous to an Executor, except Administrator is the term used for the person with the responsibility over an Estate when the Decedent did not sign a Will. Usually this is a surviving spouse or child if there is no spouse. If these people have not commenced Probate proceedings, other heirs, or even creditors interested in collecting their debts may do so.

COLLECT GENERAL COURT DATA

To ease the process, collect and organize the basic data you will need for each Court. Although generally there will only be one Court, if the Decedent owned real estate in another state you will have another Probate proceeding in that state which is secondary to the primary proceeding in the state of the Decedent's Domicile (called Ancillary Probate).

NOTE: The following sample summary chart is useful for organizing information. Contact each Court by telephone and record on the chart basic data—name, address, telephone number, and so on—that you will refer to throughout the process. Request copies of all current forms necessary. Set up a folder or loose-leaf binder tab for each Court. Keep the blank forms as well as copies of all filed documents in the separate folder or behind a separate tab in the loose-leaf binder for the Estate. Tape or note the summary data on the front of each file folder or tab so it will be readily available.

Sample Chart—Court Proceedings: General Data Summary

	Primary Probate Court	Ancillary Probate No.	Comment
Court Name			
Court Address			There may be a different address for mail and overnight carriers.
Court Address			
Court Telephone No.			
Contact Person			
Alternate Contact Person			
Date/Time of First Appointment			When you call, ask the Clerk what the procedure is for the first appointment and whether the Estate attorney must come.

	Primary Probate Court	Ancillary Probate No.	Comment
Beneficiaries Notified of Executors Appointment			Even if not required, consider apprising everyone of the date and status.
Date Papers Filed			Save copies. Ask the Clerk when you should hear a response.
Follow-up Date No. 1/Describe			Wait at least several days after the date you were promised. You don't want to become a pest and alienate the Clerks whose help you need.
Follow-up Date No. 2/Describe			
Letters Issued: Date/Number [ ] Testamentary [ ] Administer			Record the number on the Letters. Obtain at least 5–10. Limit how many since they often have an expiration date.
Co-Executor/ Co-Administrator Name and Address			List information and be sure he/she is informed and involved.
Advertising to Creditors			Ask the Clerk and/or the Estate attorney if you can advertise (publish) a notice to creditors to limit the time in which claims can be asserted.
Additional Letters Request			Many Estates request additional Letters Testamentary several times.
Bond [ ] No [ ] Yes: Amount/Issuer/Date			Inquire whether you need to file a bond. If not required, inquire whether it is advisable.
Inventory Filed			Some courts require a filing of an Estate Inventory. Some may accept a copy of a tax return instead.
Accounting Filed			Some courts require a formal Accounting. Inquire as to what your Estate must do. An informal accounting of some sort should always be prepared.
			Every Court and Estate has its own procedures. Inquire from the Estate attorney and Clerk. Note them here.

SMALL ESTATE EXPEDITED PROBATE PROCEEDINGS

If the size of the Estate is less than an amount set by state law, the Estate may qualify for a simplified proceeding for small Estates. The amount permitted can range from $5,000 to as much as $70,000 in some states. Depending on the state, there may be additional requirements as to who the surviving heirs are and what types of assets are involved. These proceedings can be completed with less paperwork, less need for professional assistance, more quickly, and at less cost. If, for example, the Decedent attempted to avoid Probate and managed to retitle most of his assets to a Revocable Living Trust or joint ownership (all of which pass on death without Probate), Small Estate Probate may be available as a simple solution to the few assets that were missed.

Once you have assembled a balance sheet of the Decedent's assets, call the Surrogate's Court to find out the maximum size Estate that can qualify for a small Probate proceeding. If the Estate meets the size requirement, request the necessary forms from the Court. Complete the forms and follow the instructions provided by the clerk.

You should also go to your local library and look up the table of contents for your state's Probate statute. Look for "Small Estates," "Summary Probate," "Streamlined Probate," "Affidavit Probate," or similar terms. You should be able to find the law. Many statute books are annotated with summaries of relevant cases; many even include sample forms. Be sure to look in the back of the book. Publishers update many legal books by periodically adding a new paperbound supplement stuck into a slot in the back cover.

Always have an Estate attorney review any documents before you file them with the Court or send them to others.

Filing an Affidavit in Lieu of Probate

In many states, the Small Estate Probate procedure is based on completing a document signed by the heirs, under oath ("Affidavit"). This is the quickest and easiest approach, if available. Instead of having any type of Probate proceeding, all that is required is the Affidavit by the heirs claiming the Decedent's property. These would be the persons named in the Will or those people who would receive the property under state law if the Decedent died without a Will (Intestate). The process should go smoothly if all the people named in the Will, and any who would receive the assets had there not been a Will, sign the Affidavit agreeing to how the property will be distributed. If there are bumps in the road, at least consult with an Estate attorney.

Once the Affidavits are completed and filed with the Surrogate's Court, the heirs can use the Affidavits to gain control over the Decedent's assets, pay debts, and transfer the remaining assets.

Summary Probate for Small Estates

If the Estate exceeds the dollar cap for Small Estates, or includes any assets that disqualify the Estate for the Small Estate Probate proceeding, state law may still permit some type of expedited proceeding, often called Summary Probate. For the states that permit this, a form (Petition) will have to be filed, heirs and other interested parties given notice, and so on. The Summary Probate proceeding is a simplified version of the formal Probate proceeding described in this chapter. Because the rules, and even the availability, of Summary Probate differ from Court to Court, you should contact the appropriate Court for sample papers and instructions. Also, review the information available at your local library.

FORMAL PROBATE PROCEEDINGS

Formal Probate is often necessary because either the Decedent did not plan to avoid Probate, or as is often the case, the Decedent attempted to avoid Probate with joint assets, a Revocable Living Trust, and other steps, but significant assets were not handled properly. If the Small Estate Probate or Summary Probate proceedings are not available, then a formal Probate is necessary. Formal Probate generally begins with filing a form with the Surrogate's Court, often called a Petition.

AFFIDAVIT AND BASIC DOCUMENTS TO BEGIN THE PROBATE PROCESS

Who Should Complete the Petition?

These forms, which will vary in name, content, and complexity from Estate to Estate and Court to Court, are an essential part of the first step of beginning the Probate process. These will generally be prepared by the Estate attorney and/or you as the Executor. In some jurisdictions, however, the Court Clerk will prepare the documents for you. You may not need to prepare much more than a simple form listing all heirs, family members, Executors, Witnesses who signed the Will, their addresses, and other pertinent information (see the Sample Probate Court Data Sheet in this chapter). In these cases, it may not be advantageous to pay an Estate attorney to complete this work. Before making the decision, however, ask the attorney how these types of forms are billed. Many Estate attorneys have paraprofessionals or Probate secretaries who can complete the forms in a fraction of the time that you can, may know how the Court's clerks like certain nuances handled, all at a small percentage of the fee the attorney would charge. In any case, it's almost always advisable to have an Estate attorney review any forms you prepare.

If you are working with an Estate attorney, ask if it will save time for you to pencil-in a Petition for the attorney as an easy way of making available all the current addresses and other information the Petition requires. Doing so may be the best approach. You can save legal fees by assuring that the attorney's paralegal or associate has the correct information at hand, yet you will still benefit from an experienced professional reviewing the Petition before filing. Again, as suggested throughout this book, the preferable way to handle Probate matters is to use an Estate attorney but minimize the costs by handling as much of the routine, administrative, and basic work as is feasible.

Getting the Forms

If the Court does not provide forms (and even if it does) you may want to go to a local office supply store that sells legal forms for your state and the specific Court (generic forms are unlikely to be accepted by many courts). Try to obtain a catalog of forms since it will include a listing of all the forms available. Purchase the ones you know you will need, and if they are sufficiently inexpensive, purchase the ones you think you might need to save a trip back to the store. Inquire whether the store (or publisher of legal forms in your state) has a package of all probate forms, or the most commonly used probate forms; then you will not have to pick out individual forms. See the earlier suggestions for locating the state law concerning Probate—many of the legal books containing state laws also include sample forms. Again, it's advisable to have any forms you prepare reviewed by an Estate attorney before use.

How to Prepare the Petition

Make photocopies of any forms before completing them. First fill in the photocopies in pencil to make it easy to make corrections and changes later. Once you have completed the rough copies, then neatly type the proposed final forms.

Be sure all the exhibits and other attachments the clerk requires are attached to the forms and properly labeled. It is best not to have any loose papers that do not reflect the Decedent's name and the Probate File Number. The File Number will generally be assigned after you file the Petition so you can leave blanks "File No. _____" on pages so it can be added later.

Once the Estate lawyer has approved the completed forms, make several copies of these before signing. The Court may want more than one copy and it is advisable that each Executor have an original signed Petition in his files.

What Documents and Exhibits Typically Have to Be Attached to the Probate Petition

The original documentation required may include an affidavit signed by the persons who witnessed the Decedent's signature on the Will. Whether such an Affidavit is required depends on local law and the manner in which the Will was executed. Many states permit the use of a Self-Proving Will. This simply means that the Will includes certain representations, often signed again by the Witnesses and perhaps the Testator as well, so that the Witnesses do not have to appear in Court or provide an Affidavit.

Petitions also typically require disclosure of asset information. Since you will probably only have just begun the process, you will have to make estimates. Simply indicate which figures are estimates. Also, ask the clerk if you need to amend the Petition when more exact figures are available. The asset data may be necessary to determine the filing fee involved (it is also necessary for determining whether Affidavit Probate or Summary Probate is available).

The Court procedures may require that specified persons receive formal notification in writing that the Decedent died and the Will is being submitted with a Petition for Probate (to be discussed). The forms to be used to complete these Notices may have to be submitted with the Petition.

The end result of the Petition process is that the Court will issue a statement (Order) that the Will be admitted to Probate and that the Letters Testamentary be issued. Often, the Order the Court is being asked to issue should be completed for the Court and submitted with the Petition. This way, once the clerks and Court are satisfied that all the papers are in order, the Judge can merely sign the Order. If the Court will decide whether the Executor has to post a Bond with a Surety company to assure the Executor's performance (if the Executor absconds with Estate assets, the Surety company that issued the Bond will have to pay) documents concerning this may also be filed with the Petition.

The sample on pages 88 and 89 shows the type of data sheet and schedule many Courts require along with the Probate Petition. The Data Sheet requires a listing of all family members by relationship. The attached schedule lists only those named in the Will. The difference, if any, between the two listings may highlight a potential problem. If all people must receive Notice of the Will and the Probate, it assures the family members not actually listed in the Will an opportunity to challenge the Will should they choose to do so.

Filing the Petition

Once the initial documents are prepared, and an Estate attorney has reviewed them, who takes them to the court? Depending on the jurisdiction, they may be filed by the Estate attorney or the Executor. If you have the time and there is no particular advantage to having the attorney handle the filing, you can do so. Although this will save costs, it may not be advisable if issues are involved that could require the attorney's presence. In some jurisdictions where the Probate process has been simplified, you will almost never need the attorney to file. In other jurisdictions, even if it is permissible to handle the filing on your own, it may not be advisable. If you are not sure, ask the Estate attorney. If he says that he should handle

SAMPLE PROBATE COURT DATA SHEET

Check One:

Administration: _____

Probate: _____

Appointment Time: _____

Date: _____

Name of Decedent: _____

Address: _____

Place of Death and Date: _____

Date of Will: _____

Next of Kin	Relationship	Address
_____	_____	_____
_____	_____	_____
_____	_____	_____
_____	_____	_____
_____	_____	_____
_____	_____	_____
_____	_____	_____
_____	_____	_____
_____	_____	_____
_____	_____	_____
_____	_____	_____
_____	_____	_____
_____	_____	_____

Name and address of Executors or Administrators:

1. _____

2. _____

Names of Witnesses: Commission to:

_____   _____

_____   _____

_____   _____

Bond Amount $ _____

Type of Letters/Documents to Be Issued:
  _____ Short Certificates
  _____ Advertising to creditors
  _____ Pages to Will
  _____ Appraisers required
  _____ Trusteeship required

Miscellaneous requirements of Estate:

1. _____

2. _____

Name of Estate Attorney, Firm and Address:

_____

_____

Estate of Dan Decedent
File No.:

SCHEDULE OF PERSONS NAMED IN WILL

The names, relationships, and addresses of all distributees and fiduciaries, designated in Decedent's Will, all of whom are of full age of majority and of sound mind and under no disability, are:

Name	Relationship	Address	Description of Legacy, Devise, or Other Interest, etc.
Susan Spouse	spouse	123 Main St. Anytown, USA	Distributee, primary executor, beneficiary of specific bequest, beneficiary of residuary estate
Cindy Child	daughter	456 Bow St. Anytown, USA	Distributee, successor Executor
Cal Child	son	111 Big Ave. Somewhere, USA	Distributee, successor Executor

All other fiduciaries, legatees, and devisees who are of full age and sound mind and under no disability, or which are corporations or associations, are as follows:

Name	Address	Description of Legacy, Devise or Other Interest, etc.
Sammy Successor	111 High Street Bigtown, USA	Successor Executor

the filing, ask why. If you are still in doubt, call the Surrogate's Court yourself to confirm.

The next step is Filing the documents, which means showing up at Court with a check or money order for the Court fees, the original Will, an original Death Certificate, and the required Court papers completed and signed (often notarized). Ask ahead of time what type of payment will be accepted for the Court fees: personal check, attorney's check, money order, or cash. If the particular Court has a policy as to the type of payments it will accept, it will not make an exception for you. Also, bring extra checks as a precaution. Sometimes there are nominal additional charges, such as for additional Letters Testamentary, which it will be convenient to pay for. Even if the Court policy is to accept only a money order or bank check for the filing fee, the clerk may have the latitude to accept a personal check for a small incidental matter.

You should not delay in filing the Will. Until the Will is filed, there is always the risk of it being lost or destroyed by fire or otherwise. Also, some states require that the Will be filed within a specified time period of death. Finally, the sooner you begin the Probate process, the sooner you will have Letters Testamentary and be able to use them to gain control over assets.

NOTICES

Most states require that some type of notification be given in writing to persons named in the Will, or not named in the Will but who logically might be interested in being informed of the Probate. This notification is referred to as Notice. Notice may be given after the Will is filed, but before (and as a condition to) Letters Testamentary being issued.

In other states, the sequence of the Notice procedures differs. You may first have the Will admitted to Probate, and the Court gives the Notice. In such cases, the Notice should include an indication of a hearing that the Court will have to determine whether anyone is going to object to the Probate of the Will.

A typical Notice would include a copy of the Will, a copy of the Death Certificate, and perhaps a copy of the Probate Petition. To prove that the Notice was received (even if the Court does not require this), you should consider sending all of the Notices by certified mail return receipt requested. When you receive the return receipts back from the post office, staple them to the copies of the Notices that you retained. File these in a folder marked "Notices," or in the Probate loose-leaf binder behind a tab "Notices." This could be invaluable if someone ever objects to the Will and tries to claim that he or she was not notified.

Who are the persons who should receive Notice? Although the rules vary by Court, or the Estate attorney may advise you of a different approach, it generally includes:

- *People named in the Will.* This could include primary Beneficiaries, Beneficiaries who receive assets only if the primary Beneficiaries die or do not want them (called Contingent or Remainder Beneficiaries) and depending on the state, Executors and Trustees. These could be included because of the potentially significant fees they may be entitled to as well as the responsibility and authority that they have. For example, if the first Executor were not to serve, the next person named to serve as Executor (the Successor Executor) would serve. This would give the successor the right to Executor Fees and the authority to make the decisions permitted under the Will. Thus, a Successor Executor may want to challenge your appointment as primary Executor.

- *Persons who would inherit had the Decedent died Intestate.* This is logical and important because if the Will were fraudulent, and the Decedent had really not signed a Will, then these people, who are listed as Beneficiaries under state law, would inherit. For example, the Will leaves all assets to Decedent's current girlfriend, and little to his children. If the Decedent had died without a Will, since he had no spouse, his children would inherit most or all of his estate. Since it is possible that the Decedent's girlfriend influenced him to sign a Will naming her, the children should get Notice. In most cases, the people named by state law are generally the people the Will names so problems are unusual. However, with the increasing frequency of blended families, nontraditional families, unmarried partners, and so on, the likelihood of differences between those named in the Will and those named under state law, will continue to increase. State law typically names the Decedent's spouse, children, and known creditors as entitled to Notice.

It can sometimes be difficult to locate the people required to receive Notice. Start with a review of the Decedent's telephone book, personal records, and documents left with the Estate attorney. There are computer and Internet services available for name searches. As a last resort, businesses can be hired to locate missing heirs, although the cost is likely to be significant. Always document the steps you have taken to identify anyone entitled to receive Notice. If you send letters by certified mail that are returned, save them unopened to prove your efforts. The post office notations on the envelope could be helpful in demonstrating to the Court the good faith efforts to make contact. If reasonable efforts fail to locate the persons, the Court may be willing to waive the requirement for that particular individual. It is best to confirm this with an Estate attorney so that you can take steps to avoid a later challenge by the person who is not notified.

If there is a doubt as to whether a particular person is entitled to Notice, it may be best in many cases to give Notice to avoid any risk of a challenge for failing to give the required Notice. However, Notice can invite unwanted questions, scrutiny, and even lawsuits including but not limited to a Will challenge.

If anyone who receives Notice has suspicions about the validity of the Will (e.g., that the Testator was under Undue Influence when he signed the Will), the person advises the Court or shows up at the specified hearing (the date is usually indicated in the Notice). Once the Notice is signed, the Court typically requires the Executor to file an affidavit stating that the Notices have been given. Copies of the Notices are often required to be filed. Remember, always save a copy of anything you file.

The following sample illustrates a Notice sent by the Estate's attorney to a beneficiary. Once Notices have been sent to all, the Estate attorney or you as Executor (whoever handled the sending of the Notices) may have to file a statement under oath (an "Affidavit") with the Court stating that all required Notices were sent. This is also illustrated with a sample form.

SAMPLE NOTICE TO BENEFICIARY

BIG RICH & HOWE
ATTORNEYS AT LAW
666 LEGAL WAY
SOMEWHERE, USA

VIA CERTIFIED MAIL—RETURN RECEIPT REQUESTED P 113 333 001
January 3, 2001
Barry Beneficiary
111 Rich Avenue
Goldmine, USA

Re: *Estate of Dan Decedent.*

Dear Mr. Beneficiary:

We are the attorneys for the Executors named in the Last Will and Testament of Dan Decedent. You are an heir of Dan Decedent and you were named beneficiary of the Dan Decedent's Last Will and Testament (and Revocable Living Trust, EIN No. 00-111111). By the laws of the State of Somestate, you are required to receive notice of the Probate of the Last Will and Testament in Whereisit County Surrogate's Court, on April 1, 2000, and a copy of the will. Enclosed with this letter are: a copy of the Last Will and Testament of Dan Decedent for your records; a copy of the death certificate; and a copy of the Data Sheet filed with the Surrogate.

The name and address of the Executor is as follows:

Elliott Executor
111 Main Avenue
Anytown, USA

Kindly acknowledge receipt of this letter, by signing and dating the second page of this letter, inserting your Social Security number and returning the same to me.

If you have any questions regarding the above, please call.

Sincerely,

Big, Rich & Howe, P.C.

By: _____
      Larry Lawyer, Esq.

enc.
cc: Elliott Executor-w/enc.

I acknowledge receipt of this letter this _____ day of _____ , 200 _____ .

My Social Security Number is _____ .

_____   _____

Barry Beneficiary   Date

SAMPLE COVER LETTER TO
COURT AND AFFIDAVIT

BIG RICH & HOWE
ATTORNEYS AT LAW
666 LEGAL WAY
SOMEWHERE, USA

January 13, 2000

VIA CERTIFIED MAIL—RETURN RECEIPT REQUESTED P 117 818 335

Whereisit County Surrogate Court
Justice Center
100 Main Street
Anytown, USA

    RE: *Estate of Dan Decedent*
            Date of Death: January 1, 1999
            Late of Whereisit County

Dear Sir/Madam:

Enclosed for filing are an original and one copy of Affidavit of Notice of Probate in the above named estate.

Enclosed is our check in the amount of Six ($6.00) ($3/page) representing the filing fee for this service.

Please file same and return the copy to our office marked "filed" in the envelope provided.

Sincerely,

Big Rich & Howe, P.C.

By: _____
      Larry Lawyer, Esq.

enc.
ALS:las
cc: Elliott Executor, w/enc.

IN THE MATTER OF THE ESTATE OF

Whereisit County Surrogate's Court

Case No. 111111

Dan Decedent, Deceased

AFFIDAVIT OF NOTICE OF PROBATE

a. Pursuant to rule 9:80-6, on January 3, 1999, I the undersigned, mailed a notice in writing that the Will of the decedent, Dan Decedent has been Probated, the place and date of Probate, the name and address of the personal representative, and that a copy of the Will shall be furnished upon request, to all of the following beneficiaries under the Will and all other heirs and next of kin of the decedent at their addresses, as follows:

(1) Barry Beneficiary, 111 Rich Avenue

Goldmine, USA.

(2) Barbara Beneficiary, 1333 Main Avenue

Some Town, USA.

b. Upon information and belief, at the time of the Decedent's death he was survived by two children. Their names, addresses and ages, as of the Decedent's date of death are as follows: [Listing Omitted].

c. Upon information and belief, none of the Decedent's children predeceased the Decedent.

d. I certify that the foregoing statements are true. I am aware that if any of the foregoing statements made by me are wilfully false, I am subject to punishment.

_____

Date

_____

Larry Lawyer, Esq.
Attorney at Law State of SomeState

Sworn to before me
this ____th day of
_____ , 2001

_____

Notary Public

REJECTION AND RESUBMISSION

Probate is not like school term papers. You turn the paper in, the teacher gives you a grade, and the process ends. With Probate, everyone must get 100 percent. If the Petition or related documents are not adequate, the clerks will either return them to you for correction, or hold them and request that you submit additional documents to supplement what you filed. Do not be alarmed. And do not assume that if you are paying an Estate attorney, rejection should never occur. It will. Rejections can occur for many reasons. The forms filed may have been updated or laws or procedures changed since the blank forms were obtained. Courts do not have the resources to track down and notify anyone with a Probate pending as to the changes. So the only way to find out is by filing a Petition or other documents that are rejected. Many rejections are for what appear to minor technicalities. You may assume that some minute technical correction is absurd, but clerks see thousands of Probate matters each year. They may be sensitive to issues that you are unaware of. They may have learned of the importance of certain fine points from problems that have occurred in an unusual case or two. In many situations, the clerks are aware of how the Judge who must issue an order wants the paperwork prepared. It is certainly preferable to have the clerk identify the problem so you can correct it before more time is spent having incorrect documents await the Judge's rejection.

LETTERS TESTAMENTARY

Once the Petition has been filed, Notices given, and other Court or state law requirements complied with, if there is no challenge to the Will or proceeding (see Chapter 6), the Court will issue Letters Testamentary authorizing you to act on behalf of the Estate. You should generally order 5 to 10 (more for a larger or more complex Estate) originals. Almost every bank, brokerage firm, or other person you will ask to transfer assets of the Decedent to the Estate will require an original (as well as a Death Certificate). Many Courts date the Letters Testamentary so that they expire after a brief time period. This is why it is better to order them in batches as you need them. If you are to serve as a Trustee of a Trust formed under the Decedent's Will (e.g., a Bypass Trust, a Trust for minor children), the Court will also issue you Letters Trusteeship to authorize you to act on behalf of the Trust.

ADVERTISING AND NOTICE TO CREDITORS AND OTHERS

Most states have a procedure for you, once you are officially appointed as Executor, to Advertise (publish) in official newspapers to put any creditors and other persons who may have an interest in the estate on notice that you are the Executor and that the Decedent's Will has been admitted to Probate. If you undertake this Advertising or notification (often you must), be certain to comply with the specific requirements of the statute so that the Advertising and/or notice will be effective to cut off any claims against you to the maximum extent permitted by state law. For example, if proper Advertising and notice is given to alert creditors, state law may provide that after six months, creditors cannot assert a claim against the Estate. If the law in the state where you are probating the Decedent's Will follows this approach, you might not want to make any significant distributions to any Beneficiaries until the expiration of this six-month time period. The Advertising procedures can be used to identify missing heirs. If the Beneficiaries need funds (e.g., minor children) before this time, ask the Estate attorney how to handle immediate distributions.

BOND

Fiduciaries may be required by state law to be Bonded. A Bond is insurance that provides financial security to the heirs and assures performance of the Fiduciary's responsibilities. The Surrogate's Court can provide information and a listing of Bonding or Surety companies in the area where you are serving, or you can consult with the attorney representing the Estate.

CONCLUSION

This chapter has reviewed the general requirements for having the Will admitted and accepted by the Court, as well as the related documents and procedures you typically must address to obtain Letters Testamentary authorizing you to act on behalf of the Estate. The steps in this chapter constitute what is technically Probate, although as explained in Chapter 1, all the stages discussed throughout this book, from collecting assets to filing tax returns, constitute what most people think of as Probate in lay terms. Although horror stories abound, the process—as this chapter illustrates—is not that difficult in most cases. In the occasional situation where the Probate of the Will becomes costly, requires long time delays, and creates tremendous aggravation, it is because of one of the unusual circumstances described in Chapter 6.

6 SPECIAL SITUATIONS

Most Probate cases are uneventful. Except for the annoyance of identifying certain assets, completing tedious paperwork, or deciphering an arcane tax regulation, and the like, most Probate matters roll along until completed. Occasionally, however (and this is where Probate has been tagged with its often undeserved evil reputation), you may encounter difficulties—and sometimes nightmares. Many of the more common pitfalls are the subject of this chapter. If any of them develop, you are really advised to hire an Estate attorney. Again, that does not mean huge fees and total involvement of the attorney. It means meeting with the attorney, fully apprising him of the issues and considering his advice as to what aspects of the Probate matters, and the thorny problems discussed in this chapter in particular, the attorney should handle.

INTESTACY—WHEN THERE IS NO WILL

If the Decedent died without a Will (Intestate), state law provides rules to determine who the Executor or Administrator is and to whom and how (outright, in custodial accounts for minors, or to a Guardian if the Beneficiary is incapacitated) the Decedent's assets will be distributed. The typical distribution scheme is to provide for a fixed dollar amount, and a significant percentage of the remaining assets to the surviving spouse, with the remainder to be shared between the children. If there is no spouse or children, the assets will be distributed to more distant relatives in order of the nearness of the family relationship (Consanguinity). Although the rules differ from state to state, grandchildren, then parents, then siblings, then nieces and nephews may take in that order.

Intestacy can create additional costs, problems, and delays compared with probate with a Will. If you are at the stage of having to administer the Decedent's Estate, there is nothing that can be done to change the situation since it is a bit late for the Decedent to sign a Will.

When there is no Will, the procedures will be similar to those described in Chapter 5 for filing a Petition, and so on. However, the terminology and some of the forms will change. The person appointed to manage the Decedent's Estate may now be called an "Administrator" instead of an Executor.

The Court may issue "Letters of Administration" instead of Letters Testamentary. When following the directions for requesting forms indicated in Chapter 5, be certain to advise the Court clerk that there is no Will. Similarly, if you go to a local office supply store to purchase forms, purchase forms for an Estate Administration and not a Probate of a Will. When you go to your local library to look up the state laws that apply, be certain to identify the special rules for Intestacy.

WILL CHALLENGES

The large transfers of wealth that are now occurring are generating more Will challenges in part because of increasingly complex family structures. Blended families, nontraditional families, second, third, and later marriages, are becoming more common than the *Leave It to Beaver* families many politicians would have you believe are the norm. These demographic changes are compounded by the litigious nature of many baby boomers who are the Beneficiaries of these wealth transfers. If you are serving as an Executor, you should become familiar with basic Will challenges and some of the steps you can take to address such a problem if it arises.

A Will challenge can be triggered by hurt feelings: "Why didn't Mom give me as much as my sister?" When a Beneficiary receives less than expected, a Will challenge may result. If a parent disinherits a child, that child might seek to challenge the Will. Whether the challenge is primarily to assuage the hurt of a Will clause confirming a parent's lack of love ("For reasons best known to me I leave nothing to my son John"), or for the money, a challenge is nevertheless likely.

In many instances, a Will challenge is undertaken because of problems that occurred with the Will itself. The Will may not have been signed with the proper formality required by state law. It may have lacked the requisite language in the document, not had the proper number of Witnesses, or the Witnesses may have been disqualified (e.g., the Witnesses may have all been Beneficiaries). In some instances, fraud or duress may have occurred in the signing of the Will. Fraud could have occurred if the Will signed was not the one the Decedent intended (a switch was intentionally made). Duress could occur if the Decedent was intimidated into signing a Will that he or she did not really want to sign. If the Decedent did not have sufficient understanding of what he or she was doing to sign the Will, a challenge may result.

Why challenge a Will? If someone succeeds in challenging the Will they may be able to convince the Court to write their name in the Will where it was arguably forgotten. For example, your three siblings were listed as sharing equally in a $100,000 distribution. Your name was not listed. Perhaps it was a matter of the Testator's merely forgetting your name. Perhaps your estranged siblings conspired in influencing the Testator to leave your name out of the Will so that their shares would be larger. Perhaps your wife, the Testatrix, left you out of her Will in favor of her new boyfriend. You may want to challenge the Will to assure an inheritance (although, as discussed later in this chapter, in this latter situation the exercise of a spousal right of election might be preferable).

What happens when someone challenges the Will and succeeds? In most situations, you as Executor in consultation with the Estate attorney will probably negotiate a settlement with the person, obtain a Release and consent to the Will being admitted, in order that you may proceed to complete the Probate of the Estate. Settling may also be advantageous for you as Executor if the settlement is less costly than the Estate attorney's estimates of the likely costs of fighting the lawsuit. Be certain to discuss with the Estate attorney whether you should obtain the approval of any Beneficiaries or other people affected by the outcome of the suit and settlement. You do not want to later be sued by the very Beneficiaries you thought you were protecting with the settlement.

In other cases if the Will challenge is successful, the entire Will you were assuming applied may be thrown out. If this happens, you may no longer be able to serve as Executor (actually, you probably would never be officially appointed as an Executor because your appointment would be held in abeyance by the Surrogate's Court pending the conclusion of the Will challenge). In some cases, it may be possible to have the Court issue Preliminary Letters authorizing you to take limited actions pending resolution of the Will challenge. If the Will is disregarded, if the Decedent had signed a Will prior to the Will just challenged, the next most recently signed prior Will may be reinstated. If there was no prior Will, then it will be as if the Decedent died intestate. Then state law will determine who receives how much of the estate (see preceding discussion). If a person would inherit under the state law Intestacy statute, but the Will gave him or her nothing, then a successful Will challenge could provide a windfall.

If you even suspect a Will challenge, be extra cautious in making distributions and taking other actions to have the distributions and actions approved by those affected. Also, try to secure and save any prior Wills, and notes concerning the Testator's conduct when the prior Will was signed. These prior Wills, and the background information to substantiate them, might be useful.

On what basis can someone challenge a Will? Among the most common justifications for a Will Challenge is the mental incompetency of the Testator. If the person signing the Will did not have a sufficient frame of mind to understand and knowledgeably sign the Will, it cannot be valid. The second typical basis for challenging a Will is the existence of Undue Influence. This is when someone coerces or even forces the Testator to sign a Will. These two reasons are often, but not always used together when a potential heir attacks a Will. Although the Decedent could have been incompetent but not subject to Undue Influence, usually the Decedent's mental incapacity makes him or her more likely to fall prey to Undue Influence.

How does the challenger prove Undue Influence? For Undue Influence, the initial Burden of Proof is on the person challenging the Will. This means the challenger must prove it occurred. However, the Courts understand full well that Undue Influence often occurs in secrecy. No potential heirs, unless they are on the Jerry Springer Show, are going to advertise in public that they are threatening old Aunt Jane if she does not add them to her Will. The threats are more typically at Aunt Jane's isolated vacation home where the nearest neighbor is farther away than her screams can carry. This is why many courts will allow a shift of Burden of Proof if the person challenging the Will can demonstrate that a confidential relationship existed between the Testator and the person exercising the Undue Influence under suspicious circumstances. A confidential relationship exists if the Testator was dependent on the person exercising the Undue Influence. For example, Nephew Tom threatened housebound Aunt Jane that he would stop doing her food shopping unless she increases his share under her Will. Shifting the burden of proving the case is important because the person who has the burden to prove the case is more likely to lose.

How do you defend the Estate and the Will against a challenge? First, do not try without competent legal assistance. A Probate attorney or Estate planner may not have the expertise. You want an attorney who specializes in Probate and Estate litigation and has considerable experience. Often, this will be a specialist other than the specific attorney who has assisted you with planning and Probate matters.

If the Will challenge is based on the Decedent not having sufficient mental capacity, to protect the integrity of the Will you will have to prove that the Decedent had sufficient capacity. Competency means that the Decedent understood the nature and extent of her assets. Did she know what she owned? Did the Decedent understand the natural objects of her bounty? This usually includes family members. This does not mean that the Decedent had to name family members as Beneficiaries, but she must have understood who her family members were and that they were not being named. The Decedent must have understand the purpose of her executing the Will. She must have understood that by executing the Will she was directing where her assets were to be distributed on her death.

Competence of the Decedent is usually done through witness testimony. What did the lawyer who supervised the Will ask the Decedent at the Will signing? What did the Decedent answer? What was the recollection of the Witnesses to the Will? Did the lawyer prepare a memorandum to the file or other notes demonstrating the Decedent's condition? You could next find out about the Decedent's typical practices and activities. Ask the people that had regular daily or weekly contact with the Decedent for their thoughts, observations, and opinions about the Decedent at or about the time period when the Will was signed. Try to develop a description and picture about the Decedent and her life. Who were the important people in the Testator's life? What motivated the Decedent to favor one Beneficiary over another? You want to find out about the problems the Decedent had with the persons who were left out of the Will or not favored in the Will. Was the Decedent under the care of a physician? If so, the physician who treated the Decedent might be in the best position to testify about the Decedent's competency. This is because the physician may have seen the

Decedent on a regular basis and may have asked a series of relatively common questions on medical history, lifestyle, and so on. If the Decedent was taking medication, the physician may have asked numerous questions to be certain that the Decedent understood when and how to take the medication. This can be persuasive proof in a competency test. Bear in mind that the competency determination is at the time the Will was signed. Even if the Decedent was not competent sometime after the Will was signed, so long as it can be demonstrated that the Decedent was competent when signing the Will, it can sustain the challenge. It is not uncommon for a Decedent to have a lucid, competent interval between periods of incompetence. However, it can be difficult to prove this.

HOLOGRAPHIC WILL

Holographic Wills are handwritten Wills. The rules vary between states. The writing and the circumstances must comply with state laws. A holographic may be valid if the material provisions are in the handwriting of the Decedent and the Will demonstrates what the Decedent intended to have happen to his property. You may need a handwriting expert to prove that the Will is the Decedent's handwriting if there is any challenge. Holographic Wills, however, frequently create problems concerning interpreting their intent because they are not drafted with the level of precision that a lawyer provides when preparing a Will. If there is a holographic Will or any written note which might be one, be certain to consult with an Estate attorney.

LOSS OF ORIGINAL WILL

The original Will might be lost. If there is a photocopy (e.g., the attorney who drafted the Will gave the Decedent a photocopy, or retained a photocopy and gave the Decedent the original) the Court may permit a proceeding to admit the photocopy of the Will in lieu of the original. If this is not done, and the determination is that there is no Will, any of the benefits of the Will would be lost. These could include Trusts to hold assets bequeathed to minor children. Trusts typically are more flexible, and run much longer, than a custodial account available if a minor inherits from an Intestate Estate. Very important for larger Estates, the tax planning benefits could be jeopardized. For example, the most common estate tax planning technique is for the first spouse to die to bequeath assets to a Bypass Trust. This benefits the surviving spouse but is not included in her Estate. Without a Will, this important benefit is lost. The following sample forms are excerpts from Affidavits to file with the Court in a proceeding to have a photocopy of a lost Will admitted. The statements that have to be made in the Affidavits highlight the issues and problems you must overcome to achieve this objective. As with any Court proceeding, with a lost Will you really have to hire an Estate attorney.

SAMPLE AFFIDAVITS TO ADMIT PHOTOCOPY
OF LOST WILL FOR PROBATE

January 2, 2001

Amy Attorney, Esq.
1111 Ripoff Road
Anytown, USA
(999) 999-9999
Attorney for Plaintiff

SUPERIOR COURT OF SOMESTATE
CHANCERY DIVISION-ANY COUNTY
PROBATE PART
DOCKET NO.

In the Matter of
the Estate of

Dan Decedent

_____ Deceased.

Civil Action

AFFIDAVIT

State of Somestate   )
) ss:
County of Any   )

Sally Spouse, of full age, being duly sworn according to law, upon her oath deposes and says:

1. I am the surviving spouse of Dan Decedent, deceased.

2. The decedent died on December 1, 2000, a resident of Any County, Somestate. He left a Last Will and Testament, dated April 1, 1999, in which I was named Executrix.

3. The decedent's original Will has been lost and has not been found in spite of due and diligent search. The decedent did retain a photocopy of his original Will.

4. This Affidavit is being made in support of my Complaint in Action for the probate of the photocopy of decedent's Will and grant of Letters Testamentary to me as Executrix of decedent's estate.

5. I consent to serve as Executrix of decedent's estate.

6. At the time Dan Decedent executed his Will he had two children living, and no other issue, and no child was born to him or adopted by him thereafter, and no issue was born to or adopted by either of his children thereafter.

7. The circumstances surrounding the loss of decedent's original Will are as follows:

a. The original Will was left in the hands of attorney Freddy Fire with an address then of 100 Main Street, Anytown, USA.

b. The attorney Freddy Fire's office was destroyed by a fire on November 1, 1999 and all the contents of such office were destroyed in said fire. The said fire was reported to the police and a copy of the police report is attached hereto. The loss of all contents of Freddy Fire's office was reported to his insurance carrier, Big Insurance Company, and a copy of said report is attached hereto.

c. The family of the deceased contacted Freddy Fire to try to obtain the original will of Dan Decedent. Freddy Fire has stated that the original will cannot be located and was presumably destroyed in the Fire. An affidavit of Freddy Fire is attached hereto.

8. I have reviewed the foregoing petition and the facts stated therein are true to the best of my knowledge, information, and belief.

_____

Sally Spouse, Executrix

Subscribed and sworn to
me before on January 2, 2001

_____

Notary
Commission Expires:

January 2, 2001
Amy Attorney, Esq.
1111 Ripoff Road
Anytown, USA
(999) 999-9999
Attorney for Plaintiff

SUPERIOR COURT OF NEW JERSEY
CHANCERY DIVISION-ANYCOUNTY
PROBATE PART
DOCKET NO.

In the Matter of
the Estate of

Dan Decedent

              Deceased.

Civil Action

AFFIDAVIT

STATE OF SOMESTATE   )
)   ss:
COUNTY OF ANYCOUNTY)

Cindy Child, being duly sworn according to law, upon his oath deposes and says:

I am the daughter of Dan Decedent, deceased.

I recognize the photocopy of the Will of Dan Decedent which is offered for probate in this court as a true copy of the original Will of Dan Decedent dated April 1, 1999.

I request that this Court accept the photocopy of the Will of Dan Decedent in lieu of the original Will which has been lost.

I have reviewed the foregoing Affidavit, and the facts stated therein are true to the best of my knowledge, information, and belief.

_____

Cindy Child

Subscribed and sworn to
me before on January 2, 2001

_____

Notary
Commission Expires:

GUARDIANSHIP FOR INCOMPETENT BENEFICIARY

When a Beneficiary Is Incompetent

What if an adult Beneficiary is incapacitated and mentally incompetent. To whom does the Executor distribute the bequests made to the incompetent Beneficiary? Someone who is incompetent cannot receive property. The Court may have to appoint a person to act on behalf of the mentally incompetent person to protect his or her interests and to periodically report to the Court so that the Court can be certain that matters are being handled properly. This person is called a Guardian, Committee, or Conservator. The nuances of each and the terminology used will differ from Court to Court.

To be subject to a guardianship, the person must be demonstrated, in accordance with the provisions of the statute and the applicable Court rules, to be a mental incompetent. A mental incompetent is defined as a person who is impaired by reason of mental deficiency to the extent that he lacks sufficient capacity to govern himself and manage his affairs. This can also apply to a person who is impaired as a result of a physical illness or disability. This determination may be made without a jury.

To be classified as a mental incompetent, there must be more than a mere impairment of the mind. However, the incapacity need not be total. This is important because even an incompetent person can have periods of lucidity. The key focus should be whether the individual involved is incapable of governing himself and managing his affairs, or is unfit for self-control.

The Court Proceeding to Determine Incompetency

This type of action is generally instituted by a spouse or next of kin. The Venue for an action for the appointment of a Guardian is the county where the incompetent was domiciled at the commencement of the action. This may not be the same county, or even the same state, in which the Executor commenced the Probate proceeding.

The process is begun by filing a legal document with the Court called a Complaint. The Complaint will typically include the following:

- Name, age, Domicile, and address of the person bringing the action, such as the spouse. This person is referred to as the plaintiff.
- Relationship of plaintiff and her interest in the action.
- Name, age, Domicile, and address of the alleged incompetent Beneficiary.
- The name, Domicile, and address of the spouse and all children and other next of kin. If any of these persons are deceased, it should be noted.
- The name and address of the institution presently providing the care for the Beneficiary. If a particular administrator or doctor is responsible, include that party's name and telephone number.

- The period for which the Beneficiary has been incompetent and under the care of institutions. Dates, names, and addresses of institutions, and names and telephone numbers of primary responsible doctors or administrators for each institution should be indicated.

- Affidavits and exhibits attached to the Complaint providing proof of incompetency and supporting the statements made in the Complaint. The allegations in the Complaint and the Affidavits must be verified in the manner provided for in the statute. Typically, at least two physicians having the qualifications required by the state's statute must submit Affidavits. The Affidavits must be made with personal knowledge and may only state facts that the person making the Affidavit could testify to. This means that Affidavits by physicians must be made by attending physicians who have examined the Beneficiary personally and not by physicians who have merely reviewed his records. Neither physician can be a relative, or a proprietor, director, or chief executive officer of the institution where the Beneficiary is being cared for, or financially interested in that institution. The Affidavit should state that the physicians have made personal examinations of the Beneficiary within a specified number of days of the date of their Affidavits. The physicians' Affidavits must conclude that the Beneficiary is unfit and unable to govern himself and to manage his affairs and they must say in detail the circumstances and conduct of the Beneficiary upon which they base their conclusions. This discussion of the Beneficiary's condition must include a discussion of the history of his condition. The Affidavits must provide examples of acts and expressions evidencing that the Beneficiary has an unsound mind.

- An Affidavit as to the nature, location, and fair market value of the incompetent's assets. The amounts of insurance and other assets must be stated. Where such information cannot be obtained, this fact must be stated and the reasons why it cannot be obtained must be stated. For example, a recent federal income tax return, and copies of any bank statements may be attached as exhibits.

What Happens When the Court Determines the Beneficiary Is Incompetent?

Where the Court finds the Complaint and Affidavits are acceptable, the Court will enter an order fixing the notice that must be given for a hearing. This notice must be given to the alleged incompetent, family members, and the person responsible for his care. The Court will also order the appointment of counsel for the alleged incompetent. The incompetent is entitled to be represented by an attorney of his own choosing.

The Court may also order that the alleged incompetent submit to an examination.

The Court has the power to appoint a temporary Guardian. This is sometimes done where the alleged incompetent is wasting assets.

The Court is permitted to proceed even where the alleged incompetent cannot attend the hearing. This can occur where the person is temporarily absent from the state so that it would be impossible for a judge to see him. However, an affidavit must be submitted demonstrating that the alleged incompetent has been afforded every opportunity to appear, and that he has been given every opportunity and assistance to communicate with his family.

The Court may then make a determination as to incompetency. The Court must also determine the extent of the incompetent's assets. The Court will also identify the nearest of kin and heirs. The burden of proof for establishing incompetence, however, is quite high. It must be demonstrated by clear and convincing proof that the Beneficiary is incompetent.

The final step after the Court makes the preceding determinations, is for the Court to appoint a Guardian.

SPOUSE'S RIGHT OF ELECTION AGAINST THE ESTATE

What Is a Spousal Right of Election?

A Spousal Right of Election, particularly as a result of the increase in second and later marriages and the growing divorce rate, can be important in determining how any Decedent's assets will ultimately be distributed.

The laws of almost every state recognize that the surviving spouse should be entitled to some minimum portion of the deceased spouse's estate. The rationale for this is that state legislatures believe that it is in the public's interest to protect surviving spouses. Many states, but not all, assure the surviving spouse at least one-third of the estate, subject to various conditions, limitations, and other requirements.

The spousal Right of Election laws of a particular state generally apply to any married person who dies domiciled in that state. Determining the state of domicile is important because the laws differ considerably from state to state. Domicile is generally defined as a place of permanent residence to which you ultimately intend to return. The determination as to which state is a person's Domicile is a facts and circumstances analysis.

Not every surviving spouse is entitled to the protection of this rule. A surviving spouse may be denied the Right of Election where the couple was living separate and apart in different homes, or where the couple had ceased to cohabit as husband and wife under circumstances that would give rise to a cause of action for divorce (or nullification of the marriage) from the Decedent, prior to death. Mere separation does not defeat the Right of Election.

Even if the right is available, it is not always obvious what it will amount to. In some states, any transfer under which the Decedent retained the possession or enjoyment of, or right to income from, the property, at the time of death, will make those assets subject to a Spousal Right of Election.

How Does a Revocable Living Trust Affect the Spousal Right of Election?

Generally, a Revocable Living Trust should not impact this right. The logical theory behind this result is that Courts have viewed Revocable Living Trusts, because of the control by the Grantor, as illusory. Therefore, they have subjected assets of the trust to Elective Share rights. Surprisingly, depending on state law, the use of a Revocable Living Trust might affect this important right. In some states, the surviving spouse may not have the right to elect against assets in a Revocable Living Trust. The determination of who (e.g., a Revocable Living Trust) should own an asset can affect the extent to which a surviving spouse may be able to exercise a Spousal Right of Election to obtain a portion of that asset.

What Is a Surviving Spouse Typically Entitled To?

A typical state spousal Right of Election law guarantees the surviving spouse a one-third share of the estate. Not only may the percentage vary from state to state, but the definitions of what is included in the Estate will vary considerably. Prior gifts may be included in the calculation, there may be subtractions for assets owned by or given to the surviving spouse, and so on. Assets held in different types of Trusts may be included, or excluded, depending on the nature of the Trust and state law. For example, an interest in a Trust created by the Decedent spouse during his lifetime may be excluded from the calculation of the Estate against which the election can be made. If a Trust is set up for the surviving spouse under the Will, such as a marital or QTIP Trust under the deceased spouse's Will for the benefit of the surviving spouse, it may only be partially counted towards fulfilling the Right of Election. Another common Right of Election issue is to what extent property to be held in other Trusts for the benefit of the surviving spouse and others (e.g., children) will be counted toward meeting her Elective Share (the amount the surviving spouse is entitled to). In many states, property in Trust is only counted at 50 percent in value and only if the spouse is the only Beneficiary. In some states, a Life Estate (the surviving spouse is given the right to use property, such as a house, but does not own it) and interests held in a Trust do not qualify as satisfying the surviving spouse's Right of Election at all.

EXAMPLE: Husband dies in 2002 leaving a $2 million Estate. $500,000 are joint assets that pass to the deceased husband's child from a prior marriage. The Probate Estate consists of $1.5 million of securities. The Will leaves $800,000 in a marital Trust, a QTIP, for his surviving spouse. The remaining $700,000 assets are distributed to a Bypass Trust, protected from estate tax by the Applicable Exclusion Amount. The surviving spouse and the Husband's children from a prior marriage are all Beneficiaries of the Bypass Trust. Under state law the Bypass Trust is included in the calculation of the Estate but does not count as an asset paid to the surviving spouse. Under a typical state statute, assets in a QTIP Trust will count

50 percent as meeting the spousal right of election. If the joint property is included in the Estate for calculating the spousal right of election under state law, then the surviving spouse has a right of election against a $2 million Estate. A one-third elective share is $666,666. The only bequest that counts toward satisfying the spousal right of election is the QTIP Trust of $800,000. This only counts at a 50 percent rate, or as if the surviving spouse received $400,000. Thus, the surviving spouse would be entitled to an additional $266,666 [$666,666 – $400,000] if she elects against the Estate.

To prevent an end-run around the Spousal Right of Election laws, many state laws permit the surviving spouse to obtain a percentage of assets given away just before death. For example, in some states, any gifts can be reached by the spouse if made within two years of death of the Decedent, if the gifts to any one donee in either of the two years exceed $3,000. However, if the surviving spouse gave a written consent to the transfer, or joined in the transfer, the property transferred may not be reached.

Another complication in applying the Spousal Right of Election rules is that they often permit the surviving spouse to inherit a specified percentage of the value of the Decedent's Estate. Thus, all assets must be valued. If real estate or closely held business interests are involved, this can be complex and can lead to arguments between the surviving spouse and the Beneficiaries named to receive the property under the Decedent's Will.

Be Certain That the Surviving Spouse Did Not Waive the Right

In many situations, when the Testator's Will is to provide the surviving spouse less than the amount of the statutory election, the surviving spouse will be requested to formally waive his or her Right of Election. This is done specifically to prevent the surviving spouse from using the election to upset the dispositions provided for under the Testator's Will. The method of assuring that the dispositive scheme will be respected is to have the spouse waive her Right of Election. It may be completed prior to, or after, the marriage. To be effective, the waiver of the Right of Election must meet specified requirements under state law. The rules will vary from state to state, but might include the following.

The waiver must be in the form of a written contract or agreement signed by the spouse waving the right. The waiver will only be effective if there is full disclosure of all assets in the estate. It would be unfair for a spouse to be able to effectively waive his or her rights under state law without knowing the assets involved. How can you agree to forgo what you do not know? The waiver must be both clear and certain. A waiver in a prenuptial agreement or divorce property settlement agreement can be effective if properly done.

When you are serving as an Executor, if the surviving spouse exerts her Right of Election, be certain to confirm whether a Waiver was ever signed. If so, the next step is to consult with the Estate attorney to determine if the waiver is effective. Also, if the surviving spouse is provided less under the

Will than the Spousal Right of Election would provide, you should not distribute assets of the Estate until the issue of whether the Election will be asserted is resolved.

CONCLUSION

This chapter has summarized a number of special situations and problems that can affect an Estate. When you are serving as Executor and any of the situations discussed could arise, or even appear to be an issue, be certain to obtain professional legal advice. Also, be careful because the law differs considerably from state to state. Also, be certain to keep the Beneficiaries, other Fiduciaries, and other persons interested in the Estate apprised of the status of these situations because they all can add time delays and cost to the Probate process.

Part Three

NUMBERS AND PAPERS: ORGANIZING, BUDGETING, AND INVESTING

7 GETTING ORGANIZED AND HANDLING ACCOUNTING

Organization is critical for managing any Estate. Even for a modest and simple Estate, there can be a considerable number of transactions and correspondence. For any Estate, there is always the risk that a Beneficiary or other person may question your actions. Thus, you should take steps to organize correspondence and other paperwork, keep records of all financial transactions, calendar key deadlines (see Chapter 2), and review checklists to monitor the progress of the Estate settlement. This chapter provides practical tips on addressing these matters.

CORRESPONDENCE AND COMMUNICATION

One of the most important things for you to do as Executor is to be certain to keep everyone involved with the Estate fully informed of what is happening. This is important to ensure that each of the professionals working on Estate matters is aware of what every other professional is doing. This is vital so that nothing gets dropped because a professional assumed you or another professional was handling a matter that he should have handled. It is also important to keep all the Beneficiaries fully informed. Many of the problems that affect Estates are a direct result of Beneficiaries becoming anxious because of a lack of information. The following sample form can be adapted for your Estate. Type up a transmittal form with all key information. Forward any information, forms, reports, and so on that you receive, to each of the appropriate persons. This can save considerable time over typing formal letters for each piece of communication. Be certain to set up a file for correspondence and save copies of all correspondence to or from yourself in chronological order. This should be done even if it is a duplication of many of the items that you have filed in other files or tabs in the Estate loose-leaf binders you set up. There are simply too many situations where having the chronological order of documents, or the duplication when another file is misplaced (or you can not determine which other file you put a particular document in), not to do this.

Although much of your communication will be by telephone, try to get anything important in writing to document the steps you have taken. Considering jotting down brief notes of each telephone call in the Estate appointment calender you were advised to maintain in earlier chapters.

SAMPLE TRANSMITTAL FORM
ESTATE OF DAN DECEDENT

SENT FROM:

[   ]   Elliott Executor, 123 Main Street, Anytown, USA. Telephone 999-123-4567.
[   ]   Tina Trustworthy, 456 Big Street, Somewhere, USA. Telephone 999-456-7890.
[   ]   Barbara Banker, Big Bank & Trust Co., 1000 Finance Way, Sometown, USA. Telephone 999-111-1111.
[   ]   Alice Attorney, Esq., 100 Main Street, Anytown, USA. Telephone 999-222-2222.
[   ]   Amy Accountant, CPA, 400 Anchor Way, Bigcity, USA. Telephone 999-333-3333.

SENT TO:

[   ]   Elliott Executor, 123 Main Street, Anytown, USA. Telephone 999-123-4567.
[   ]   Tina Trustworthy, 456 Big Street, Somewhere, USA. Telephone 999-456-7890.
[   ]   Barbara Banker, Big Bank & Trust Co., 1000 Finance Way, Sometown, USA. Telephone 999-111-1111.
[   ]   Alice Attorney, Esq., 100 Main Street, Anytown, USA. Telephone 999-222-2222.
[   ]   Amy Accountant, CPA, 400 Anchor Way, Bigcity, USA. Telephone 999-333-3333.
[   ]   Betty Beneficiary, 789 Route 1, Somewhere, USA. Telephone 999-444-4444.

DOCUMENT ENCLOSED:

[   ]   Bills:

Vendor Name	Address/Description/Comment	Amount

[   ]   Other Documents:

Description	Comment	Date

ACTION REQUIRED:

[   ]   Pay bill.
[   ]   For your files.
[   ]   File with appropriate tax, or government agency.
[   ]   Review and call with any comments.
[   ]   Take action indicated by attached document.

[   ]   Other: _____

CHECKLIST

The following checklist will assist you in handling the Estate. The checklist is not all inclusive. Be certain to review the steps you need to take with the accountant, attorney, and other professionals you hire:

- Verify information on death certificate. If it is not accurate, order corrected certificates.

- Locate and secure the original Will. It must be filed with the Surrogate's Court with the Probate Petition.

- Open an Estate checking account and route every transaction through the account to assure records of all transactions are in one place. Also, carefully explain each transaction to facilitate proper categorization and to assist in addressing any questions raised by Beneficiaries or an IRS audit.

- Search the Decedent's apartment or house to identify and secure assets.

- Write all banks and brokerage firms Decedent dealt with (not just where there are current accounts) to identify other accounts or assets, safe deposit boxes, margin accounts, debts, and so on. Also, obtain date of death values for any assets.

- Review the Wills and any Trusts of relatives for Powers of Appointment in favor of the Decedent. These are rights given to the Decedent under a Will or Trust for the Decedent to designate in his Will where the property governed by the other person's Will or Trust should be distributed. Review the tax consequences of these with the Estate's attorney.

- If an estate tax return may have to be filed, write each broker, bank, and so on for the Alternate Valuation Date (six months following the Decedent's death) balances to determine whether the Estate would be valued lower at the Alternate Valuation Date.

- Determine accrued interest on any bank accounts, bonds, or other interest-paying assets. This is interest earned on the account but not paid to the Decedent before death.

- Contact the Veterans Administration and the Social Security Administration concerning benefit information and to notify them of Decedent's death so that future payments will be stopped.

- Contact Decedent's employer (and possibly former employers) for benefit information, severance pay, death benefits, accrued vacation pay, and so on.

- Obtain appraisals for all material assets such as real estate, business interests, jewelry, and so on.

- Maintain insurance on assets during administration. Have all existing coverage reviewed to be certain that it is up to date and that the Estate is properly listed as the insured.

- Invest idle cash balances in a diversified and safe manner that is consistent with the Estate's overall investment objectives.

- Identify and obtain property in hands of bailees (jewelry for repair; clothes for cleaning; etc.). One way to identify these is to scan the Decedent's checkbook. Then contact local service and repair businesses to which checks have been written in the past to determine whether they are holding any of the Decedent's property.
- Write charities (see prior Form 1040, Schedule B; review old checkbooks) to identify outstanding pledges.
- Write closely held businesses for stock subscriptions outstanding, shareholder (operating or partnership) agreements. Review them for any obligations or rights.
- Write attorneys used by the Decedent to request information concerning outstanding claims, litigation, and so on.
- Write any real estate brokers with whom the Decedent dealt to determine whether there are any outstanding realty contracts.
- Verify that the Decedent has received any refunds due on prior federal and state income tax returns received. Review the old returns, and/or speak with the Decedent's accountant, to identify the refunds. Then review the Decedent's checking and other accounts to determine whether a deposit in that amount was made.
- Verify that any premiums or refunds due on insurance policies were received.
- Review Decedent's records and contact Decedent's family to inquire as to any jointly owned property with the Decedent.
- Make an inventory of any of Decedent's safe deposit boxes.
- Inventory assets in any vacation or second home.
- Inventory any cash on hand. If there is significant cash, have a witness on hand and consider videotaping the counting.
- Pay funeral and other administrative expenses.
- Set up ledger of all receipts and related items for every expense.
- Pay taxes and utilities on all real property.
- File Decedent's final individual income tax returns after carefully reviewing with the CPA being used any elections, special provisions governing a final return, the allocation of expenses between the Decedent's final income tax return and Estate tax return.
- Verify whether any reportable gifts were made by the Decedent (or the Decedent's spouse in which the Decedent agreed to gift split) prior to death. Were these reported on gift tax returns filed? Are gift tax returns due?
- File the Estate's federal and state income tax returns.
- File estate's federal and state estate and inheritance tax returns.
- Obtain additional Letters Testamentary or Letters of Administration if necessary.
- Obtain additional death certificates if necessary.

- Make claims for any life insurance policies and obtain Form 712 from each insurance carrier.
- Make claims for any employer-provided death benefits.
- Make claims for any inheritances under other Wills, Trusts, and so on of people making bequests to the Decedent. Consider whether Disclaimers should be filed for any.
- Make claims for veteran or other government benefits.
- Make claims for pension or other retirement assets, arrange for any rollovers before the deadlines. Contact your accountant and the bank or brokerage form to confirm these deadlines.
- Apply for a tax identification number on Form SS-4 for the Estate and any Trusts set up under the Decedent's Will.
- File Form 56 with the IRS notifying the IRS where tax information should be sent.
- Value all assets at date of death and value all assets at the Alternate Valuation Date, if appropriate.
- Determine whether the Estate received any Income in Respect of the Decedent (IRD) under Code Section 691.
- File personal property tax returns if applicable.
- Contact the post office and arrange to have all mail forwarded to you as Executor. Carefully review all mail to identify bills to pay (if the Estate is required to do so), assets to gain control over (e.g., an interest or dividend payment could indicate a bond or stock that you had not previously been aware of).
- Terminate Decedent's lease for residential property if required or if permitted and advantageous. If not, investigate a sublease. Review the lease provisions to determine the rights you have as Executor.
- Obtain all prior gift tax returns since these will be necessary to properly complete the Estate's tax return.
- Determine whether Ancillary Probate is necessary to address real estate located in different states.
- Obtain evidence corroborating any debts or claims and then determine if the Estate must pay them. If debts must be paid, address them in the budget (cash flow analysis).
- Review any unpaid medical expenses of the Decedent and determine if insurance will cover them, and if not, whether they have to be paid by the Estate.
- Verify who can legally use Decedent's car; verify insurance coverage.
- Cancel credit cards.
- Cancel videotape rental, library, and other courtesy cards.
- Notify Decedent's banks that they should permit outstanding checks to clear.

- Obtain prior three years' bank records and income tax returns as they will probably be necessary in the event of an IRS tax audit.

ASSEMBLE THE DOCUMENTS

One of the first steps any Executor should take is to obtain and review, with legal counsel if necessary, all the pertinent legal documents that may affect the Estate. The following is a list of many of these. Although some of these documents are discussed elsewhere in this book, they are listed here to provide a single comprehensive list of documents:

- Living Will; Health Care Proxy. These may provide important information as to burial requests, funeral services, and so on. Unfortunately, if you have not previously found them, it may be too late.
- Powers of Attorney. Powers lapse on death. However, if a third party in good faith and without notice of death completed a transaction under the authority of the power of attorney, it may still be valid. If any significant transactions were completed near the time of the Decedent's death, you may want to investigate them.
- Will. This is usually the primary document governing the Estate (see Chapter 4).
- Revocable Living Trust. If a Revocable Living Trust exists then the Trust, in combination with the Will should govern most transactions. Be alert for any issues that may arise because of the use of two documents. They are not always used in the format of a simple Pour Over Will with everything in the Trust.
- Letter of Instruction. Any personal notes to provide guidance to you as to how the Decedent would want you as Executor, and any Trustees, to handle matters can be quite helpful, even if not legally binding.
- Personal Property List. Many Decedents assemble a listing of how their personal property should be distributed. This is commonly done even if the Will is silent. Attempt to locate such a list and follow it to the extent you can. Be cautious; if the list is not prepared in a manner that makes it legally binding (most are not), then while you may want to carry out the Decedent's wishes because of your moral obligation to do so, you must be constrained by the legal provisions of the Will.
- Insurance Trust. A common estate planning technique is to have a Trust own insurance on your life (or the joint lives of you and your spouse). On your death (or on the death of the last of you and your spouse in the case of joint life, also called second to die, insurance), the insurance trust may receive substantial proceeds that may be used to fund loans to the Estate or to purchase assets from the Estate to provide liquidity. The Trust cannot pay the Decedent's Estate Tax directly.

ORGANIZING ESTATE FINANCIAL MATTERS

Record keeping is one of the most important functions of an Executor. You have a fiduciary responsibility to assure that you identify all assets (Chapters 10–14), account for all assets and funds received (Chapter 7), invest those funds prudently (Chapter 9), pay all expenses and claims (Chapters 15–17), and ultimately distribute the remaining funds to the Beneficiaries designated in the Decedent's Will and provide some type of Accounting supporting the amounts distributed (Chapters 19–20). Even for a relatively small Estate, setting up basis accounting and record keeping procedures is essential. With a few simple techniques and tips, the process should not be that difficult. This chapter provides you with that background.

USING LOOSE-LEAF BINDERS TO ORGANIZE THE ESTATE

Set up four loose-leaf binders (or file folders if you prefer) to organize estate records. If you can simply file documents in a rational order as you receive them, it will give you considerable control over the entire Estate and the Probate process. Using the procedures described here will help:

1. *Correspondence Binder.* This should be a chronological file that includes a copy of all correspondence concerning the Estate in date order, whether sent or received by you or other key persons.
2. *Estate Tax Return Binder.* If the Estate will have to file a federal (or just state) estate tax return, set up an Estate Tax Return Binder.

TABS: The following are common tabs for a Probate Estate Tax Return binder:

[1]   Correspondence with Tax Authorities
[2]   Final Federal Estate Tax Return
[3]   Final State Estate or Inheritance Tax Filings
[4]   Real Estate (Form 706-Schedule A)
[5]   Stocks and Bonds (Form 706-Schedule B)
[6]   Cash (Form 706-Schedule C)
[7]   Insurance (Form 706-Schedule D)
[8]   Property Jointly Held with Spouse (Form 706-Schedule E, Part I)
[9]   Property Jointly Held with Non-Spouse (Form 706-Schedule E, Pt II)
[10] Miscellaneous Property (Form 706-Schedule F)
[11] Revocable Transfers (Form 706-Schedule G)
[12] Funeral Expenses (Form 706-Schedule J)
[13] Debts (Form 706-Schedule K)
[14] Marital Deduction (Form 706-Schedule M)
[15] Tax Waivers
[16] Decedent's Last Income Tax Returns
[17] Miscellaneous

---

3. *General Probate Binder.* For any Estate, set up a General Probate Binder.

TABS: The following are common tabs for a General Probate Binder:

[1]   Correspondence with Courts
[2]   Probate Petition
[3]   Death Certificates
[4]   Letters Testamentary
[5]   Letters Trusteeship
[6]   Miscellaneous Court Filings
[7]   Bond
[8]   Inventory
[9]   Will (copy)
[10]   Revocable Living Trust (copy)
[11]   Accounting Matters

---

4. *Probate Banking Binder.* For all Estates, set up a Probate Banking Binder.

TABS: The following are common tabs for a Probate Banking Binder:

[1]   Correspondence—Financial
[2]   Decedent Bank Accounts
[3]   Estate Checking Account—Permanent Information
[4]   Estate Checking Account—Check Vouchers and Supporting Documents
[5]   Checking Account Statements
[6]   Estate Brokerage Account—Permanent Information
[7]   Estate Brokerage Account—Supporting Documents
[8]   Brokerage Account Statements

HANDLING ESTATE FINANCIAL TRANSACTIONS

Basic Rule

The basic rule of maintaining proper financial records for an Estate is to document absolutely everything. The greater the detail, the more substantiation, the better. Its always easier to document and describe a transaction when it occurs than at a later date when someone is questioning the transaction.

Selecting a Bank

Many Executors simply continue to bank where they have had their personal bank accounts or where the Decedent maintained bank accounts. Although this may be adequate, there may be no compelling reason to continue using either institution for the Estate. Evaluate the Estate's banking and financial needs and interview not only previously used institutions but others as well. Estate financial matters create different needs and can benefit from different services and departments than personal banking needs. Inquire as to what specific trust and estate services various institutions offer, how they price them, and what specifically they can do to assist you in handling the Estate. Many larger institutions have extremely sophisticated trust departments that can assist you in arranging financing, consolidating accounts, investment management, and so forth. These services may help you hold down legal and other fees.

Accounts in Estate Name

All transactions should be run through the Estate's name and under the Estate's tax identification number. Other than minor exceptions for necessary initial expenditures by you prior to the Estate account being opened (each of which should be carefully documented) never commingle Estate funds with your personal funds, Beneficiary funds, and so on.

Safety Checks

Purchase safety checks for all Estate payments. These checks have a carbonless check voucher attached. Each time you write out a check a carbonless second sheet records the transaction. Take this second sheet (called voucher copy of the check) and staple the bills or other documents supporting the payment to them. Then file these in the Probate Banking Binder in check number order.

Document All Cash Payments

If you choose to advance your own funds to cover an Estate expense, make a copy of the check and attach copies of the supporting documents (e.g., the bill). When the Estate checking account is open, you can then reimburse yourself and use the previously assembled backup to support the check.

Run All Financial Transactions through One Estate Checking Account

You can vastly simplify the record keeping for the Estate by running all payments and deposits through a central or single Estate checking account and brokerage account. Any proceeds of any nature received should be deposited in one Estate checking account. Each deposit slip should be saved and the source and nature of the deposit clearly explained. Even if the Estate receives a large settlement that you will invest pending distribution, first deposit it in the central Estate checking account and thereafter transfer it to the Estate brokerage account for investment. All investments should likewise be made in street name in a single brokerage account (unless the Estate is so substantial that the insurance limits on the account will be exceeded).

All payments should be made from the same account. Similarly, each check should clearly document the purpose of the check.

Carefully describe every deposit, check, credit/debit memo, or other transaction. Detailed descriptions will make it much easier for you, or your professionals, to identify transactions, prepare accountings, and complete tax returns.

CONCLUSION

This chapter has provided an overview of how to organize estate documents and financial transactions. Get started right. Organize and control all documents and transactions. It will greatly simplify the entire Probate process and provide you greater protection if any of your actions are later questioned.

8 BUDGETING

Budgeting, whether formal and detailed, or somewhat informal, can be important for many Estates. The most significant item to budget and plan to meet for many Estates is the federal estate tax which is generally due within nine months of the Decedent's death. Budgeting may be necessary to help you determine if lines of credit should be established, property sold, and how to invest Estate cash balances. Budgeting steps will make it easier to later prepare an Estate Accounting or to prepare an Estate Inventory.

EMERGENCY CASH

Use the following template to identify possible emergency cash needs.

Template for Emergency Cash Needs

Procedure	Document Reference/Comment	Person Responsible Date Completed	Estimated Amount	When Needed
Inquire of immediate family/dependents re: cash/ financial demands.			$	
Verify expenses currently being paid to protect assets (rent; utilities; insurance).			$	
Other immediate cash needs.			$	

ASSETS: ANALYSIS OF POSSIBLE CASH PROCEEDS

To help budget funds that will be available, list assets of the estate, the estimated values, and when you expect to receive them. Most importantly, is it appropriate or advisable (for reasons other than cash needs) to liquidate any of these assets? If so, then estimate a liquidation date and the costs of liquidation. Be conservative because, if a cash shortfall is indicated, it will be safer to have lines of credit ready or other options addressed, than not to. If you still project a cash shortfall, then consider, in order of priority, which assets should be sold to raise cash. Be certain to address other options to sale, such as using the assets as collateral for a loan or to secure mortgage financing. The chart below shows a useful way to list assets.

Template for Estate Liquidity from Various Estate Assets

Item/Description	Expected Sale Date (Hold=No Imminent Sale)	Estimated Value Less Costs to Sale	Can Asset Support A Loan?	Planning Comment
Total				

TEMPLATE TO ORGANIZE ASSETS AND THE STEPS TO TRANSFER THEM

Use the sample charts on pages 123–128 to organize and manage the Estate's assets, liabilities, expenses, cash flow, and so on. The more details you complete on these matters, the lower your professional fees will be. Just don't be penny wise and pound foolish. Be sure to have the Estate attorney and accountant review everything. Identify each asset and its ownership. Indicate whether the asset is a Probate Asset or nonprobate asset. Determine where the asset is to be transferred. For example, a joint account would be transferred to the joint owner if the joint owner is living and has not Disclaimed. Assets in a Revocable Living Trust should be distributed without Probate as directed in the Trust. Assets subject to Probate will be distributed as provided in the Will. Stock in a closely held business may be governed by the buyout provisions in the shareholder agreement. Determine what has to be done to complete the appropriate transfer. You can review this process with the Estate attorney and determine which transfers you can appropriately handle, and which should be handled by the attorney. For example, you may contact insurance companies and obtain payment on insurance policies by sending them the original policy, a death certificate, and any completed forms they need (be sure to save copies of everything and obtain Form 712). On the other hand, you may prefer to have the attorney handle the completion and filing of a deed to transfer real estate.

Template for Asset Control Summary Sheet

Type of Asset	Description/ A/C No.	Probate/ Nonprobate	Date of Death Value	Where to Transfer (List Will or Trust Reference)	Steps Required to Transfer

Template for Expenses: Summary Schedule

Item/Description	Estimated Payment Date	Estimated Amount to Pay	Planning Comment
Total			

Template for Liabilities: Summary Schedule

Item/Description	Estimated Payment Date	Estimated Amount to Pay	Planning Comment
Gross Estate			

PRO FORMA CASH FLOW STATEMENTS BASED ON PRECEDING DATA

Template for Pro Forma Statement of Cash Expenditures

Date: Page 1 of : _____

Item Description	Mo.1 Death	Mo. 2	Mo. 3	Mo. 4	Mo. 5	Mo. 6	Mo. 7	Mo. 8	Mo. 9 706	Post Return
Legal										
Accounting										
Utilities										
Medical										
Insurance										
Property Upkeep										
Specific Bequests										
State Taxes										
Federal Taxes										
Total cash outlay										

Template for Pro Forma Statement of Cash Flows

Date: Page _____ of : _____

Item Description	Mo.1 Death	Mo. 2	Mo. 3	Mo. 4	Mo. 5	Mo. 6	Mo. 7	Mo. 8	Mo. 9 706	Post Return
Interest										
Dividends										
Sale of property										
Sale of business										
Loan from insurance trust										
Total cash inflow										

Template for Pro Forma Statement of Cash Available for Investment

Date: Page _____ of : _____

Item Description	Mo.1 Death	Mo. 2	Mo. 3	Mo. 4	Mo. 5	Mo. 6	Mo. 7	Mo. 8	Mo. 9 706	Post Return
Cash Inflow Total										
Other nonscheduled sources										
Cash outflow										
Other nonscheduled sources										
Net Cash Position										
Preliminary Distributions										
Reserve for tax audit										
Other Reserves										
Rationale for reserves										
Net available for investment										
Considerations affecting time frame for investment										
Investment decision on excess cash										

Template for Pro Forma Statements of Cash Flow Signature Page

RECEIVED AND ACKNOWLEDGED:

EXECUTORS:

Estate of Dan Decedent

_____

Elliott Executor, Executor

BENEFICIARIES:

_____

Betty Beneficiary

_____

Barry Beneficiary

TRUSTEES OF TRUSTS TO BE FORMED:

Credit Shelter Trust f/b/o Sue Survivor

By: _____

    Jane Jones, Trustee

CONCLUSION

This chapter has provided an overview and sample templates to help you budget estate income, asset sale proceeds, expenses, and the like. This will be useful in planning asset sales, financing, and investments.

9 INVESTING ESTATE ASSETS

Investing estate and trust assets is a key responsibility of most Executors and Trustees. Failing to invest wisely can defeat the Decedent's objectives, create financial hardship for Beneficiaries, and even expose you to personal liability. If you violate the law governing the investment of Estate or Trust assets, a Court might require you to personally make up the losses. To avoid these results, you must familiarize yourself with the following, even if you hire someone to manage the investments for you:

- *The Will.* Most Wills include several provisions governing investment of Estate and Trust assets. The rules may be different for different situations. For example, the investment standard for the Estate may be different than the investment standard for a Trust formed under the Will for a minor child.

NOTE: The Will may include a significant exception to the concept of having a diversified portfolio. This is common where stock in an S corporation may be a significant asset and where interests in a family business or investment are intended to be held by the Fiduciary. The Will may incorporate guidance or specific investment standards desired by the Decedent for these assets.

As a Fiduciary, you may not be liable to a Beneficiary to the extent that you acted in reasonable reliance on express provisions of the governing instrument, the Will. This means you must be very familiar with the terms (see Chapter 4).

- *State law.* The state law will govern the assets you invest. The laws can differ significantly from state to state. Also, these investment laws, often referred to as Prudent Investor laws, are changing. Many states are adopting versions of the law that address modern portfolio theory, described later in this chapter. Other states still have antiquated rules that favor capital preservation as the primary objective. Be certain you understand your state's rules and the interplay of those rules and the Will governing the Estate or Trust for which you are responsible.
- *Specific circumstances of the Estate or Trust.* If you are the Trustee of a Trust for three children, one child might be age 30 and have a steady

income and little need for Trust distributions; whereas another child, also a beneficiary of the same Trust, might be a 19-year-old college student with no income. Obviously, you must have some understanding of the Beneficiaries to invest Trust assets properly.

- *Tax laws.* Different Beneficiaries and different Trusts have widely different tax rules that affect them. You must understand these rules to know how to invest. You must get professional tax advice on these matters.

Even if you hire a professional money manager, or use an investment service of a mutual fund family that helps you determine the appropriate investments, you as Fiduciary are still responsible. You can delegate investment decisions, but you must still maintain vigilance. This chapter helps you understand how to do this.

HOW INVESTMENT THEORY SAYS YOU SHOULD INVEST

The modern portfolio theory has been a widely accepted concept in measuring risk and return. Asset allocation is an essential component to any thorough Probate. Asset allocation can address many important planning goals, including:

- Minimize the risk investment assets are exposed to, thus giving greater security to the Estate.
- Improve total return on Estate assets thus, over the long term, maximizing income and capital gains and asset values.
- Provide direction and guidance to Fiduciaries where the documents (Will, Trust, etc.) provide an indication of the Grantor/Decedent's risk tolerance and investment philosophy.

What is asset allocation? It is the process of identifying the asset classes in which a particular investor will invest, and then allocating the investor's capital to those asset classes through an analysis of rates of return and risk tolerance. The basis of this is modern portfolio theory. The investor must provide personal guidance to the financial planner or money manager as to the fundamental question: "How much risk are you willing to endure to achieve the return you desire?" As a Fiduciary you must make this type of analysis in light of the Will and Trust provisions, Beneficiary needs, state law, and other relevant facts and circumstances.

Modern portfolio theory, in very general terms, assumes that the investment markets are efficient. Therefore, the decision as to which asset categories to which investor capital is allocated is more critical than picking specific assets (e.g., stocks) within any particular category. A key aspect to investing is diversification, both within an asset category and between different asset categories. Selecting asset categories that have negative correlation (e.g., when one rises the other tends to fall) can minimize risk while achieving the desired level of return. For example, stocks carry a higher risk than Treasury bills, but at the same time, stocks have greater potential for higher returns. Thus, in creating a portfolio one may want to combine these two assets. Once a portfolio is created, the main concern of the investor is no longer the expected return and the standard deviation of each individual asset, but it is the expected return and the standard deviation of the portfolio as a whole.

Studies have demonstrated that more than 90 percent of the risk of a portfolio can be explained by the allocation of assets. Where a portfolio is diversified among asset categories, approximately 90 percent of the risk can be viewed as market risk; whereas only 10 percent or less of the risk of that portfolio will be specific risk of a particular stock. The ultimate level of optimization will be achieved when all specific, or nonmarket risk, is eliminated. Finally, in identifying and investing in asset categories, the categories should reflect the diverse global economy and not merely U.S. equity markets.

Modern portfolio theory holds that the "potato chip method" simply is not the most efficient method of selection. When we eat potato chips, most of us reach into the bag of chips and attempt to pick the biggest chip. According to this theory, seeking in the same way to identify the hottest stock is not an appropriate approach. Neither is selecting asset categories that alone exhibit only modest risk (the approach often used under older versions of the prudent man rule). With investments, the more mundane but statistically proven superior method of allocating assets and committing to long-range strategies is preferable to market manipulation, timing, and individual security picking.

FACTORS A FIDUCIARY SHOULD CONSIDER

When investing Estate or Trust assets, you should consider the following factors:

- *Prudent investor.* As a Fiduciary, you should invest and manage trust assets using the guidelines of a prudent investor; consider the purposes, terms, distribution requirements, and other circumstances of the Will or Trust.

- *General economic conditions.* These may affect the current Beneficiary and the Remainder Beneficiary (the person who receives assets after the current Beneficiary) differently.

- *The time period involved.* A Trust that is formed under the Decedent's Will to fund education of the Decedent's child who is 3 years old should be invested much differently than for a child who is 19.

- *The possible effect of inflation or deflation.* This is why assets that are to be held for a long period should be invested in a broader range of assets—not merely cash, money market accounts, or Treasuries.

- *Expected tax consequences of investment decisions or strategies.* For example, preserving the Stepped-Up Basis on death for low-basis assets is important (see Chapter 18). Consider buying lower yielding tax-exempt securities for high-bracket taxpayers. If it is feasible try to identify the income, estate, and generation-skipping transfer tax status of all Beneficiaries. Ideally, you should obtain income tax return and balance sheet information, as well as basic input about the intent of each Beneficiary. This is not always practical, however. How much information can you require the Beneficiaries to provide?

If there is a QTIP Trust, income must be paid out annually (or more frequently) to qualify for the marital deduction. What about the tax bracket of the spousal beneficiary? If a Dynasty Trust is established to continue for many generations, the GST tax is of paramount importance. What of the income tax brackets of the many potential Beneficiaries. If a Pot Trust for many Beneficiaries is used, the tax brackets of the various Beneficiaries could differ dramatically. Where a Trust distributes income in the year it was earned to the Trust's Beneficiaries, the Trust is generally treated as a conduit for that income, and the tax cost is passed to the Beneficiary receiving the income. This result is achieved by giving the Trust a tax deduction for the income actually distributed (or required to be distributed) to the Beneficiary. If a total return concept is used in setting Trust distributions, will the "or required to be distributed" test fail? Must a prudent Fiduciary obtain annual tax projections from an accountant? The laws are new and may not be fully clear. There are also significant differences from state to state. Be sure to consult with both an Estate attorney and investment adviser.

- *The role that each investment or course of action plays within the overall trust portfolio.* No class or type of investment is per se imprudent. Thus, an investment that might be imprudent alone may not be imprudent as part of an overall portfolio and strategy. A Trust whose main purpose is to support an elderly widow of modest means will have a lower risk tolerance than a Trust to accumulate for a young scion of great wealth.

- *Other resources of the Beneficiaries.* How is the Fiduciary to know the "other resources" of each Beneficiary? What level of diligence is necessary? Must the Trustee request a financial statement? Balance sheet? Income tax return? Is the Fiduciary obligated to look beyond the face of such items? How often must the Fiduciary request updated information? Part of the answer will be Fiduciaries taking additional steps to protect themselves.

- *The need for liquidity, for regularity of income, and for preservation or appreciation of capital.* What are the ages, lifestyles and needs of each Beneficiary? What criteria for distributions does the Will and/or Trust include? Did the grantor express any wishes for how distributions should be made?

- *Asset value.* Consider an asset's special relationship or special value, if any, to the purposes of the trust or to one or more of the Beneficiaries as, for example, an interest in a closely held enterprise, tangible and intangible personalty, or real estate. Where a family business is involved, if the Will does not specifically address retention, at minimum obtain the approval of all Beneficiaries and seek the guidance of an Estate attorney.

The Fiduciary is generally required to diversify the investments of the Trust unless it is reasonably determined that because of special circumstances the purposes of the Trust are better served without diversifying. This is really a two-part test. It must be determined when special circumstances apply. For example, interests in a closely held family business may be owned by a Trust. But this is not the entire analysis. The second step is that not diversifying the holding must result in the purposes of the Trust being better served. If a Trust is established for a minor child, the purposes of the Trust may properly (absent express proof to the contrary) be best served by assuring the maximum total return until the child/Beneficiary attains college age, at which time liquidity to meet college tuition and living expenses may be of paramount importance. For the family unit as a whole, however, maintaining control over a family business may be a primary Estate and financial planning goal. Suppose the trust owned 5 percent of the equity in the family business and the family unit as a whole owned 51 percent of the business. If the 49 percent nonfamily partner offered a substantial premium for the 5 percent equity held by the child's Trust, what should the Trustee do? It may be clear to the Trustee that the sale would undermine the family's financial stability and business control. However, if only the child is a Beneficiary of the Trust, is that relevant to the purpose of the Trust? The result could be a pressure on a Trustee to take action consistent with the purposes of the Trust but in direct conflict with anything the grantor may have intended for the family as a whole.

EXAMPLE: Diversification may not be appropriate when:

1. A tax-sensitive trust owns an underdiversified block of low-basis stock. The tax cost of recognizing the gain may outweigh the advantages of diversifying the holding.

2. The wish to retain a family business.

- *Impartiality.* The Fiduciary is required to act impartially in investing and managing the Trust assets taking into account any differing interests of the Beneficiaries.

- *Limitations of appropriate costs.* A Fiduciary, carrying out investment and management decisions, may only incur costs that are "appropriate" and "reasonable" in relation to the assets, the purposes of the Trust, and the skills of the Fiduciary. If you delegate investment management you must control the overall costs. For example, you may have to reduce the amount of commissions you receive with respect to Trust assets if investment responsibility has been delegated. For example, consider what fees are built into the cost of a mutual fund? The duty of the Trustee to monitor investments is not avoided by the delegation of investment management. Thus, how much of a reduction is appropriate? Dollar for dollar (i.e., reducing the Trustee's fees by each dollar of management fees paid to the money manager) would seem inappropriate. What of a investment manager or financial adviser who earns brokerage commissions? If these commissions would be paid in any event, should there be a reduction? Does this mean that Trustees will shop for advisers who simply earn commissions rather than separately stated fees (such as a percentage of assets under management)? How should this be addressed in the typical Fiduciary compensation provision in a Trust? Discuss these issues with the Estate attorney to avoid problems for yourself at a later date.

CONCLUSION

This chapter has provided an overview of some of the many decisions you must address in determining how to invest Estate funds. These decisions should be made in conjunction with the budget information discussed in Chapter 8.

Part Four

ASSETS

10 SAFE DEPOSIT BOXES, CASH, BANK ACCOUNTS, E BONDS, AND MARKETABLE SECURITIES

Although cash, bank accounts, marketable securities and similar assets are among the most common assets, they can raise many issues. The first step is to collect the detailed information necessary to gain control over cash and other liquid assets and the valuation data necessary to report them on an Estate tax return. You also must determine how the accounts should be distributed.

How do you assure that you have identified all of the Decedent's marketable securities, cash, and so on? First, obtain the Decedent's most recent income tax return. Schedule B of the return lists every person paying the Decedent interest or dividends. Also review the Decedent's state income tax return, which may provide additional detail as to Treasury and other securities. You can also write to every bank and brokerage firm suspected of holding an account.

Marketable securities may be in the form of actual stock, bond, or other certificates held in the Decedent's home or safe deposit box, or book entry securities held at a brokerage firm. It is generally advisable to locate all securities physically held by the Decedent and transfer them to a brokerage account to be held in street name to avoid any liability you have for the original certificates. This will also simplify the record keeping you must undertake.

Many people provide varying degrees of trading authority to money managers or brokers. Consider whether these should be terminated immediately. If so, give written notice to avoid any issues as to what was done. Until you have opened Estate accounts and formulated an appropriate investment strategy, it might be inadvisable to permit continued trading without your approval.

CORRESPONDING WITH BANKS AND FINANCIAL INSTITUTIONS

An early step in many Estates is to write each bank and brokerage firm to request confirmation of accounts, balances, and other relevant information. The following sample letter can serve as a starting point:

SAMPLE LETTER TO BANK
OR BROKERAGE FIRM

ELLIOTT EXECUTOR
123 MAIN STREET
ANYTOWN, USA

November 8, 1999
Big Bank Corp.
222 Wind Avenue
Sometown, Somestate

RE: *Estate of Dan Decedent*
     Date of Death: April 1, 1999
     Social Security No: 000–00-0000

Dear Sir/Madam:

I am the Executor of the above named estate. Enclosed are a certified copy of the death certificate of Dan Decedent and Letters Testamentary issued for the above estate. During his lifetime,
Dan Decedent held the following accounts with your institution:

Certificate of Deposit no. 1111111
Certificate of Deposit no. 2222222
Certificate of Deposit no. 3333333
Checking Account No. 000–11-3333

In order for us to proceed with the administration of the estate, please provide us with the following information:

Exact title of each account.
The balance of each account on the date of death.
Accrued but unpaid interest as of the date of death.
Verify the type of account involved (e.g., IRA, CD).

Please provide us with the requisite documents that are necessary to close out the above
accounts.

Any margin accounts or open orders for the purchase and sale of securities of any nature are can-
celled effective immediately. No trading authority shall remain in effect for any of the Decedent's accounts unless confirmed specifically otherwise in writing by the executor.

In addition, please advise if there are any other accounts that Dan Decedent (Social Security
Number 000–00-0000) may have with Big Bank Corp., either individually, jointly, or as custodian for another party.

Your kind attention to this matter is appreciated.

Sincerely,

Estate of Dan Decedent

By: _____
    Elliott Executor

CERTIFICATES OF DEPOSIT

Certificates of deposit can be difficult to manage because if they mature and are not withdrawn in a specified time period, say 10 days, they automatically renew. Once a certificate of deposit has renewed, there are typically penalties for withdrawing it prior to maturity. However, the death of the depositor can waive the early withdrawal penalty. Thus, the Estate should be able to receive interest to the date of your terminating the certificate, without the normal penalty. Review this with the institution in which the deposit is made. Depending on the cash position of the Estate (see Chapter 8 concerning budgeting), it may be advisable to cash in the certificate and deposit the funds in a money market account, short-term Treasury, and so on. Remember, the investment decision should be made in light of the overall objectives, cash needs, and tax position of the Estate and the Beneficiaries.

HOW DIFFERENT TYPES OF ACCOUNTS AFFECT PROBATE AND THE DECEDENT'S ESTATE TAX RETURN

An important matter to address concerning bank and other financial institutions is determining the account title and what it means to the Probate. Many people, especially senior citizens, may establish a joint account to facilitate management of that asset (e.g., to enable a younger family member to assist by paying bills). In some instances, the intent of such an account is to pass assets on the death of the transferor (i.e., for the account to serve as a Will Substitute). In other instances, the intent of establishing a joint account is to make a gift (e.g., parent wants to give child money but may believe it advisable to keep parent's name on the account to facilitate making future gifts, or helping the child make investments).

For the following discussion, assume that Parent Taxpayer is the person establishing the account and placing funds in the account. Junior Taxpayer is the child of Parent Taxpayer.

Junior Taxpayer

Where Parent Taxpayer opens an account solely in the name of Junior Taxpayer, the funding of the account should constitute a completed gift for gift tax purposes. Junior owns and controls the account. This may have been required to be reported on a gift tax return and thus may have reduced the Applicable Exclusion Amount available on the Decedent's Estate Tax return. Since Junior owns the account, there should be no further steps you need to take.

Parent Taxpayer in Trust for Junior Taxpayer

In these instances, Parent Taxpayer may want the funds to be transferred to Junior's control only on Parent's death. Thus, Parent Taxpayer likely has the right to revoke, in whole or part, the account at any time simply by withdrawing funds from the account. This type of account should likely not constitute a completed gift until such time as funds are spent on Junior Taxpayer's benefit, or Parent Taxpayer dies resulting in a transfer to Junior Taxpayer of the balance of the account. Unlike the joint account to be discussed, a completed gift should not occur because the nature of this account should not permit Junior the powers to withdraw without Parent's approval or act. In almost all situations, Parent possesses the exclusive right to control or withdraw funds while alive. Although this type of account should not constitute a completed gift on formation, cases have arisen where the Beneficiary attempted to demonstrate that the depositor intended a completed gift.

This type of account is often called a Totten Trust. This account name derives from a landmark case which held that the fact that the depositor could withdraw funds at any time, thereby revoking the gift, did not serve to revoke the arrangement and thereby deny the survivor (Junior Taxpayer) from receiving the balance on Parent Taxpayer's death.

This type of account will pass outside the Will as a nonprobate asset. However, it will be included in the Taxable Estate. Junior will probably have to submit the bank book and a death certificate to obtain the funds. If Junior is a minor, contact the institution about setting up a custodial account.

Parent Taxpayer and Junior Taxpayer, Jointly, with Right of Survivorship

In this type of account, funds can generally be withdrawn by either joint tenant. The rules, however, differ between states. This is perhaps the most common structure for a joint bank account. Parent Taxpayer likely has the right to revoke, in whole or part, the account at any time simply by withdrawing funds from the account. This type of account should likely not constitute a completed gift until such time as Junior Taxpayer withdraws funds, funds are spent on Junior Taxpayer's benefit, or Parent Taxpayer dies resulting in a transfer to Junior Taxpayer of the balance of the account.

The Uniform Probate Code provides that while both joint tenants are alive the presumption is that the account balance is owned in the proportion of the contributions of each joint tenant to the account. In the preceding examples, this would result in Parent Taxpayer owning the entire balance of the account until death.

On death of Parent Taxpayer, Junior Taxpayer succeeds to the entire property interest. The deceased Parent Tenant has no right to transfer the joint account by Will or otherwise. Thus, this type of ownership has been used as a Will Substitute. It is, however, included in Parent's Taxable Estate. Review the tax allocation clause of the Will with the Estate attorney to determine if there is any impact. You may have to provide Junior with a Death Certificate and bank book. Determine the value of the account to report on the Estate tax return.

Parent Taxpayer and Junior Taxpayer

This type of account is likely an unartful attempt to establish the type of account referred to previously; a joint account with right of survivorship (Parent Taxpayer and Junior Taxpayer, Jointly, with Right of Survivorship). Courts have held that the fact that the depositor/Parent could control the right of withdrawal from the account did not invalidate the intended survivorship feature. For purposes of the Estate, the comments concerning survivorship account above will apply.

Parent Taxpayer, Payable on Death to Junior Taxpayer

This type of pay on death account, often called a POD for short, is not a completed gift. The account balance should be included on Parent's Estate Tax return and should be transferred outside Probate directly to Junior at such time. You may have to provide Junior with a Death Certificate and the bank book.

Issues Affecting Various Types of Bank Accounts

Controversies can arise where on the death of the depositor, Parent Taxpayer, both the Estate of Parent and the survivor (Junior Taxpayer) claim the funds. The fact that an account is a type of joint account (e.g., Parent Taxpayer and Junior Taxpayer) is not always conclusive that Junior Taxpayer should inherit the balance existing in the account on Parent Taxpayer's death. As discussed earlier, Parent may have set up the account merely as an administrative convenience, and not with the donative intent necessary to make a gift or even an ultimate transfer on death, to Junior Taxpayer. Overcoming the presumption of Junior's inheritance, however, is likely to be a difficult task.

Similar concepts have been applied to assets other than bank accounts, such as securities.

The bottom line is that you must review all account documentation and if anything is unclear discuss it with the Estate attorney.

TRAVELER'S CHECKS

If the Decedent left uncashed traveler's checks, call the issuing company. They may cash the checks if you send a Death Certificate and Affidavit.

They may also request Letters Testamentary. If you have probated the Will, this is not a problem. If you have not, however, inquire whether they will accept an affidavit by the next of kin as sufficient. Don't forget to report this on the Estate tax return.

SAFE DEPOSIT BOXES

Importance of an Inventory

Safe deposit boxes are often a key source of information for Executors. Boxes often hold surprising and important documents, assets, keys, and the like.

Finding the Decedent's Safe Deposit Box

Locating a safe deposit box is not always a simple matter. Given the important information and assets a box may contain, many people keep the very existence of a box quiet. Consider the following steps to help find undisclosed boxes:

- *Lawyer's file.* When anyone prepares a Will or other Estate-planning documents, the attorney will request financial information. Although not all clients reveal the location or even the existence of a safe deposit box, some may. If the files can be located, request the information.
- *Federal income tax return.* Although an income tax return will not list safe deposit boxes, it can contain two important clues. First, Schedule B (and sometimes the detailed schedules attached to it) include a list of all bank accounts. Most banks require the presence of an account to open a safe deposit box. Thus, the listing of accounts provides a list of banks to write to inquire as to the existence of accounts or boxes. You will have to await Letters Testamentary for the banks to respond to your inquiry. Tax returns also list each payer of interest and dividends. If you identify names of stocks or other accounts for which you have not been able to locate the original certificates, the likelihood is that they are in the Decedent's as yet unlocated safe deposit box. Look for annual bills for rental renewal.
- *Banks near the Decedent's residence.* If the Decedent moved in the few years prior to death, check with banks located near the prior residence as well. Most people tend to take out safe deposit boxes near their homes. The elderly, who may prefer not to drive or have difficulties getting around, are even more likely to have safe deposit boxes within close proximity.
- *Close family members.* Ask, in writing, if they were aware of any safe deposit boxes (or other assets) that you have not located. Save your letters and their replies to demonstrate your efforts in the event assets

later turn up, or your actions are questioned. This could be important if the later discovered boxes are found to have had some of their contents taken before you identified them.

Procedures to Gain Access

Generally, to enter a safe deposit box, the owner must sign an affidavit stating that he is an owner of the box and that all of the owners are alive. If the owner (or often any owner) has died, Probate is necessary. If the safe deposit box is jointly owned, the surviving joint owner may be permitted access in some states. In many states, however, the joint owner will have to await Probate of the Will and the authority of the Executor to enter the box. Some states require that notification be given to the state tax department so that the contents of the box can be inventoried to assure payment of any state taxes. Some people give ownership of their safe deposit boxes to corporations or other entities in which they own interests. In such cases, if the entity does not terminate on the death of the entity's owner (a general partnership will terminate, a corporation won't) then the surviving officers or other principals of the entity who were listed as having access to the safe deposit box can access it without Probate proceedings.

Regardless of how you as Executor obtain access to the contents of the safe deposit box, carefully consider how you will demonstrate that all of the contents of the box have been accounted for. If the box contains substantial cash, jewelry, or similar valuable items, how can you prove later what it did, or more likely, what it didn't, include. Consider having one or more witnesses (such as Beneficiaries or independent advisers such as the attorney or accountant for the Estate) present to witness the opening and most importantly, the inventorying, of the box contents. In some cases, a videotaping of the box opening may be advisable. If you anticipate challenges by any family, friends, or other heirs, consult with an Estate attorney before opening the box.

Opening the Safe Deposit Box Once Found

The actual steps to physically gain access to a safe deposit box may be as follows:

1. Obtain the documents that the bank requires for access to a safe deposit box. They may be a Death Certificate and Letters Testamentary.
2. Prepare the forms the bank requests as a prerequisite to providing entry to the box.
3. Secure the key to the safe deposit box. If the key is not available, ask the bank for the name of a locksmith to drill the lock on the safe deposit box. Confirm the appointment date so that the appropriate bank

officer, you as Executor, and the locksmith will all be available at the same time.

4. Notify the state tax department, if required.

5. Complete any required state forms that may have to be filed to obtain access to the box. These forms may have a title like "Application for Release of Safe Deposit Box."

6. Arrange for a witness to sign off on the inventory of the safe deposit box to prevent later claims that contents are missing. Consider video-taping the entire process in case someone later asserts that valuable assets are missing.

Checklist of Contents

The following checklist may be helpful to use when opening the safe deposit box. If the items are present, provide a brief description. If not present, so indicate.

- Deeds
- Mortgages
- Army Release
- Original Social Security Card
- Birth Certificate
- Marriage Certificate
- Divorce Documents
- Stock Certificates
- EE Bonds
- Naturalization papers
- Coin Collection
- Jewelry
- Cash
- Stamp Collection
- Insurance Policies

CHECKING ACCOUNTS

You should notify the banks where the Decedent had checking accounts of the Decedent's death and request that they honor any checks written prior to the Decedent's death. You should verify whether there were any over-draft lines of credit tied to the account, automatic deposit features (and what items were so deposited), and any automatic deductions. Cancel any lines of credit and confirm any outstanding loan balances. Terminate any automatic payments or transfers. Be certain to arrange for appropriate payments to be continued by payment from the Estate. Inquire whether any investment accounts are linked.

Another important use of the Decedent's checking account is that it can provide a great checklist of things you should consider:

- Payments to cleaners, shoe repair stores, and the like can indicate places where the Decedent may have assets stored.

- Payments for periodic monthly expenses can provide a listing of expenses you might need to protect property.

- Payments or transfers to brokerage or investment accounts may lead you to those accounts.

- Payments to family members may indicate gifts made that you can review to see whether any of the gifts exceeded the $10,000 (to be indexed) annual gift tax exclusion thus triggering gift tax filing requirements.

- Payments for property taxes may help you identify real estate investments. Property tax bills may also be useful in valuing the properties.

- Medical and other payments may help you identify outstanding debts or claims. These can also be analyzed to avoid duplicate charges appearing on current invoices.

- Payments to state and federal tax authorities can be used to determine current tax payments for reporting on the Decedent's final income tax return.

- Pension or retirement proceeds deposited to the account may help you identify additional payers to contact to advise of the Decedent's death and to cease payments.

CASH

If there are cash balances be certain to count, and safeguard the cash by depositing it in an Estate account. If the cash amounts are significant, consider having a bank representative present when the safe or other container holding the funds is opened. It may be advisable to retain a professional videotaping company to tape the counting of the cash. Record in the daily log or calendar (see recommendation in Chapter 2) the identification of the cash and the counting. If the amounts are significant, discuss the possible income tax implications with an accountant.

GOVERNMENT SECURITIES AND SAVINGS BONDS

The U.S. government issues three types of securities. Treasury bills are short-term debt instruments issued for $10,000 or greater amounts at a discount from their face value. Treasury Notes are longer term securities with maturities from one to ten years. Treasury Bonds have the longest maturities of 10 years or longer. Zero coupon and other variations are available.

Series EE Savings Bonds are issued at 50 percent of their face value with interest paid at maturity. EE Bonds can be owned as co-owners (e.g., joint tenants with right of survivorship), individual ownership, or Beneficiary ownership. EE Bond interest is reported upon redemption. Alternatively, EE Bonds can be exchanged for Series HH Bonds which pay interest periodically.

Exercise caution in determining the tax consequences of Savings Bonds. The Decedent may have made a special tax election to report the increase in the value of the Bonds as taxable interest each year. If this was done, the face value would not be the tax basis and the excess of the proceeds over the initial purchase price on redemption would not all be taxable. Consider the benefits of reporting all accrued Savings Bond (both EE and HH) interest on the Decedent's final income tax return (see Chapter 17).

The amount of Savings Bonds to be included in the estate is based on redemption tables published by the United States Treasury. You can call 1–800–US–BONDS to obtain the necessary information.

MARKETABLE SECURITIES

Marketable Securities Generally

As noted, you should identify all securities, gain control over them, and then obtain valuations for tax and distribution purposes.

Place certificates for which you have physical custody into street name in the Estate brokerage account. Remember to save copies of any certificates turned in. Be certain to record the details of any sales, trades, or transfers in detail. When corresponding with brokerage firms, money managers, or financial planners, consider the advisability of canceling any trading authority that they have until you have had time to evaluate the accounts, Estate cash needs, and investment strategy. If you do not have adequate professional investment expertise, hire a financial adviser for the Estate to confirm the strategies and steps you take.

Next, securities must be valued. This could be important for distributing assets and reporting the securities on a federal Estate Tax return. For example, if the Will divides the remaining (Residuary) Estate among three siblings, you may require a valuation of the securities to equalize the bequests. You should also determine whether actual securities should be distributed to Beneficiaries or the securities should be sold and cash distributed. If the Beneficiaries will reinvest the funds in securities in any event, it may be more economical not to sell securities, thereby saving the commissions and other transfer costs of the sale and reinvestment.

The price at which securities should be valued is based on the date of death values and the alternate valuation date, which is the date six months following the Decedent's death. For over-the-counter securities, the value is the average of the high and low value of such shares on the date of death. If the date of death was a Saturday, an average of the values for the Friday prior to and the Monday after the date of death are used. If there were no sales on the date of death of the securities involved, then the value is determined by the weighted average of the means between the bid and ask prices on the nearest date before and the nearest date after the date of death. Determine the value of the dividends declared prior to death, but payable after death, and whether such stock was trading ex-dividend on such date.

Similarly, for bonds the bid and ask price for the bonds held are used for valuation purposes. In addition, the date on the accrued interest on such bonds must be obtained. This information is often obtainable in the *New York Times* or *The Wall Street Journal* for the date of death.

Note: Save a copy of *The Wall Street Journal* with security data as of the date of death (this may be the paper for the next business day) and as of the six-month alternate valuation date in the Estate records.

You must also determine whether the publicly held securities were trading ex-dividend on the date of death, or whether dividends were declared to holders of record prior to death, but paid after death. This information is available in Standard & Poors or other dividend declaration books, which should be in the reference section of the library.

CONCLUSION

Cash, bank accounts, marketable securities, CDs, and so on are some of the most common assets found in Estates. These assets raise a host of issues which you must deal with. These assets must be identified, secured, valued, budgeted, and reinvested. This chapter has provided an overview of how you can deal with many of these issues. Never minimize the importance of retaining on behalf of the Estate a financial professional to assist you with these matters.

TIP: Merely consolidating securities at one brokerage firm in street name will not only dramatically simplify record keeping, but will put the firm's services at your disposal in valuing and transferring securities. Finally, having a financial professional involved can provide you with guidance as to any securities that should perhaps be sold immediately.

---

11 TANGIBLE PERSONAL PROPERTY

Tangible personal property includes jewelry, artwork, guns, coin and stamp collections, furs, cars, boats, and the like. Although these are generally (but certainly not always) a modest percentage of the entire Estate, they often represent the most emotionally charged assets in the Estate.

EXAMPLE: Dad's Will directs the Executor to distribute Personal Property. Simple but very vague. The Executor gives art valued at $25,000 to daughter, and Dad's favorite pocket watch valued at $1,000 to son. Daughter blows up. The pocket watch means far more to her than the far more valuable art. The watch represents her memories of important close times shared with her father.

Personal Property can also be some of the most difficult to value. While appraisals are common, they can be expensive and time consuming (in identifying the appropriate skilled persons to use), and can vary dramatically from appraiser to appraiser because of the subjectivity often involved.

LOCATING AND SECURING PERSONAL PROPERTY

What are the steps to take concerning personal property? First, identify it and secure it. Personal property can be located in the Decedent's home, on his person at the time of death, in a vacation or second home, in a safe deposit box, and elsewhere. Once located, it must be secured. This could mean transferring it to an Estate safe deposit box or to a firm that will hold it in safe keeping pending a later sale or auction of the items. Insurance is critical to address.

TIP: Take pictures of everything.

The sample chart on page 149 can be used to manage personal property. Address whether and to what extent the item is insured in the "Insurance Status" column. Attach bills, appraisals, photographs, and other

Sample Personal Property Summary Chart

Item/ Description	Insurance Status	Date of Death Valuation	Alternate Valuation Date and Value	File Reference to Detail Attached	Form 706 Schedule/ State Schedule
Total					

supporting data and reference it in the "File Reference to Detail Attached" column. The final column assumes that the Estate will be filing a federal Estate Tax return. If not, leave it blank. If the Estate will be filing, this last column will help you verify that all personal property has been reported on the Estate Tax return.

INSURANCE, SHIPPING, AND OTHER SAFETY MEASURES

Obtain as quickly as possible the Decedent's homeowners insurance and review the scheduled property for an indication of Personal Property to find. Call, and confirm in writing, with the insurance company that the insurance remains in force (if not immediately secure insurance) and verify that the Estate is named as an insured. Be certain that the Personal Property is insured for its full fair market value. Often, people underinsure and skip insuring small items completely, to minimize the annual insurance premiums. Whereas the Decedent could choose to intentionally underinsure his Personal Property, you do not have that luxury in a Fiduciary capacity. Insure, or you can be held personally liable.

When shipping any Personal Property, make sure that it is properly insured. Check the Will for any provisions saying who should pay what costs. If amounts are large, consult with the Estate attorney. If the amounts are significant, discuss with the Estate attorney whether the Estate or the Beneficiary pays the insurance and shipping costs. For small costs, it may be just as reasonable to insure them unless anyone objects. However, if the costs are significant, such as shipping a piano cross country, get a firm decision before sending it.

INTERPRETING THE TANGIBLE PERSONAL PROPERTY CLAUSE IN THE WILL

Many different clauses can be used in a Will for the distribution of Personal Property. Read the Will carefully and be certain that you understand exactly what the provisions require. Some Will provisions leave it to your discretion as Executor to simply divide Personal Property. If this is the case, consider any instructions that the Decedent communicated to you. You should consider having the property appraised and ask the Estate attorney about the merits of having all of the Beneficiaries sign off on a document which lists all Personal Property, its appraised values, and how you have distributed it. Some Wills require that the value of Personal Property be equalized by a cash distribution. Using the previous example, the son would receive a $24,000 cash distribution to equalize the value he received ($1,000 watch) compared with the $25,000 artwork the daughter received.

Some Wills refer to, or actually incorporate by reference, a listing the Decedent made for distributing his Personal Property. Be certain that you have the current and only listing before making any distributions.

NOTE: Consult with the Estate attorney to determine what actions you have to take to be certain that the list of property you found is the list referred to in the Will.

HOW THE TAX ALLOCATION CLAUSE MAY AFFECT TANGIBLE PERSONAL PROPERTY

Personal Property is generally, but not always, exempt from paying its share of Estate Tax. Many Wills have the Estate Taxes paid "off the top" as an administration expense, or from the Residuary (what's left). In these cases, distributions of Personal Property should not be affected. If the Will is silent, however, state law may require that all Beneficiaries bear their respective pro rata shares of tax. This could require a contribution from those Beneficiaries receiving Personal Property. The Will may intentionally require that Beneficiaries of Personal Property pay their fair share of estate and other taxes. Having Beneficiaries of Personal Property pay a share of taxes can be quite burdensome if the same persons are not also receiving other bequests under the Decedent's Will. This is because the Personal Property is not cash, but cash is needed to pay the tax.

AUTOMOBILES, MOTORCYCLES, BOATS

Expedited Procedure for Transfer

If the Decedent owned a car, motorcycle, or boat, there should be a certificate of ownership indicating the registration number and other basic information. In some instances, depending on the state and the value of the vehicle, there may be an expedited procedure available to transfer title to a surviving spouse or child without the need for Probate. The department of motor vehicles would still require an original Death Certificate, the original registration or title for the vehicle, and most likely some type of affidavit as to your relationship and right to inherit it.

If the vehicle was owned by the Decedent and another person as joint tenants, the surviving joint tenants should receive title to the vehicle on death. The vehicle will still have to be reported on the Decedent's Estate Tax return.

Formal Procedure to Transfer

If this exception does not apply, you will have to contact the local department of motor vehicles and inquire as to their procedures. Generally, they will require a Death Certificate, Letters Testamentary, and the original registration and title for the vehicle.

Valuation of the Vehicle

You can generally value vehicles by looking up the year, model, and sometimes condition in an industry value guidebook. Check with your local library. If the vehicle is unusual, a collector's item, or not listed in the standard books, you should obtain a formal appraisal.

CONCLUSION

Personal Property is found in almost every Estate. Even when people endeavor to entirely avoid Probate by using a Revocable Living Trust, they commonly overlook Personal Property when transferring assets to such trusts. These assets involve their own unique issues, which vary from estate to estate.

12 REAL ESTATE AND BUSINESS INTERESTS

Despite being diverse, real estate and business assets have been grouped in this chapter because they present several common problems that you will have to deal with. Unlike marketable securities, they are difficult to value. Further, once real estate and business interests have been appraised, it is important to address the controversial issues of additional valuation discounts for lack of marketability and lack of control of partial ownership interests. Discounts are beyond the scope of this book and should be addressed by the accountant and attorney hired by the Estate. In most cases, you should also hire an appraiser to work with the accountant and attorney to determine the appropriate discounts. Many people balk at the costs of a formal appraisal. But if the Estate is large enough to be taxable, it should be carefully considered.

Real estate and business assets often present management and succession issues that do not affect other assets. Who will manage the real estate? Who will operate the businesses?

If there are co-owners (partners, shareholders, or members) they may also have significant rights. There may be an agreement (partnership, shareholders, or operating) governing the transfer of ownership interests. A buyout agreement may govern what the Estate must do with the ownership interests.

NOTE: See Martin M. Shenkman *Starting a Limited Liability Company* (New York: John Wiley & Sons, Inc., 1996) for sample agreements and clauses.

Liability exposure can be a significant concern for real estate and business interests, especially if they are not properly structured.

These and other issues are briefly addressed in this chapter.

PERSONAL REAL ESTATE ASSETS

Residential real estate, whether a principal residence or vacation home, presents issues different than commercial rental real estate. If the Decedent is survived by family or others who reside in the house (or condominium or apartment), the use of the house is unlikely to change. If the Decedent is not survived by anyone using the house, the property should be secured.

TIP: Consider installing an alarm and central station, hard-wired, smoke/fire detection system. This is especially important if the property will remain vacant for any significant period.

Selling the House

If the house is to be sold, arrange for a listing with a real estate broker. You may also want to have the house independently appraised to avoid any challenges by the Beneficiaries that you eventually sold the house at less than was appropriate.

Holding the House Pending Sale

What if the house has not been sold by the time the Estate Tax return is to be filed? For Estate Tax purposes, the Estate Tax return may have to be filed based on an appraisal of the house. Should the ultimate sale occur at a different price, the return can be amended. The alternative would be to leave the Estate open until such time as the house is actually sold.

The deductions for the house could affect three tax returns: the Estate's Estate Tax return, the Estate's income tax return, and the Beneficiaries' personal income tax returns. The expenses associated with maintaining the house as an investment pending its sale may be deductible. If the house is distributed to the Beneficiaries in kind, the Beneficiaries may be able to deduct such expenses on their personal income tax returns. If the house is not being rented, the expenses would be Schedule A itemized deductions, categorized as miscellaneous investment expenses. This may provide a deduction. If the house is rented, it should be reported on the Beneficiaries' Schedule E. However, should the deductions remain in the Estate for income tax purposes, they could offset the income earned by the Estate for a period of time.

Life Estate

Some Wills grant a particular Beneficiary a right to live in or use a particular property for a certain number of years or for life. This might be done in say a second marriage. The wife who owned the house may grant her second husband the right to live in the house for five years following her death. After that five-year period, the house may then be given to her children from her prior marriage. If this is done, the second husband may be required to reasonably maintain the house and prevent damage. If so, how can the children as eventual Beneficiaries of the house (referred to as Remainder Beneficiaries), or you as an Executor, demonstrate whether the house was reasonably maintained? One consideration is to obtain a thorough appraisal. A complete appraisal might be useful in proving what the condition of the house was at the inception of the life estate. A thorough appraisal will generally include a physical description and photographs. A home inspection report might also be helpful. A comprehensive home inspection report will usually include a written description of the condition of every room, major systems, and so on.

Estate Tax Considerations and the House

If the Estate is taxable a portion or all of the house may be used to fund the Bypass Trust. This might require a Disclaimer. Be sure to address these technical details with the Estate attorney.

INVESTMENT REAL ESTATE ASSETS

If commercial rental real estate is involved, be certain that the property is properly insured for reasonable maximum limits for liability and damage. If the property is not fully leased, it is your obligation as Executor to attempt to make the property productive. Consider hiring real estate leasing agents to lease up any vacancies. If you do not have adequate real estate management skills, consider hiring a professional management company. If there are qualified family members who can manage the property, consider hiring them. However, be certain that they are qualified, that the terms of their being hired are comparable to what unrelated persons would charge, and that everyone interested in the property agrees to the family member being hired. Discuss this matter with the Estate's attorney to determine whether any other steps should be taken. Also discuss how the activities of family members may affect the Estate's qualification for special tax benefits such as Estate Tax deferral, special use valuation, or the deduction for family business interests.

Obtain copies of all relevant documents. This includes the deed, leases, mortgages, insurance policies, and management and maintenance agreements. If you are not skilled in reviewing these, have real estate counsel (not necessarily the Estate attorney) review the documents and advise you of any issues to be addressed.

If there are other partners, obtain copies of any agreements between the owners. If there are buyout provisions, determine whether insurance has been taken out to fund the purchase.

Real estate presents a potentially substantial financial risk—environmental contamination. If you are serving as an Executor—or Trustee—and have any option in accepting real estate assets, do not accept the transfer until you have first had a professional inspector perform an environmental evaluation of the property.

As the Executor, you must be concerned with the liability the Estate faces. You should take reasonable steps to protect the Beneficiaries. If the property involved was owned by the Decedent individually (or with other family members), or in a general partnership form, or in a limited partnership form if the Decedent was a general partner, any suit or claim concerning the property could expose all of the Decedent's assets to liability. One of the most common liability protection techniques for real estate is to transfer each individual property to an entity called a limited liability company (LLC). When this is done, any claims arising after the transfer should only be able to collect a judgment against the entity, and not against any other assets of the Estate. Discuss with the Estate attorney whether you should undertake to restructure the ownership of any of the Decedent's real estate.

If the Decedent owned interests in a partnership or limited liability company that owns depreciable real estate ask the Estate's accountant or tax consultant to review and explain to you a technical tax benefit called a "Code Section 743(b) Adjustment."

If real estate was owned directly by the Decedent in another state, Ancillary Probate may be required.

BUSINESS ASSETS

Business assets are closely held businesses usually owned by a small group of people, a family, or even the Decedent alone. These present many unique and difficult problems compared with ownership of stock in a publicly traded company. Closely held business interests may not be passive investments. You may have to arrange for their management. Valuation may be more art than science. Legal documents and other formalities you would never consider for a publicly traded stock become important to follow up on.

Issues to Address Concerning the Entity Owning the Business

Businesses are frequently owned in corporate, partnership, or LLC form. You should obtain copies of any key business records: certificates filed to form the entity, corporate or company kits (include minutes and other documents), agreements governing the relationships between the owners, and recent tax returns. Determine whether any required buyout procedures bind the Estate. What are the rights and obligations of the Estate? Are there others who are managing the business? Can you monitor the performance of the business, or would a sale or negotiation of another arrangement work? In most cases, it is recommended to have a corporate/business attorney review these documents and advise you. The matter may be as simple as confirming that there is an automatic insurance-funded buyout. In many cases, however, the business documents are incomplete or nonexistent. In these situations, addressing any gaps in the legal documentation for the entity may be important to assure that the limitations on liability for the Estate remain intact.

Legal Documents Required for Business Interests

Once it is determined that the Estate will sell its interest in the closely held business and the terms are negotiated, the corporation or other entity, and its owners should confirm the terms of the agreement. Bylaws, minutes, and other basic business records may have to be updated. Documentation removing/replacing the Decedent as an officer or director may be necessary. You may then sign, as Executor, documents permitting the transfer of the Decedent's business ownership interests back to the business or to the other owners. You may sign a Release to the business and other owners acknowledging that the Estate has no further claims against them. You should request a similar Release back from the entity and other owners confirming that they have no claims against the Estate. The following sample corporate minutes and stock power (p. 157) illustrate some of the documents used. A Release is illustrated in Chapter 20.

SAMPLE MINUTES FOR BUYOUT

WALLY'S WIDGETS, INC.
UNANIMOUS CONSENT OF SHAREHOLDER AND DIRECTOR
IN LIEU OF MEETING
TO REPURCHASE STOCK, RECOGNIZE SHAREHOLDER'S DEATH, ETC.

The undersigned, being the sole surviving director and shareholder of the Corporation, hereby takes the following actions:

RESOLVED, the Corporation acknowledges Dan Decedent died on April 1, 1999, and that 100 shares constituting his entire interest in the Corporation have been purchased on the date hereof, by Sally Shareholder pursuant to the provisions of the Shareholders' Agreement dated June 1, 1995. The Corporation hereby cancels stock certificate No. 2 from Dan Decedent, pursuant to authorization of the Executor of the Estate of Dan Decedent (Letters Testamentary attached hereto), and to then issue stock certificate No. 6 to Sally Shareholder in the amount of 100 shares.

RESOLVED, that the Corporation is hereby authorized to issue general releases to the Estate of Dan Decedent and to Elliott Executor.

RESOLVED, that the Three (3) Promissory Notes payable to Dan Decedent by the Corporation [$11,000 dated March 1, 1997; $22,000 dated January 10, 1998; and $9,000 dated February 22, 1999] are hereby canceled as part of the transaction by a net adjustment of $12,753 the agreed fair valve of said notes against the amount due the Estate of Dan Decedent for the purchase of the stock held by the estate.

RESOLVED, that Dan Decedent's positions as officer and director are terminated effective April 1, 1999.

RESOLVED, the following persons are elected to serve as officers of the Corporation until their successors are elected and qualified:

President	- Sally Shareholder
Vice President	- Sally Shareholder
Secretary	- Sally Shareholder
Treasurer	- Sally Shareholder

RESOLVED, the corporation hereby adopts any and all acts heretofore done or undertaken by the Directors of the Corporation since the last meeting or consent of the Directors.

RESOLVED, that the officers are directed and authorized to undertake any acts necessary to carry out the above resolutions.

Dated: December 13, 1999   CORPORATE SEAL:

_____

Sally Shareholder, Shareholder
  and Director

ACKNOWLEDGE AND AGREED
Estate of Dan Decedent

By: _____
       Elliott Executor, Executor

SAMPLE FORM FOR STOCK POWER

FOR VALUE RECEIVED, The Estate of Dan Decedent hereby sells, assigns, and transfers unto Sally Shareholder who resides 220 Highview Avenue, Anytown, Somestate, 100 shares of the Capital Stock of Wally's Widgets, Inc., standing in the name of Dan Decedent on the books of said Corporation represented by Certificate No. 2 herewith, and do hereby irrevocably constitute and appoint Arlene Attorney, Esq. as attorney to transfer the said stock on the books and records of said Corporation with full power of substitution in the premises.

Dated: December 13, 1999

SHAREHOLDER/TRANSFEROR
ESTATE OF DAN DECEDENT

By: _____   Witness: _____
       Elliott Executor, Executor

Business Valuation Issues

The value of any closely held business should be determined from analyzing all of the facts and circumstances and confirmed in a written appraisal report that should be attached to the federal Estate Tax return. A value may be determined under a number of different valuation methods such as discounted cash flow, comparable businesses, a net asset value calculation, monthly net revenue multiplier method, or other methods.

The history of the business should be reviewed and analyzed. The shareholder or other agreements governing the relationship of the owners should be reviewed to determine their implications to the value. Was a set price for buyout provided for? Was it arm's length? Relevant provisions of bylaws and the certificate of incorporation should be reviewed.

Revenue Ruling 59-60 provides a comprehensive list of factors each of which should be analyzed in context of valuing the Decedent's interest in the business. Although the valuation analysis should not necessarily be confined to the factors in that Ruling, each factor cited should be addressed. Revenue Ruling 59-60 does not prescribe any one valuation method or formula; it merely acknowledges that no valuation method will be generally applicable to the facts in every situation. The factors are (1) the nature of the business and the history of the enterprise; (2) the economic outlook both generally and for the specific industry; (3) book value of the stock and the financial condition of the business; (4) earning capacity; (5) dividend paying capacity; (6) the existence of any goodwill or other intangible value; (7) stock sales and the size of the block of stock to be sold; and (8) the market price of publicly traded corporations in similar businesses, whether such trading is on an exchange or over the counter.

How Shareholder or Other Agreements Affect the Estate's Dealing with Business Interests

Almost an unlimited number of different approaches to structuring a buyout can be used. Some common ones include (1) the three appraiser method, (2) the right of first refusal method, (3) the Dutch auction method (and variations thereof), and (4) the fixed price method.

In addition to determining the method of establishing a buyout price, consideration must be given to the overall structure of the transaction. Who will actually consummate the buyout, and how will the buyout be funded? There are two general approaches: (1) The partnership, LLC, or corporation redeems the Estate's interests (a redemption); or (2) the various partners, members, or shareholders repurchase the Estate's interests (a cross-purchase arrangement). There are a number of tax consequences to these approaches.

Where a stock redemption approach is used, the proceeds received by the Estate on account of the Decedent's death will not create taxable income. If the redemption constitutes a complete termination of the Estate's interests in the corporation, which it should in most circumstances (or meets selected other requirements), the Estate will report the excess of the amount received in the redemption, over your adjusted basis (cost), which is generally stepped up to fair value at death, in the stock, as a capital gain.

Where a cross-purchase arrangement is used to buy out the terminated interest of the Decedent in a closely held corporation, the proceeds the other shareholders receive as a result of the Decedent's death will not be taxable. The Estate should not recognize any gain for income tax purposes on the sale since the shares will have received a step-up in basis to their fair market value on either the date of death or the Alternate Valuation Date. The shareholders purchasing the Estate's shares will receive an increase in Tax Basis, which will reduce their taxable gain on a later sale.

Where the valuation used for the buyout provides a reasonable value, it will be a factor considered by the IRS in valuing the Decedent's interest in the business for Estate Tax purposes. Where the buy-sell agreement is the result of voluntary action by the stockholders and is binding during life as well as the death, the agreement may or may not, depending on the circumstances of each case, fix the value for Estate Tax purposes. However, the agreement is a factor to be considered, with other relevant factors, in determining fair market value. It is always necessary to consider the relationship of the parties, the relative number of shares held by the Decedent, and other material facts, to determine whether the agreement represents a bona fide business arrangement or is a device to pass the Decedent's shares to his heirs at a discounted Estate Tax cost.

Where a buy-sell agreement is a realistic arm's-length valuation of the business, it can be an important factor in determining the value of the interest in the business for Estate Tax purposes. However, several requirements must be met for the IRS to give much credit to its terms. It must be a bona fide business arrangement and not a device to transfer property to the Decedent's family at artificially low Estate Tax rates. Its terms must be comparable to buyout agreements used by unrelated people. Discuss "Chapter 14" of the Internal Revenue Code with the Estate attorney.

S Corporation and Qualified Subchapter S Trust (QSST)

S corporations are regular corporations for which the shareholder made a special tax election to be taxed in a manner similar to a partnership. This means that most income and expenses are not taxed to the corporation, but rather are passed through to the individual shareholders and each reports his pro rata share on his personal tax return. To preserve this favorable tax treatment for the corporation and its shareholders, a number of requirements must be met. Of particular concern is the limitation on who can be a qualified shareholder of an S corporation. Ownership by an unqualified shareholder can ruin the tax-favored S election. If the Decedent owned any stock in an S corporation, confer with the accountant and attorney for the Estate to determine how to proceed. Many Trusts typically formed under Wills do not qualify as S corporation shareholders. If you as Executor distribute S corporation stock to these Trusts, you could destroy the tax-favored status. Instead, other Trusts may qualify as recipients of the S corporation stock or alternative arrangements may have to be made. Many Wills and Trusts include special provisions to convert Trusts into qualified S corporation shareholders. These Trusts are called Qualified Subchapter S Trusts (QSSTs).

The shareholder agreement for the corporation may contain a restriction on transferring stock to a Trust that does not qualify:

Notwithstanding anything herein to the contrary, any Shareholder may transfer any portion of his shares of stock in the Corporation to a Trust for the benefit of his immediate family. If the Corporation shall elect to be taxed as an S corporation, then such Trust must meet the requirements of Section 1361(d) of the Internal Revenue Code of 1986, as amended (a QSST Trust). Further, any Trust agreement governing such Trust shall make such Trust subject to all of the restrictions and requirements of this Agreement.

A typical Will provision may include language similar to the following:

With respect to any part of the Trust Estate of any Trust formed under my Will which is stock in a corporation electing under the provisions of Code Section 1362 of the Code of 1986 to be taxed as an S corporation (S corporation Assets), such Trust is intended to be a Qualified Subchapter S Trust, as such term is defined under Code Section 1361(d) of the Code. Notwithstanding any provision to the contrary in my Will, my Fiduciary shall, with respect to such stock, operate such part of any such Trust in a manner consistent with such requirements. All provisions of my Will which affect such part of any such Trust shall be construed consistently with the requirements of a Qualified Subchapter S Trust.

Be certain to review the provision of the shareholder agreement and the Decedent's Will with the Estate attorney to determine what other actions must be taken.

CONCLUSION

Business and real estate interests raise complex and potentially serious issues for you as Executor. When significant business or real estate interests are present in the Estate, hire the appropriate professionals to assist you.

13 INSURANCE, PENSIONS, RETIREMENT ASSETS, AND ANNUITIES

Insurance, annuities, and retirement assets are increasingly large parts of many Estates. An important issue for you as Executor is that these assets generally pass outside Probate and without regard to the Will under the Beneficiary designations listed by the Decedent, often many decades before. Because these are nonprobate assets, issues may arise as to whether the Beneficiaries of these assets should pay their fair share of any Estate or other taxes. State law will often direct that they do. In either case, these assets are often beyond your control.

INSURANCE

The first step is to collect basic information on all insurance policies on the Decedent's life. Many will have named Beneficiaries and will pass to them outside your control. That does not mean, however, that you cannot have indirect access to the funds so provided. For example, life insurance Trusts are intended to work in this very manner. The insurance proceeds pass to the Trustee of the insurance Trust. The Trustee can loan the Estate money or purchase assets from the Estate. In either case, the result is liquidity that the Estate otherwise would not have. Other policies may be tied into business buy-sell arrangements (see Chapter 12). Insurance payable to the Decedent's Estate will generally provide you quick and available cash resources. This may have been done intentionally so that the insurance can be used to fund a Bypass Trust. The Decedent may also have owned insurance policies on the lives of other people. For these policies, it is the cash value that is included in the Decedent's Estate. In all cases, obtain information on every insurance policy and evaluate the implications to the Estate. The sample chart on page 162 will be helpful. Ideally, obtain copies of each policy and a current report from the insurance company confirming any policy loans, the current Beneficiaries, and so on.

Insurance professionals can provide no-cost, helpful assistance in analyzing insurance data, collecting policy proceeds, and planning for future

Sample Chart for Recording Insurance Information

Insured's Name	Owner of Policy	Beneficiary of Policy	Cash Value of Policy	Death Benefit of Policy	Insurance Carrier/ Policy No.	Implications to Estate
			$	$		

insurance needs. To collect policy proceeds, you must complete the claim form provided by the insurance company. This may require information to help confirm that the insured Decedent had not committed suicide within the specified period, and that the insured did not die of an illness during the contestability period (usually one or two years) that was not properly disclosed in the insurance application. The claim form should also help demonstrate whether the Decedent died from an accident that could trigger an additional accidental death benefit payment. Finally, the claim form may contain a listing of the available settlement options for payment of the insurance proceeds.

In addition, the insurance company will typically require an original Death Certificate. The original of the insurance policy should be provided. Be certain to retain a copy of all items sent for your files. Always request in the cover letter sent to the insurance company that they provide you with Form 712, the information that is necessary for you to properly report the insurance proceeds on the Decedent's federal Estate Tax return. Your letter forwarding the claim form and related documents should be sent certified mail return receipt requested so that you have proof of filing.

If the insurance is paid to the Estate, it will provide cash for you to pay Estate Taxes and other expenses. The remaining funds may be used to fund a Bypass Trust under the Will (see Chapter 18).

When insurance is payable to an Estate, the creditors of the Estate will be able to reach it as an asset to satisfy their claims. If the insurance is instead payable to a named Beneficiary, such as a child or surviving spouse, then the Estate creditors may be hard pressed to assert any claim against it. But the cash may not be as available to the Estate.

QUALIFIED PLANS AND IRA ACCOUNTS

General Rules for IRAs and Qualified Plans

Individual Retirement Accounts (IRAs) and qualified pension and other plans are a major asset for many people. Often, these assets need to be used to fund a Bypass Trust (see Chapter 18) to protect the Applicable Exclusion Amount of the first spouse to die (previously, loosely referred to as a credit shelter Trust) because there are inadequate other assets. Complex Estate Tax rules are compounded by the even more complex income tax rules that apply to IRAs, pension plans, and other qualified plans. To properly plan for the use of Applicable Exclusion Amount and pension assets, some basic pension tax and distribution concepts must be considered.

Distributions from certain plans and IRAs must begin by the Required Beginning Date (RBD). The Required Beginning Date is April 1 of the year following the year in which the Decedent reached age 70½. This rule, however, is modified for participants who are working at age 70½ so that distributions would be postponed until the Decedent retired. IRAs are subject to the qualified plan distribution rules.

When the Decedent reached (if he reached) the Required Beginning Date he had to either: (1) take a lump sum distribution of the pension plan balance on that date; or (2) start to receive yearly installments of at least the plan's account balance (as of December 31 of the prior year) divided by his then life expectancy. If the Decedent had a Designated Beneficiary on his plan on the Required Beginning Date, he could then have used a joint life expectancy (the life expectancy for both the Decedent and the Designated Beneficiary) in the preceding calculation (instead of his life expectancy alone). This will lengthen the time period over which withdrawals have to be made, thus maximizing the amount of the plan balance that can continue to grow on an income tax deferred basis.

If the Decedent died prior to reaching his Required Beginning Date, then the following steps should be taken. The Decedent's plan balance must be distributed within five years of death. There are two exceptions to this rule. First, if the Decedent had named a Designated Beneficiary for the plan other than his spouse, and distributions begin within one year of the Decedent's death, distributions may be made over the life expectancy of the Designated Beneficiary instead of the five-year default period.

If the Decedent's surviving spouse is the Designated Beneficiary of his plan, then any Estate Tax is deferred. Income tax on distributions will be due only when the Decedent's spouse receives distributions.

When this occurs, the Decedent's surviving spouse has several options for receiving distributions:

1. If payments begin by the later of December 31 of the year following the year in which the Decedent died, or December 31 of the year the

Decedent would have reached age 70½, then payment of his plan balance may be made over the life expectancy of the Decedent's surviving spouse.

2. The Decedent's surviving spouse can roll over the Decedent's plan balance into a rollover IRA account set up by her. Distributions from that rollover IRA would have to begin when the Decedent's spouse reaches age 70½. His spouse could also designate Beneficiaries for that rollover IRA account.

3. The Decedent's surviving spouse can treat the Decedent's IRA as if it were her own IRA. Thus, any distribution options that the Decedent may have had under his IRA, his surviving spouse can elect to have as well.

What happens if the Decedent's spouse dies after his death? If the Decedent's spouse dies prior to distributions of the Decedent's plan balance beginning, then the payments of the Decedent's plan balance is made over the life expectancy of the Designated Beneficiary. If instead the Decedent's spouse dies after payments to her of the Decedent's plan balance had begun, the distribution options will depend on whether she had elected to have her life expectancy recalculated annually to determine payments. If the Decedent's spouse's life expectancy was recalculated annually, distributions of the Decedent's plan balance must be completed within five years of the Decedent's spouse's death. If the spouse's life expectancy was not recalculated, distributions may continue for the duration of spouse's life expectancy. The fact that the Decedent's spouse is no longer alive does not affect this latter distribution plan.

What happens if the Decedent dies after the Required Beginning Date. The distribution of his plan balance to the Beneficiaries must be made over a period as least as short as the Decedent's lifetime distribution. If the life expectancy of the Decedent and his spouse was recalculated every year, the entire balance must be distributed by December 31 of the year following the death of the last to die of the Decedent and his spouse.

Designated Beneficiaries are determined as of the Required Beginning Date. Generally, only individuals can be Designated Beneficiaries. If the Decedent's Estate is the Designated Beneficiary (e.g., the Decedent's IRA application indicates that on his death the plan balance should be paid to his Estate), then the plan balance will be subject to income tax within five years of the Decedent's death. No rollover of the Decedent's plan balance will be permitted. The tax allocation clause in the Decedent's Will (the provision that says which Beneficiaries and which assets should bear the Estate Tax burden) should identify which assets will bear any tax due.

If the Decedent named a Trust as the Designated Beneficiary, it is the actual people (i.e., the Beneficiaries of the Trust, not the Trust itself) who may be the Designated Beneficiaries. To qualify for this treatment, however, several requirements must be met at the later of the Required Beginning Date and/or the date the Trust is named Beneficiary. These requirements are an important part of the steps necessary to use qualified plan assets to fund a Bypass Trust or QTIP Trust. The Trust must be valid under state law except for the fact that there are no current assets (corpus). The Trust Beneficiaries must be identifiable and must be individuals. The Trust must be irrevocable on the later of the date it is designated as the Beneficiary of the plan, or the Required Beginning Date. You must provide a copy of Trust document to the plan administrator.

For some Decedents, the maximum $650,000 (1999) of assets that can avoid Estate Taxation as a result of the Applicable Exclusion Amount are not available to fund a Bypass Trust. When this occurs, consider having the surviving spouse Disclaim some portion or all of the IRA or pension assets to the extent that the secondary Beneficiary designation and/or the Decedent's Will result in the assets passing to the Bypass Trust.

If this latter approach is to be used, the qualified plan or IRA must meet the minimum distribution rules. The minimum amounts required to be distributed are measured by the life expectancy of the Decedent's spouse, if his spouse is the oldest eligible Designated Beneficiary. The Trust could include a requirement that the Trustee withdraw from the qualified plan or IRA the minimum distribution amounts which are required to be withdrawn. Once these amounts are received by the Bypass Trust, the terms of the distributions from the Trust to the Beneficiaries are based on the provisions contained in the Bypass Trust provisions in the Will.

The Trust could divide plan proceeds into two shares: one share could pass to a QTIP (marital) Trust for the Decedent's surviving spouse (or outright to the spouse); and the second share could be planned to use up any remaining Applicable Exclusion Amount available to the Decedent's Estate (i.e., to fund the Bypass Trust).

There are two ways to have a Bypass Trust, or other Trust, qualify as the recipient of IRA and qualified plan assets. First, is the direct approach. Using this approach, the Trust is named as the Designated Beneficiary of the qualified plan or IRA. The second alternative is for the Decedent to have named his spouse as the primary Beneficiary of the IRA and the Bypass Trust as the secondary Beneficiary. Thus, if the Decedent's spouse disclaims (renounces, files papers in court stating that she does not want the inheritance provided) the interests in the Decedent's IRA or qualified plan assets would then be distributed into the marital QTIP Trust or into the Bypass Trust under the Decedent's Will. A number of additional rules will apply if a Trust is so used:

- The Decedent's spouse cannot roll over plan assets into a rollover IRA account.
- The measuring life for determining the period over which payments must be made is the Decedent's spouse's life expectancy, if the spouse is the oldest Designated Beneficiary.
- The balance payable after the death of the Decedent's spouse is paid to the remainder Beneficiaries over the balance of the spouse's life expectancy.
- Estate Tax can be deferred and avoided through the application of the Decedent's Applicable Exclusion Amount against the plan assets transferred to this Trust.

Surviving Spouse Can Roll over Plan

A surviving spouse is entitled to roll over the plan or IRA benefits into an IRA and defer the income tax consequences. The rollover should be completed within 60 days. The surviving spouse is thus able to treat the Deceased spouse's IRA or plan proceeds as if they were her IRA benefits. The following sample letter illustrates the surviving spouse rolling over IRA benefits to take advantage of this rule after her children Disclaimed their interest in the IRA (Disclaimers are discussed in Chapter 18). This scenario would be necessary if the Decedent husband had named the children as primary Beneficiaries of the IRA with no secondary Beneficiary so that the proceeds would then be payable to the Estate.

IRA and Qualified Plan Assets and the Nonspouse Beneficiary

IRA benefits are generally included in the Decedent's Gross Estate for federal Estate Tax purposes. If the benefits are payable to the surviving spouse, she can roll them over into an IRA account in her name preserving the income tax deferral for as long as possible. If, however, the plan or IRA benefits are payable to the Estate, the surviving spouse cannot qualify to roll over the plan benefits into her IRA.

From an income tax perspective, the excess of a lump sum distribution of an IRA over the Decedent's nondeductible contributions is taxable to the Beneficiary of the IRA as income in respect of a Decedent (IRD). As the Beneficiary receives distributions, income is taxable to him. The Beneficiary, however, is entitled to a tax deduction on his income tax return for the Estate Tax attributable to the plan benefits taxed in the Decedent's Estate. This provides a partial offset for the income tax cost to be paid by the Beneficiary.

If a Beneficiary other than the Decedent's spouse is named Beneficiary of an IRA account, he or she can elect to defer the payment (and hence taxation) of the IRA inheritance. Various restrictions and requirements, however, may apply. Where the Decedent died prior to having any of his entire interest in the IRA account distributed (i.e., distributions had not commenced prior to death), the general rule is that the IRA will have to be paid out over a five-year period. If the following requirements are met, however, the nonspouse Beneficiary may qualify for a lengthier deferral:

- The portion of the IRA involved is payable to the nonspouse as a Beneficiary designated under the plan.
- The portion of the IRA that the Beneficiary is entitled to will be paid out to her over the nonspouse Beneficiary's life expectancy.
- The distributions begin not later than one year after the date of death.

Where the Decedent died after having commenced distributions of his interest in the IRA account, the distributions to the Beneficiary, as described

SAMPLE LETTER TO ROLL
OVER IRA BENEFITS

SALLY SPOUSE
123 MAIN STREET
ANYTOWN, SOMESTATE

November 1, 1999

Big Bank Corp.
1000 Financial Way
Bigtown, USA

RE: *Rollover of IRAs of Dan Decedent.*

Dear Sirs:

I am the surviving spouse of the late Dan Decedent, sole residuary beneficiary under the Article Tenth of the Last Will and Testament of Dan Decedent (dated September 1, 1999) and sole Executrix of the Estate under Letters Testamentary dated October 5, 1999.

I am beneficiary of the following IRA accounts of Dan Decedent as a result of the renunciation/disclaimer of all interests in such accounts by my children (Charles Child and Cathy Child) who were named primary beneficiaries on the accounts. As a result of such renunciation/disclaimer, the disposition of such assets is governed by the will of Dan Decedent. As residuary beneficiary under such will, all such assets pass to me.

1. CD No. 833389.
2. CD No. 443339.
3. CD No. 999322.
4. CD No. 443322.

I hereby accept the receipt of the above assets as beneficiary of the residuary Estate result of the renunciations/disclaimers executed by my children. I acknowledge that the Bank has not made any representation concerning the tax effect of this rollover or the renunciation/disclaimer. I agree to hold Big Bank Corp. harmless for any tax consequences of the transactions contemplated herein.

Please roll over each of said accounts into an IRA established in my name, Sally Spouse, Social Security Number 000-00-0000.

The aforementioned transaction is permissible in accordance with IRS Private Letter Rulings: 8635043, 8623054, 8450068, and 8909065.

Please use the address above for your records.

Sincerely,

Estate of Dan Decedent

By: _____
    Sally Spouse, Executrix

_____

Sally Spouse

_____

Charles Child

_____

Cathy Child

earlier, must be at a rate that is at least as rapid as that rate used by the Decedent.

All of the above rule are very complex. Be certain to review all pension and retirement assets, and any steps you as Executor may take as well as any steps the Beneficiary may take with the Estate attorney, accountant, and the firm holding the plan assets.

ANNUITIES

An annuity is a type of insurance product where the Decedent may have contracted with an insurance company to receive payments for a specified period for himself or another designated Beneficiary. Many variations are available. A variable annuity may pay a return based on investment returns to the insurance company. An annuity could be deferred so that it will only start payments at some future date. An annuity may pay for life, or for a fixed number of years. A hybrid approach may also be available with payments for life, but for not less than some minimum number of years.

Many charitable organizations have arranged for the sale of charitable gift annuities. Under these arrangements, the Decedent may have transferred appreciated property to the charity in exchange for an annuity for part of the value, and a charitable contribution for the balance.

If the Decedent purchased an annuity arrangement for both himself and another Beneficiary, there will be a gift to that other person based on the value of the annuity to that person at the time the annuity was purchased. The annual $10,000 (indexed) gift tax exclusion is not available. If the second Beneficiary was the Decedent's spouse, however, the unlimited Marital Deduction would be available (assuming the spouse was a U.S. citizen).

For income taxes purposes, a portion of each annuity payment paid to the Decedent is taxed as interest income, and a portion is treated as a return of his investment. This interest portion can result in accrued interest to be reported on the Decedent's Estate Tax return.

The amount to be included in the Decedent's Taxable Estate, if any amounts are to be paid to any other Beneficiary under the annuity arrangement as a result of the Decedent's death is based on the value of the payments to be made to that Beneficiary following the Decedent's death. If the Estate receives a refund under the annuity arrangement this amount will also be taxable in the Decedent's Taxable Estate.

CONCLUSION

Pension and retirement assets are a common asset in most Estates, and are becoming a significant, if not the dominant asset, in many Estates. Annuities are common investment assets. Therefore, the planning issues relating to these assets must be addressed. Often, your accountant may be in the best position to address the income tax considerations.

14 MISCELLANEOUS ASSETS: POWERS OF APPOINTMENT, CERTAIN TRUSTS, LOANS, OTHER TRANSFERS

The preceding chapters have provided an overview of some common assets you are likely to encounter as an Executor. There are, however, many different types of assets, each with its own unique legal, practical, and tax considerations. This chapter highlights only a few of the additional, perhaps less common, assets you may encounter.

POWERS OF APPOINTMENT

A Power of Appointment is a right granted to the holder of the power to determine who should receive beneficial ownership of property owned by the grantor of the power and not the holder of the power. Where the holder of the power has the right to direct the property that is subject to the Power of Appointment to himself, his Estate, his creditors, or creditors of his Estate, the Power of Appointment is considered a General Power of Appointment and the holder is taxed as if he had actually owned the property transferred. Where the Power of Appointment is not broad enough to include these enumerated categories, it is a deemed a *limited* Power of Appointment and generally has no tax consequences. If the language creating the power is vague, state law must be consulted to ascertain whether the power is a general or limited one. Other exceptions can also apply to prevent a limited Power of Appointment from being characterized as a General Power of Appointment. For example, where the power is subject to an ascertainable standard, it is not considered to be a General Power of Appointment. Where the asset can only be appointed for health, education, support, or maintenance, it is subject to an ascertainable standard and is therefore not deemed to be a General Power of Appointment. Also, where the holder of the power can exercise it only jointly with another person who has an adverse interest, the power will not be deemed to be a General Power of Appointment.

The Estate and gift tax consequences of a General Power of Appointment are that the exercise, or release, of the power, are considered a transfer. For example, if the Decedent died holding a General Power of Appointment (whether it was specifically exercised under the Decedent's Will, or merely permitted to lapse) the entire value of the property (e.g., Trust assets) over which the Decedent could have exercised the Power of Appointment, will be included in the Decedent's Taxable Estate. An important exception is the 5%/$5,000 limited power. In such instances, only the property over which the holder of the power could have exercised the power (i.e., the greater of 5% of the Trust or other property involved, or $5,000) is included in the holder's Estate. The entire value of the Trust or other property subject to the power is not.

Many grants of Powers of Appointment require specific reference to them to exercise those powers. Some state laws may provide that a Residuary clause automatically exercises a power. The inclusion of property subject to a General Power of Appointment can have a significant effect on the tax status of an Estate. All these factors should be considered.

You should review, with the assistance of the Estate attorney, the Decedent's Will to identify provisions exercising a Power of Appointment.

SAMPLE CLAUSE:

I hereby exercise the Power of Appointment which I possess over the principal of the Marital Deduction Trust created for my benefit under Article Twelve of the Will of my late spouse, Sally Spouse, which Will has been admitted to probate on June 1, 1998, in the Surrogate's Court of Anywhere County, State of Somestate, as hereinafter provided. I direct the Trustees of said Trust to distribute such assets to my children, per stirpes.

Also, review any existing Trusts, Wills, or other documents of relatives of the Decedent (Trusts formed by the parents are often a likely place for these powers) granting the Decedent Powers of Appointment.

QUALIFIED PERSONAL RESIDENCE TRUSTS (QPRT)

A Qualified Personal Residence Trust (QPRT) provides a mechanism through which the Decedent irrevocably transfers his residence to a Trust, retaining a term interest (to be discussed) and naming family members or others as Remainder Beneficiaries when the term interest ends. The QPRT is an estate planning technique that takes advantage of the time value of money to reduce federal Estate and gift taxation. The Decedent would have transferred his residence (his principal residence, or one other qualifying residence or vacation home) to a QPRT and reserved a term interest in the house—the sole and exclusive right to use the residence for a specified term of years. On the expiration of the specified term of years, if that Decedent had lived, the house would have then distributed to the Remainder Beneficiaries (the other heirs or family members, typically the children).

An important characteristic of the QPRT is that the Decedent must have survived the retained term of years for the house not to be taxed in his Estate. If the Decedent did not survive the term of years, then the house is taxed in the Decedent's Estate at its then fair market value, thereby rendering this Estate-planning technique unsuccessful. As a result, it is generally recommended that the QPRT document include a provision stating that if the Decedent died during the term of his retained interest, the house reverts back to his Estate. Having such a provision in the QPRT documents would have supported a further discount on the value of the gift ultimately going to the Decedent's Beneficiaries (i.e., the remainder interest) had he survived. The rationale for the discount is that there is a possibility that the remaindermen will never receive the property. If the Decedent died before the Trust ends, this is in fact what has occurred. The value of this reversion is based on the age of the Decedent when the QPRT was formed and the use of actuarial tables to determine the likelihood of his death during the retained term of years.

If the Decedent died before the end of the QPRT, you must coordinate the reversion of the house to the Estate and the distribution of the house under the terms of the Decedent's Will. You may assist the Trustee of the QPRT in winding up and terminating the QPRT.

NOTE: For details on rights the Decedent may have had under other types of Trusts, see Martin M. Shenkman, *The Complete Book of Trusts* (2nd ed.) (New York: John Wiley & Sons, 1997).

MORTGAGES AND LOANS

If the Decedent owned interests in any loans whether secured by mortgages on real estate or other assets, obtain and secure the original signed note or other loan documents. There should be only one original signed note for each loan. Review the terms of the loan and related documents. In the calendar where you are tracking Estate matters (see Chapter 2), list the dates interest and principal should be received. If any payments are late, review the loan document to determine what rights the Estate has as the successor in interest to the Decedent. Determine what steps you are required to take to protect those rights. For example, a default may be prohibited unless you have given the borrower a written demand for payment. There may be a limited number of such demands you are required to make over the life of the loan. Find out how many demands the Decedent made before his death.

Be wary of improperly documented loans. Frequently—especially when the borrower is family—loans are not properly documented. This could be problematic. If the borrower has financial problems, and the loan is not properly documented and the security arrangements perfected by filing a mortgage or taking other steps, strangers may end up with greater rights than the family.

Family loans present another common situation, forgiveness. In many cases, loans to family members are intended to be forgiven at the death of the person lending the funds. A typical Will clause might read as follows:

> If I am a mortgagee on any mortgage on the real property located at 123 Main Street, Anytown, USA, and Charles Child has an equity interests in such property, then an amount equal to the value outstanding balance due to me or my estate from such person under such mortgage shall be transferred to such person for repayment of said mortgage and such mortgage shall be canceled. In the event that there is any transfer of value under the preceding section, then a transfer of an equal amount shall next be made to my other Children, per stirpes, in order to equalize the amounts transferred.

Be certain to address this provision with the Estate attorney. Also, consider the equalization of the other Beneficiaries. Income tax consequences to the borrower can be triggered from the cancellation of the debt. Discuss this with the Estate's accountant.

Loans that are included in the Decedent's Estate must be valued. The value depends on the terms of the loan, the security of the collateral, and how marketable it is. If the loan cannot be assigned by the lender, the value may be negatively affected. If the interest rate is lower (higher) than prevailing market interest rates, then the value of the loan will be less (more) than the face or maturity value. Have the Estate accountant, or an appraiser, value the loan. Save the valuation report in your files. If an Estate Tax return is filed, a copy of the valuation will have to be attached.

WAGES AND FRINGE AND SIMILAR BENEFITS

If the Decedent was employed, there may be a final paycheck (or several if the employer has a salary continuation policy for deceased employees or is merely compassionate). You should also inquire, in writing, whether the Decedent was entitled to any vacation pay, bonus pay, sick pay, stock bonus or incentive plans, pension or other retirement plans, or other benefits. Be certain to obtain a confirmation of the answer in writing and save it in the Estate files. If the Decedent had signed an employment agreement or other contract, obtain a copy and have the Estate attorney review it to assure that all payments due have been accounted for. The employer may require a Death Certificate, Letters Testamentary, and perhaps an affidavit or form providing information concerning the deceased employee, your capacity to request information, and information concerning the heirs.

The Social Security Administration will have to be notified to discontinue sending benefits. In addition, you may have to return the last payment depending on how quickly notice is received.

CONTRACTS IN PROCESS (EXECUTORY CONTRACTS)

The Decedent may have signed a contract or entered into an agreement before death that has not been concluded. For example, the Decedent may have signed a contract that was not closed prior to death for the sale of his house . Review any such contracts with the Estate attorney and determine what the Estate's rights and obligations are under the contracts. If you believe there is a basis not to conclude the contract or arrangement and that it would be advantageous for the Estate not to do so, consult with the Estate attorney (a litigation specialist may be preferable) and determine how to proceed.

CLAIMS, CAUSES OF ACTION

If the Decedent had any claims that could be pursued, such as a contract that was violated or an act that led to the death of the Decedent giving rise to a potential lawsuit, you as Executor are obligated to investigate the potential claim and pursue it if appropriate. For example, if the Decedent was injured in an automobile accident six months before death, he may have considered commencing a lawsuit but died before doing so. You should have the potential claim investigated and determine whether pursuing it is feasible.

To protect the Estate's interests, and yourself from any claims of not fulfilling your responsibilities, corroborate that you have conducted a reasonable inquiry and search of the Decedent's business, investment, and other activities to identify any claims. An appropriate expert should evaluate any potential claims. If the claim is not to be pursued, consider obtaining a written opinion from the expert stating that he or she does not believe the claim is feasible to pursue.

CERTAIN TRANSFERS THAT ARE INCLUDED IN THE TAXABLE ESTATE

Several rights that the Decedent held at death are considered by the tax laws to be assets taxable in the Decedent's Estate. These rights do not look anything like assets and almost any nontax professional would overlook them. However, to properly complete the Decedent's Estate Tax return (see Chapter 18), you must not only identify these rights, but you must also determine their taxable values.

Any property that the Decedent transferred during his lifetime, but for which the Decedent retained the possession or enjoyment of the right to the income from the property, or the right to designate the persons who will possess or enjoy the property or the income from the property, is included in the Decedent's Estate for federal tax purposes. For example, the Decedent owned a home that he gave to his children several years before his death. The understanding was that the Decedent made the transfer to "remove the house from his Estate for tax purposes" but that the children would permit him unfettered access to reside in the home until death. The Decedent, in fact, continued to live there until his death. The entire value of the house is included in the Decedent's Estate.

The direct or indirect retention of the right to vote shares transferred of stock in a closely held corporation is considered to be retention of control and is cause for the stock to be included in the Estate for tax purposes.

NOTE: Mom owns stock in the family widget business, Wally's Widgets, Inc. She gives all of her stock away to her children, to remove it from her Estate. However, Mom has each child sign a voting proxy making her the child's agent to continue voting the stock until she agrees otherwise. The stock is still included in Mom's Estate.

If the Decedent transferred property prior to death, but the recipient of the gift can only receive the property by surviving the Decedent, and the Decedent retained a right to receive the property back that exceeds 5 percent of the value of the property, the entire property is included in the Decedent's Estate for federal Estate Tax purposes.

The rights discussed in this section are complex, technical, and difficult to identify. Nevertheless, they are considered "assets" for tax purposes.

CONCLUSION

There are infinite rights and interests that a Decedent may own. This chapter has highlighted several of them.

Part Five

EXPENSES AND LIABILITIES

15 EXPENSES

You must address expenses of the Estate. This may require that you budget to assure adequate cash flow to meet these expenses (see Chapter 8). If cash flow is inadequate or simply may require time to receive (e.g., you must probate the Will, obtain Letters Testamentary, and marshal the asset; only then can you sell or mortgage it), it may be necessary to arrange for lines of credit or other methods of dealing with expenses. For any expenses of the Estate, you want to assure, to the extent feasible, that they are deductible for federal Estate Tax purposes. At minimum, this requires reasonable record keeping on your part to corroborate the validity and appropriateness of the expenses involved. Finally, to the extent feasible, you have a Fiduciary responsibility to control expenses and costs. This chapter provides suggestions for addressing these issues.

CORROBORATING AND DEDUCTING EXPENSES

Administration expenses you incur in managing the Decedent's Estate may be deductible on the federal Estate Tax return. With Estate Tax rates beginning at 37 percent, the value of these deductions can be significant. An important planning issue for these expenses is whether they should be deducted on the Estate Tax return or the Estate's income tax return. This planning is discussed in Chapter 18.

Interest deductions are subject to restrictions on deductibility similar to those faced by individuals. Personal interest expenses are not deductible, only interest incurred in connection with a trade or business, investment or passive activity, or interest on a qualified residence is. Interest paid on deferred Estate Tax is not deductible for estate or income tax purposes.

Generally, any expenses that you seek to deduct for tax purposes must be reasonable. Therefore, to avoid a denial of a deduction, or perhaps worse, a charge by the Beneficiaries that you have inappropriately spent or squandered Estate funds, document every expense. If you receive a bill, be certain that the bill has sufficient detail for anyone reviewing it after the fact to understand the basis for the charges and why they were reasonable. For example, never pay a bill to an attorney or accountant that simply states "For professional services rendered." Insist on a detailed bill listing at minimum the work done and the dates involved. If you have bills for repairs, maintenance, painting, and so on, be certain that the bills are sufficiently detailed to clarify that they were for Estate property. This will avoid any claims that you have misused Estate funds to pay for repairs on nonestate property, such as property previously distributed to a Beneficiary.

CASH EXPENSES

A practical problem that confronts many Executors is the dilemma of documenting the many small cash expenses incurred. For example, a cleaning service may be hired to clean up the Decedent's apartment. A gardener may be hired to tend to the grounds. A local handyperson may be hired to help make minor repairs, pack, and move some of the Decedent's possessions. Taxi fares and tips may be unavoidable. The realities are that although it is appropriate and advisable to pay by check to assure documentation, and to obtain cash receipts, these safeguards are not always possible. Try to pay by check whenever possible, even if you must use your own personal check prior to the Estate's checking account being opened (which may require Letters Testamentary and a tax identification number from the IRS for the Estate). This assures a paper trail. Request a receipt for all payments. Any receipt you get should be stapled to the voucher copy of the check or a blank piece of paper, and then stored in check number order in a loose-leaf binder set up for tracking the details of the Estate's checking account. If you or another person has had to advance cash, seek reimbursement when the Estate checking account is opened and attach the supporting items to the voucher copy of the Estate's check used to reimburse you.

FUNERAL EXPENSES

Funeral and related items are one of the largest expenses you may pay as Executor. This can include the funeral service, religious service, casket, gravestone, and perpetual care. Because of the traumatic emotional environment in which the family may make funeral arrangements, be alert for unusual, excessive, or unnecessary expenses. If costs are not as estimated, discuss them in detail with the funeral director or other providers. If you are still concerned and cannot resolve the issues directly, consult with the Estate attorney.

MAINTAINING THE ESTATE AND ESTATE ASSETS

You have, as the Fiduciary of the Estate, an affirmative obligation to preserve its assets. Thus, you must make reasonable expenditures of Estate funds to insure assets, protect assets (e.g., repairs), and so on.

To identify appropriate repairs and other expenses, consider having an expert evaluate the property involved and issue a report of recommendations. For real estate, a home inspector can issue a report of recommendations. If the Decedent had artwork or books that are decaying because of improper care, have a restoration specialist issue a proposal for addressing the problems.

FORM TO DOCUMENT AND CORROBORATE ESTATE EXPENSES

The Form on page 180 can be used to support and organize the documentation for each expense. These should be attached to the check vouchers and filed in check number order in the Probate Banking Binder described in Chapter 7. Expenses paid in cash should eventually be reimbursed from the Estate checking account to the person paying the cash expense. This step is critical to assure that all expenses and financial transactions are recorded in one account to help you control the Estate, as well as have organized records for any IRS audit and the details to help prepare a comprehensive formal Estate Accounting if it becomes necessary. Lines have been provided for Beneficiaries to sign off agreeing in advance to the expense. Although not always necessary, if the expense is a payment to a related party, an unusual item you would prefer agreement on, or simply a payment that one of the Beneficiaries may complain about, consider having them sign off.

CONCLUSION

Proper documentation of expenses, budgeting to assure that they can be met, and diligence to assure that they are reasonable and necessary are important to protect the Estate and you personally from claims. Review any questionable items with the Estate attorney. Be sure to address any tax payments with an accountant.

SAMPLE DOCUMENTATION FORM

Dan Decedent Estate Expense Support

Payee Name Payee Address	
Amount of Expense	
Purpose of Expense	
Description of Bill, Contract, Other Items (Attached details: [ ] Yes [ ] No)	
Basis for Payment	
Other Comment	

For use by Estate attorney re: Estate Tax Return:
[ ] Deductible on 706
[ ] Deductible on 1041
[ ] Not Deductible
Comment/Explanation:

Expense:

_____

_____

_____

_____

Agree and approve of the above expense:

_____ Date:

_____ Date:

_____ Date:

16 LIABILITIES

Liabilities of the Decedent must be addressed. Common liabilities include a home mortgage, medical bills, claims or lawsuits, personal loans, credit card debt, and other items. Your initial task is to identify all liabilities. This can be done in the following manner:

- Review the Decedent's checkbook for payments to lenders, banks, credit card companies, and so on.
- When writing banks and brokerage firms to confirm account balances, as described in Chapter 10, the same letters should inquire as to any lines of credit, loans, mortgages, margin accounts, and the balances of those accounts.
- On Schedule E of a recent income tax return of the Decedent, review real estate rental properties and businesses to determine whether any loans or other liabilities exist. Contact the principals of the entities involved.
- Schedule A on a recent income tax return of the Decedent lists itemized deductions including interest payments that may indicate loans.
- See the suggestions in Chapter 12 for identifying real Estate assets of the Decedent. Since real estate so commonly is purchased with a mortgage, investigate whether any of the properties identified has a mortgage. If you remain unclear, consult a title company to order a title report to identify any outstanding liens, including mortgages.
- The final income tax return for the Decedent may have a tax liability that has to be paid.
- Continue to review the Decedent's mail following death. Most creditors bill on a periodic basis.

When you become aware of any liability, correspond in writing with the creditor to quickly advise them of the status of the Probate (whether you have been appointed, and if not, when you anticipate Letters Testamentary being received), that you are aware of the claim, and that as soon as feasible you will address the claim. Putting creditors on notice quickly and apprising them honestly of the status will encourage a more amicable resolution of the matter and will often dissuade a creditor from filing a suit to collect the debt for a reasonable period of time. However, use your discretion and judgment. Some bills, such as utilities, mortgage, telephone, and casualty insurance on the Estate's assets may warrant paying once you have determined they are legitimate. This is important to assure that essential services and protections do not lapse. However, if you pay claims prior to being officially appointed as Executor, assuring adequate Estate assets, you may end up being personally out for the money paid. Alternatively, if the claims are important to address, one or more of the Beneficiaries may be willing to advance the funds. In either case, use the recommended procedures to document the expenditures and later to reimburse them from the Estate checking account once it is set up.

DETERMINING WHETHER TO PAY A CLAIM

Once you have identified all claims, you must determine whether they should be paid by the Estate. The first step is to determine if the claim is valid. If you believe it is not, immediately correspond in writing to the creditor. Send your reasons for objecting via certified mail return receipt requested. Ask the Estate attorney whether the objection should be filed with the Court. If you delay too long in filing your objection, you may be prevented from doing so.

A common reason not to pay a liability is that the liability is being paid by another source. For example, credit or mortgage life insurance is commonly used. If a life insurance policy was purchased to repay mortgage or other liabilities, those funds should be applied before any payments by the Estate.

Even valid claims are not always required to be paid. If the Estate has inadequate assets to pay all claims, you must address how they will be paid. This can happen even in a large Estate if most assets pass outside the Probate Estate as a result of joint property or other Probate avoidance techniques.

In a smaller Estate, there simply may not be enough assets to cover expenses. If the Estate's assets are inadequate, state law will provide a listing of priorities in which claims are to be paid. Claims with highest priorities are paid first until the Estate is exhausted. The first claims to pay generally relate to the costs of administering the Estate, then funeral expenses, taxes, medical expenses, and so on. In very small Estates, state law may provide for a minimum family allowance that can be paid to family members before many creditors are entitled to be paid.

Certain legitimate creditors' claims may not have to be paid if they are not submitted to you prior to required legal deadlines. If you publish a notice to creditors (see Chapter 5), most creditors must submit their claims by the required deadline (two to eight months in many states).

If products or services were purchased using a joint credit card in the name of the Decedent and another person, the Estate and the other person may be jointly liable for the payment of the bill involved. Address the issue of who should be responsible before making payment.

CREDIT CARDS

Cancel credit cards as quickly as possible by cutting the cards up to avoid any inappropriate use. Do not throw them away, however. Write the credit card companies (see the following sample letter) informing them of the cardholder's death and the date of death. Enclose the cut-up card. Request the immediate termination of the account and a final bill. When the bill arrives, carefully scrutinize it. Are all charges in order? Were all charges incurred at a reasonable time? If the Decedent was hospitalized for weeks before dying, could the charges possibly have been legitimate? Be certain to save records of all bills paid, and to pay the final balances (if the Estate has adequate assets and is required to) with an Estate check (see Chapter 7).

If another family member was using the card (or a secondary card on the same account), apply for a new card in that user's name.

SAMPLE LETTER TO CREDIT CARD COMPANY

ELLIOTT EXECUTOR
123 MAIN STREET
ANYTOWN, USA

April 27, 1999

Attention: Customer Service
Big Bank Corp.
1000 Financial Way
Somecity, Anystate

Re: *Notice to Cancel Card/Account.*

Dear Sirs:

I am writing to you as Executor for the Estate of Dan Decedent. Please be advised that the following account/card holder has died:

Decedent's Name: Dan Decedent
Date of Death: January 13, 1999
Old billing Address: 456 Travel Way, Anytown, Somestate
Account No.: 0001-22-3333-4

Please CANCEL this card effective immediately and do not accept any transactions for processing dated after the Date of Death.

Any final bills should be sent to: Elliott Executor, 123 Main Street, Anytown, USA.

Please confirm that there is no credit life insurance on this account.

A copy of the death certificate of Dan Decedent and the cut-up account/credit card are enclosed.

Sincerely,

Estate of Dan Decedent

By: _____
    Elliott Executor, Executor

enc.

MEDICAL EXPENSES

Once medical bills have been identified, advise the medical providers of your status as Executor, that you have received the claim and are reviewing it for payment. Prior to making any payment, verify that Decedent had no medical or other insurance coverage to cover the expense. Although it might take some time to negotiate with the Decedent's health insurance company, it is preferable to exhaust insurance, employer, government benefits, and any other reimbursement options before payment. If you pay the medical bills and than discover that an insurance carrier has also paid it, or would pay it, it will likely prove difficult to obtain a refund of amounts you have previously paid to the medical provider.

Medical expenses incurred for the Decedent's benefit, and paid within one year after his death, could be deducted on his final income tax return. However, they would be subject to a restriction that they can only be deducted if they exceed 7.5 percent of his adjusted gross income. There is no limit on the deductibility of such amounts on the Estate Tax return. A decision must be made as to which approach is to be used.

CONCLUSION

Addressing claims against the Estate is essential before making distributions to Beneficiaries. Quick action to address claims can help you assure that the Estate does not pay invalid claims or claims that others can be required to pay. Use discretion in all cases to avoid jeopardizing Estate assets.

Part Six

TAXES

17 INCOME, GIFT, ESTATE, GST, AND INHERITANCE TAXES

Income, gift, estate, and generation-skipping transfer ("GST") taxes are likely to be the largest expenses of the Estate. In fact, the aggregate tax payments may be greater than the distributions to the largest Beneficiary. In addition to the substantial costs involved, there are many filing deadlines that should not be overlooked. Hire professionals with expertise in these matters. As discussed in Chapter 2, be certain that the Estate's professionals are clear as to their responsibilities. Generally, the Estate accountant should assume responsibility for filing all income tax returns. The Estate attorney should generally assume responsibility for filing the Estate Tax return. Gift tax returns may be filed by either; simply be sure that a decision is made and communicated.

When you consult with the Estate accountant and attorney, ask them for the dates the various tax filings (and payments if different) are due. Record each date in the chart provided in Chapter 2 and in the Estate calendar book discussed in that chapter. Do not assume that the professionals are solely responsible for meeting the deadlines. It is your responsibility as well. Calendar the dates and follow up in advance to insure that they are not missed.

FEDERAL TAX RETURNS FOR THE DECEDENT

Federal Income Tax Returns for the Decedent

A final federal income tax return must be filed for the Decedent. Generally it is due by the same due date that the Decedent's return would have been due (April 15). You may be able to extend the filing date by filing Form 4868 and thereafter Form 2688. Consult with an accountant.

Generally, the IRS has three years from the date an income tax return is filed to assess additional taxes. This time period can be so long that it can delay your making distributions from the Estate and winding up the Estate. You can shorten this time period to 18 months by writing to the IRS and requesting a prompt assessment of the Decedent's income taxes and filing Form 4810. This procedure is not a guarantee that taxes cannot be assessed at a later date if one of the Decedent's income tax returns included fraudulent information, was not filed, or reflected a substantial omission of income. Before making final distributions from the Estate, consider whether you should hold any cash in reserve to address the 18-month period, or the longer time periods. Think carefully since you as Executor can be held personally liable. For this reason, an additional request limiting personal liability can be made. This can be made by filing Form 5495.

If the Decedent was due a refund, file Form 1310. The sample letter on page 189 refers to the preceding items. However, the requests to limit the time periods during which the IRS can assess tax should be filed separately from the filing of the final tax return.

CAUTION: Before filing the requests to limit the time periods in which taxes can be assessed, or your personal liability as Executor, discuss with the Estate accountant and attorney how these filings may trigger an IRS audit.

When filing the final income tax return for the Decedent, the top of page one of the return should reflect "DECEASED—DAN DECEDENT." Also, you must address who should sign the return. It can be signed by you as Executor, the surviving spouse on a joint income tax return, or in some instances perhaps by the Trustee of a Revocable Living Trust if no Executor was appointed because of the Decedent having effectively avoided Probate.

Special rules and considerations apply to this final income tax return. For example, the surviving spouse can file a joint return with you as Executor. Under some conditions, the surviving spouse can file without the Executor's involvement. If the surviving spouse remarried before the close of tax year, the joint return status with the Decedent is not permitted. Before electing the joint filing status, have the Estate's accountant calculate tax as married filing separately to determine which approach is better.

Consider the tax Election available to report interest on government savings bonds (see Chapter 10).

The medical expenses incurred by the Decedent can be deducted on the Decedent's final income tax return or on the Estate's federal Estate Tax return.

Federal Gift Tax Returns for the Decedent

Review the Decedent's checkbooks and other financial records, and question the Decedent's heirs, to identify any gifts that trigger the requirement of filing a gift tax return. For example, many taxpayers sign durable powers of attorney that permit the agents to make gifts with the specific intent of encouraging gifts to be made if the Decedent's time appears limited.

SAMPLE LETTER TO
INTERNAL REVENUE SERVICE

ELLIOTT EXECUTOR
123 MAIN STREET
ANYTOWN, USA

December 13, 2000

VIA CERTIFIED MAIL P 000 000 000
Internal Revenue Service
1040 Tax Avenue
Anytown, Somestate

> Re: *Dan Decedent, Decedent*
>   *Social Security No. 000-00-0000*

Dear Sirs:

Enclosed are the following:

a. Form 1040 U.S. Individual Income Tax Return prepared by Andrea Accountant & Co. CPAs for the above named decedent.

b. An original death certificate.

c. An original certified letters testamentary.

d. Form 1310 Statement of Person Claiming Refund Due a Deceased Taxpayer, signed by the executor, Elliott Executor.

e. By this letter we request on behalf of the Decedent's Estate a prompt assessment of any additional taxes due on any of the Decedent's income tax returns as permitted under Code Section 6501(d). This request shall shorten to 18 months from the date of this letter the period during which additional tax can be assessed.

f. By this letter the undersigned Executor of the Estate of Dan Decedent hereby requests a discharge for the undersigned Executor from personal liability for the decedent's income and gift taxes as permitted under Code Section 6905. This request shall limit to nine months from the date hereof the time period in which the IRS must notify the Executor of any deficiencies if it will seek to hold the Executor personally liable.

Sincerely yours,

Estate of Dan Decedent

By: _____
    Elliott Executor, Executor

It is important to identify whether a gift tax return has to be filed because of any gift made during the last year of the Decedent's life. This is important because if any of the Decedent's Applicable Exclusion Amount was used up on the gift tax returns to offset taxable gifts, a larger Estate Tax would be due. Thus, the gift tax returns are integrally related to the Estate Tax return.

Form 56

Form 56 should be filed to notify the IRS that you are now acting as personal representative of the Estate. The filing of this form allows the IRS to contact you directly regarding any notices of tax liability concerning federal income tax or other returns filed by the Decedent.

FEDERAL TAX RETURNS FOR THE ESTATE AND TRUSTS FORMED BY THE ESTATE

Federal Income Tax Returns for the Estate

The Estate constitutes an independent taxpayer and thus must file its own income tax return. The return is Form 1041. It is required to be filed if the Estate earns more than $600 of gross income. If the Estate elects to report income on a calendar year, like most individual taxpayers, the return would be due on April 15. If the Estate decides to elect a fiscal tax year (any year-end other than December 31) the return is due on the 15th day of the fourth month following the end of the tax year. The selection of the best tax year can be a useful income tax planning technique for some estates. The year can be selected to best match income and deductions. Also, if the deductions incurred in the Estate's final year exceed income, then the Estate's Beneficiaries can deduct the excess on their personal income tax returns. When the selection of the Estate's tax year is coordinated with the distributions to Beneficiaries, income can be retained, or paid out to Beneficiaries, in a manner that maximizes the lowest marginal tax rates of the Estate and Beneficiaries to minimize tax.

Like an individual taxpayer, an Estate can delay the tax filing deadline by filing a request for an extension on Form 2758.

Federal Income Tax Returns for Trusts Formed by the Estate

Any Trusts formed under the Decedent's Will, such as a Bypass Trust, marital or QTIP Trust, or Trusts for minor children, will each require their own income tax filings on Form 1041. Even if you prepare your own tax return Form 1040, carefully consider having an accountant with trust experience help with these returns. Saving a $500 or $1,000 fee but making significant planning mistakes is no bargain.

Federal Estate Tax Return for the Estate

The most complex and comprehensive tax return is the Estate's Estate Tax return filed on Form 706. This return requires detailed disclosures, generally addressed with detailed attached exhibits. Numerous complex tax Elections (choices) must be made.

CAUTION: Never attempt to prepare and file an Estate Tax return without obtaining professional assistance. Even if you have successfully filled out and filed your own income tax return for years, do not make the mistake of filing the Estate Tax return on your own. An Estate Tax return may be the most complex of all tax filings! If your objective is to minimize professional fees, do it by assisting with collecting the detailed information for the return, but follow the directions of an expert.

To understand in general terms the Estate Tax return, a brief overview of the Estate Tax is necessary.

The Estate Tax is a transfer charge assessed on property owned by the Decedent on death. The actual tax, however, is much broader and more complicated than this simple explanation indicates. There are numerous exclusions and deductions. Also the definition of property the Decedent owned at death includes items that many people find surprising. With Estate Tax rates as high as 55 percent (60 percent when certain phaseouts are in effect), planning is important. Even though most planning had to have been completed well before the Decedent's death, considerable planning opportunities may still be available ("postmortem" planning).

The first step in the process is to identify all property and property interests that are included in what is called the Gross Estate. This are discussed in Chapters 10 through 14. Once the properties are identified, they must be valued. The sum of all assets owned by the Decedent, after reduction for certain expenses and other allowable adjustments (see Chapters 15 and 16), will be the base on which the Estate's Tax is calculated. The Form 706 Estate Tax Return (which can be obtained from the IRS; call 1-800-TAX-FORM) provides detailed charts and schedules for making these calculations.

Generally, the Decedent's Gross Estate includes all property, whether real estate (land and buildings), personal property (furniture, jewelry, etc.), or intangible property (copyright, license, etc.), to the extent the Estate Tax rules require that this property be included in the Estate. Assets included in the Gross Estate include any interest that the Decedent had in property at the time of death which is included in the Probate Estate. For example, a bonus the Decedent was entitled to at the time of death is included in his Gross Estate. If the Decedent owned insurance on the life of another person, such as under a cross-purchase buyout agreement, the value of the policy is included in his Gross Estate. Business and partnership interests are included. The fact that the Decedent's surviving spouse may have an interest under state law concepts of dower or curtesy (spouse's claim to assets) does not affect the inclusion of these assets in the Gross Estate for tax purposes.

Property interests to be included in the Estate are very broadly defined. Even property that the Decedent gave away during his lifetime can be required to be included in his Gross Estate. For example, if the Decedent transferred property, but retained the right to the income, or even the right to designate who will obtain the income, these assets can be brought back into the Gross Estate. If the Decedent transferred property to another person, but that person could only obtain the right to use and enjoy that property after the Decedent's death, the entire value of this property is includible in his Estate. If the Decedent transferred property but reserved the right to change who will have the right to enjoy that property, this will also be included in his Estate. Insurance proceeds receivable by you as Executor of the Decedent's Estate, or by any other Beneficiary if the Decedent retained incidents of ownership in the policy (e.g., the right to change Beneficiaries), will be taxed in the Estate. If the Decedent had a General Power of Appointment over property (e.g., he could designate who would get the property), the value of that property is included in his Gross Estate.

The fair value of the assets at the date of death is the amount to be included in the Gross Estate. The value to be used is called the "fair market value." This is the price at which the property would change hands between a willing buyer and a willing seller, neither being under any compulsion to buy or to sell, and both having reasonable knowledge of the relevant facts. Where a stock traded on a public exchange is included in the Estate, the value is easily found in any major newspaper. For assets such as real estate and closely held business interests, valuation can be a substantial point of contention between the Estate and the IRS.

A special valuation rule is provided for farms, ranches, and certain property used in a closely held business.

Another special rule permits you as Executor to value assets at the date six months after the Decedent's death, rather than under the general rule using the date of death. The rationale for this rule is quite simple. Had the Decedent died just prior to a stock market decline, the value of the Estate could be based on historically high stock prices. The Estate Tax would be due nine months later, following the market crash. The Estate Tax could exceed the entire value of the estate. The Alternate Valuation Date provides what can be an important degree of flexibility to address changing market conditions if it will reduce the Estate Tax. Where this date is elected, it applies to all property included in the Gross Estate that has not been disposed of prior to the Alternate Valuation Date.

The Estate is allowed deductions for funeral expenses, Estate administrative expenses, claims against the Estate, debts relating to any property included in the Gross Estate, charitable bequests, and qualifying bequests to the Decedent's surviving spouse.

If an expense could qualify to be deducted on either the Decedent's Estate Tax return, or for income tax purposes, you as Executor must select one place to claim the deduction since a double benefit is not permitted. Losses, such as a casualty loss, are also deductible. When these items are deducted from the Gross Estate, the result is the Taxable Estate.

The federal Estate Tax is calculated as follows. A tentative tax is calculated on the sum of the Taxable Estate, as determined according to the preceding guidelines, increased by the adjusted taxable gifts made by the Decedent after 1976. These are gifts made in most prior years on which the Decedent used up some of his Applicable Exclusion Amount or on which he incurred a gift tax. The idea is that since a single integrated tax structure is used for both estate and gift tax purposes, all taxable transfers, whether made during the Decedent's life or after his death, should be added and subjected to the same graduated tax rate schedule. There is no double taxation of the gifts, however, because a credit is provided for gift tax paid on those amounts. Gifts included in this tentative tax calculation are based on their fair market value when the gifts were made. If the gift wasn't adequately disclosed on a gift tax return, the IRS may be able to revalue it. This tentative tax amount is then reduced by the gift taxes that would be payable on gifts made by the Decedent after 1976. A reduction is also made for the applicable exclusion amount available to Decedent's dying in that year. The following chart can be used to determine the exclusion amount for any year:

Applicable Exclusion Amount by Year

Year of Death	Tax Credit Your Estate Receives to Assure That Amount of Assets Is Excluded (Applicable Exclusion Amount)	Assets Your Estate Can Exclude from Tax (Applicable Amount)
1999	$211,300	$650,000
2000	$220,550	$675,000
2001	$220,550	$675,000
2002	$229,800	$700,000
2003	$229,800	$700,000
2004	$287,300	$850,000
2005	$326,300	$950,000
2006 and later years	$345,800	$1,000,000

A number of credits may also be applied to reduce the Estate Tax. These include a credit for prior transfers and for death taxes paid to the Decedent's state.

In preparing the federal Estate Tax return, the preceding points will all be addressed to the extent that they apply to your Estate. In addition, many tax elections must be considered. Some of these are addressed in Chapter 18.

The sample cover letter on page 194 can be used in filing the Estate Tax return with the IRS. Always send the return by certified mail return receipt requested to prove the filing date because it can be important in determining whether the deadlines for various elections were made.

SAMPLE COVER LETTER
FOR ESTATE TAX RETURN

ELLIOTT EXECUTOR
123 MAIN STREET
ANYTOWN, USA

December 13, 2000

VIA CERTIFIED MAIL Return Receipt # 000 000 000
Internal Revenue Service
1040 Tax Avenue
Anytown, Somestate

> Re: *Dan Decedent, Decedent*
>   *Social Security No. 000-00-0000*

Dear Sir/Madam:

I am the executor of the above named estate.

Enclosed are the following:

    a. United States Estate Tax Return (Form 706).

    b. Exhibits to Form 706.

    c. Check No. 603 payable to "Internal Revenue Service."

Kindly acknowledge receipt of the enclosed by signing the bottom of this letter and return it to us in the envelope provided.

Sincerely yours,

Estate of Dan Decedent

By: _____
    Elliott Executor, Executor

IRS Acknowledgement:

Tax return and Exhibits received by: _____

    Date: _____

enc.

STATE TAX RETURNS

Many states have their own filing requirements. Because the requirements vary state by state inquire of the Surrogate's Court where you file the Decedent's Will for Probate, call the state's tax department for forms and instructions, or rely on the accountant or attorney you hire to represent the Estate.

CONCLUSION

This chapter has summarized some of the many federal and state tax filings that you will have to address as Executor. Because these forms are complex and involve many important and substantial issues, it is strongly recommended that you obtain professional guidance and assistance in preparing and filing these returns.

18 TAX PLANNING IS STILL POSSIBLE AFTER DEATH

The federal Estate Tax rate begins at 37 percent, reaches the maximum 55 percent rate quickly, and can even be higher in certain circumstances. These costs are so substantial that tax planning deserves careful attention. Although tax planning prior to death, and preferably many years prior to death, is the best way to minimize Estate and other transfer tax costs, planning after death (postmortem tax planning) can still have a tremendous impact on reducing transfer tax costs. This chapter highlights some of the many planning opportunities. Because many complex planning considerations are not addressed here, it is strongly recommended that you review these matters with both the accountant and the attorney representing the Estate.

CHECKLIST

Consider the following planning checklist:

- Select the optimal calendar or fiscal tax year for Estate.
- Determine which expenses to deduct on Estate Tax return versus the Estate's income tax return.
- Can any joint account holder prove contribution in order to reduce federal Estate Tax?
- Do Executor's fees provide a deduction on the Estate Tax return of greater value than the income tax cost to be incurred by the Executor reporting the fees on his or her personal income tax return?
- Does the deduction of administration expenses on the Estate's Estate Tax return generate more benefit than deducting them on the Estate's income tax return?
- Medical expenses incurred for Decedent and paid within one year after death can be deducted on the Decedent's final income tax return subject to a reduction of 7.5 percent of the Decedent's adjusted gross income (AGI). These expenses can be deducted without any limit on the Estate Tax return. Consider the 7.5 percent reduction and different marginal tax rates.

- If the Decedent purchased savings bonds with his own funds and registered them in his name and the name of another as co-owners, the entire value of the bonds will be included in his Gross Estate.
- Interest accrued on Series E bonds is income in respect of a Decedent (IRD). The federal Estate Tax applicable to this asset can be deducted in calculating the income tax on these E Bonds.
- Is the Estate valued at a lower amount using the six-month Alternate Valuation Date?

SELECTING THE ASSETS TO USE TO FUND DIFFERENT TRUSTS TO MAXIMIZE TAX ADVANTAGES

The Applicable Exclusion Amount enables the Decedent's Estate to avoid tax on the first $650,000 in 1999 (increasing to $1 million for Decedents dying in 2006). The manner in which this Applicable Exclusion Amount is generally taken advantage of is through the funding of a special Trust under the Decedent's Will, or Revocable Living Trust, of the first spouse to die. This special Trust is called a Bypass Trust. This name is used since the assets in the Trust bypass tax in the Estate of the surviving spouse. The income, and principal, of this Trust can be distributed to or for the benefit of any Beneficiaries. Typically, the income and principal are distributed for the benefit of the surviving spouse and any children or other heirs in the discretion of the Trustee (called a sprinkle power). Some taxpayers prefer to limit distributions to solely the surviving spouse. Read the Will carefully and review the provisions with the Estate attorney. There are many variations and you don't want to be held responsible for inappropriate distributions. On the death of the surviving spouse, the remaining assets in the Bypass Trust can be distributed to the children or other heirs. The key benefit of this planning is that the surviving spouse can have access and benefit (albeit restricted compared with outright ownership if the assets were bequeathed directly instead of in the Bypass Trust) without those assets being later taxed in the surviving spouse's Estate. The remainder of the Estate is usually distributed outright or in a marital or QTIP Trust to the surviving spouse (a QDOT if the surviving spouse is not a citizen). The marital portion will be taxed in the surviving spouse's Estate on her later death. The Bypass Trust assets will not be. Therefore, when selecting which assets to use to fund the Bypass Trust and the QTIP or marital portion, use assets most likely to appreciate to fund the Bypass Trust. This would have the growth occur outside the surviving spouse's Estate.

WILL THERE BE A BYPASS TRUST?

The possibility that a very large estate could produce little, if any Bypass Trust, surprises many. This could occur because of a bequest of an item of tangible personal property under the personal property clause to someone other than the surviving spouse where the value of the item has increased significantly from what was anticipated (e.g., a painting), or large administrative expenses, and so on.

ALLOCATING DEDUCTIONS BETWEEN ESTATE AND INCOME TAX RETURNS

Administration expenses can be deducted either on Form 706, the Estate Tax return, or on the Estate's income tax return—Form 1041. If no Estate Tax is due, as is common on the death of the first spouse when the Will includes an unlimited Estate Tax Marital Deduction sufficient to eliminate any Estate Tax, the Estate's administration expenses should not be deducted on Form 706. Rather administration expenses should be deducted on the Estate's income tax return if one must be filed. There may be a distinction between how management and transmission expenses are treated. Discuss this with the Estate attorney.

PLANNING FOR THE PROGRESSIVE ESTATE TAX RATE

The Estate Tax is a progressive tax. The higher the Taxable Estate, the greater the percentage rate at which the Estate Tax is assessed, until the maximum 55 percent rate is reached. Thus, the lower marginal rates between 37 percent and 55 percent present a planning opportunity. In some instances, it may make sense for the Estate of the first spouse to die to intentionally incur an Estate Tax to the extent that the tax is below 55 percent. A Disclaimer may have to be filed in order to trigger this tax.

MARITAL DEDUCTION (QTIP)

If the following requirements are met, the Decedent's bequest to his surviving spouse will qualify for the Estate Tax Marital Deduction: (1) The spouse is given a life estate in particular property; (2) the spouse has the right to all of the income from that property payable at least annually; (3) the property must pass from the Decedent's Estate; (4) no person has a power to appoint any part of the property to any person other than the surviving spouse; and (5) the necessary election is made by you as Executor to have the property qualify. Carefully evaluate with the accountant and attorney for the Estate what portion if any (or even all) of bequests to a qualifying Trust for the benefit of the surviving spouse should be elected to qualify for the Estate Tax Marital Deduction. The election you make on the Estate Tax return will be determinative.

TIP: Consider extending the deadline for filing the federal Estate Tax return for six months when a QTIP Trust is funded. If the surviving spouse dies during this period than the QTIP election can be made for only the portion of the Estate of the first spouse to die equal to the amount that would have been taxed at the maximum marginal tax rate. The portion of the QTIP Trust that would be taxed at the lower progressive Estate Tax rates from 37 percent to 55 percent would not be covered by the QTIP election. Thus, a tax would intentionally be incurred at the lower Estate Tax rates on the death of the first spouse.

MARITAL DEDUCTION FOR NONCITIZEN SPOUSES (QDOT)

No Marital Deduction can be claimed for property passing to a non-U.S. citizen spouse unless the property passes into a QDOT (special Trust meeting certain statutory requirements). The unlimited Marital Deduction is not available where the surviving spouse is a noncitizen unless the QDOT is used. Some offset to this tax cost is offered through a credit provision. Where one spouse bequeaths property to the other spouse, who is a noncitizen, that property transfer is subjected to the Estate Tax. However, a credit will be available to the Estate on the later death to offset the tax paid by the first spouse's Estate on the earlier transfer, which did not qualify for the Marital Deduction. Review the requirements to qualify a bequest to a surviving noncitizen spouse, possibilities of re-forming the Will so that the bequest qualifies, and the Election you must make as Executor on the Estate Tax return with the accountant and attorney for the Estate.

NOTE: See Martin M. Shenkman, *The Complete Book of Trusts* (2nd ed.) (New York: John Wiley & Sons, 1997), for a comprehensive discussion of QTIP and QDOT Trusts.

CLOSELY HELD BUSINESS AND CODE SECTION 303 REDEMPTIONS

If stock of a closely held business is redeemed (i.e., repurchased from the Decedent's Estate by the corporation) to pay funeral and administration expenses, and death taxes, the provisions of Code Section 303 can enable the Estate to qualify to treat the redemption as a capital gain. The purpose of Code Section 303 is to enable the corporation to redeem shares in a corporation that is includible in the Gross Estate, thus providing cash to pay taxes and expenses, without adverse income tax consequences. If the requirements of this Code Section are met, the distribution will be treated as a distribution in full payment in exchange for the stock redeemed and not as a dividend distribution by the corporation. If the latter treatment applied, the entire proceeds would be taxable as ordinary income.

If the requirements of Code Section 303 redemption treatment are met, then the distribution will be treated as a distribution in full payment for the stock (i.e., a sale). This benefit, however, is limited by the sum of:

1. The Estate Taxes incurred by the Decedent's Estate, including Estate Taxes payable to the federal government, state governments, and foreign countries. It also includes interest on such taxes.

2. The administration expenses of the Estate, including funeral and other expenses. The debts and losses deductible from the Gross Estate are not included in determining the limitation under Code Section 303. Administration expenses are allowable even if they are claimed on the Estate's Fiduciary income tax return (Form 1041) and are not taken against the Estate Tax.

These limitations are logical. The purpose of Code Section 303 is to give the Estate a break on receiving distributions necessary to pay taxes and expenses. Distributions above this amount do not need the tax break.

If the preceding basic requirements described are met, then the distribution is considered to be in full payment for the redemption of the stock, limited to the sum of (1) the Estate Taxes payable, and (2) the funeral and administrative expenses allowable as a deduction.

To qualify for Code Section 303 redemption benefits, the Estate must meet the following basic requirements.

- *Distribution of Property.* There must be a distribution of property to the Estate. The redeeming corporation must distribute property to the shareholder in exchange for the stock. Property is defined to include money, securities, and any other property. The term property does not include stock in the corporation making the distribution (or rights to acquire such stock). A corporation's installment promissory note has been deemed property because it does not represent an equity interest in the distributing corporation, even if the full payment will not occur until after the statutory period.

- *Included in Gross Estate of Decedent.* The redeemed stock must have been includible in the Gross Estate for federal Estate Tax purposes. If stock is acquired by the Estate, directly from the Decedent by operation of law or by the terms of his Will, then the stock may be qualify for Code Section 303 redemption benefits. However, if the stock was received by you as Executor in satisfaction of a monetary bequest, the stock may not be available for a redemption, unless you have the power to distribute assets in kind.

- *Distribution Must Redeem Stock of the Corporation.* The distribution from the corporation to the Decedent's Estate must be to redeem part or all of the corporation's stock held by the Estate. The second part of this test, that the payment from the corporation must be for something classified as stock, is rather broadly interpreted. It does not matter whether the stock is voting or nonvoting stock. Similarly, this tax benefit is not limited only to common stock. Subchapter C stock as well as Subchapter S stock can qualify. This benefit is also available to stock that was not included in the Gross Estate, if the Tax Basis of the stock is determined by reference to the basis of stock included in the Gross Estate. This could include stock received in a reorganization, in a distribution or exchange.

- *35 Percent Requirement.* The benefit of Code Section 303 is only available if the stock in the corporation which is included in the Gross Estate exceeds 35 percent of the value of the Gross Estate. For this calculation, the Gross Estate is reduced by funeral and administration expenses and the debts and losses of the Estate. If the Decedent owned stock in more than one corporation, the corporations involved can be treated as one business for the purpose of applying this 35 percent test. To aggregate corporations, 20 percent or more in value of each corporation must be included in the Estate.

- *Timing Requirement to Qualify for Redemption Treatment.* Code Section 303 redemption benefits only apply to distributions by corporations from the time of the Decedent's death until: three years and 90 days after the filing of the Estate's federal Estate Tax return, Form 706; within 60 days from the Tax Court's decision for redetermination of Estate Tax deficiency; within the time determined by the Estate Tax deferral provisions of Code Section 6166 (described later in this chapter). If a Code Section 303 redemption occurs more than four years from the date of Decedent's death, then the distribution may not be more than the lesser of: (1) the balance of the unpaid taxes and administration expenses remaining unpaid immediately prior to the distribution; or (2) the aggregate of such taxes and expenses paid within one year after the distribution.

NOTE: For more details on Code Section 303 Redemptions and planning for closely held business interests generally, see Martin M. Shenkman, *Estate Planning after the 1997 Tax Act* (New York: John Wiley & Sons, 1998), and *Starting Your Own Limited Liability Company* (New York: John Wiley & Sons, 1997).

DEDUCTION FOR QUALIFYING INTERESTS IN CLOSELY HELD BUSINESSES TRANSFERRED TO QUALIFYING HEIRS

The tax laws provide a potentially valuable deduction from the Estate Tax for bequests of qualifying business interests to heirs active in the business. This deduction is available only to qualifying family-owned business interests, affectionately called QFOBIs (pronounced Q-Fobees). The maximum amount that can be deducted is $675,000. However, the full value of this maximum deduction will not always be realized because of the interplay of the Code Section 2057 deduction and the Applicable Exclusion Amount. If the full $675,000 deduction is claimed, the Applicable Exclusion Amount available to the estate will be limited to $625,000. If the deduction for the closely held business interest is less than the maximum

$675,000 allowable, the Applicable Exclusion Amount will be by the excess of $675,000 over the amount of the deduction allowed.

EXAMPLE: The deduction claimed under Code Section 2057 for a qualifying family business interest is $550,000. The difference between this deduction amount and the $675,000, or $125,000 ($675,000 – $550,000) is added back to the amount of the Applicable Exclusion as limited by Code Section 2057(a)(3)(A) of $625,000. Thus the Applicable Exclusion would be $750,000. However, this amount cannot exceed the actual Applicable Exclusion Amount available in that year under the general Applicable Exclusion provision. Thus, for 1999, the Applicable Exclusion Amount would be limited to $650,000.

The requirements to qualify for this Estate Tax deduction are:

1. *United States Citizen or Resident.* The Decedent must have been, at the date of death, a U.S. citizen or resident.

2. *Election.* You must indicate on the Estate Tax return that this special treatment of the tax deduction is to apply.

3. *Heirs Must Sign Agreement.* Each person who has an interest in the business must sign a written agreement stating that they consent to the recapture provisions. If the QFOBI requirements aren't met, the tax that had been saved on the Estate Tax return will have to be paid. This agreement must be signed by each person who has an interest in any QFOBI property designated in such agreement. You must file this agreement with the Decedent's federal Estate Tax return.

4. *More Than 50 Percent of the Estate.* The QFOBIs must comprise more than 50 percent of the Decedent's Estate. This computation is complex. For purposes of this test it is the adjusted value of the QFOBIs plus the amount of certain gifts of such QFOBIs, made during your lifetime, that combined must exceed 50 percent of the Decedent's Adjusted Gross Estate.

Gifts of QFOBIs include gifts the Decedent made to family members during his or her lifetime that were taxable, or which used up a portion of his Applicable Exclusion Amount.

In addition, for such prior gifts to be included in determining whether the 50 percent of the adjusted gross estate test is met, the gifted QFOBIs must have been continuously held by members of such family (other than the Decedent's spouse) between the date of the gift and the date of the Decedent's death.

The 50 percent of adjusted gross estate test requires that the aggregate value of the Decedent's interest in QFOBIs that were passed to qualifying heirs is more than 50 percent of the Decedent's Adjusted Gross Estate.

5. *The Business Interests Must Be Qualified (QFOBIs).* The term QFOBI means an interest in a trade or business carried on as a proprietorship. This term also includes an interest in any entity carrying on a

trade or business if certain ownership concentration tests are met. The business must be owned at least 50 percent by one family (directly or indirectly), 70 percent by two families, or 90 percent by three families. The Decedent's family must not own less than 30 percent of the business interests.

CAUTION: A divorce settlement could destroy a family's ability to meet the ownership test. If two families own 70 percent of a business so that the requirement is met, but one son divorces and the court awards his spouse 1 percent of the stock in the corporation, the 70 percent test is failed and two families could bear a tax burden.

NOTE: Consider the need to meet these requirements in drafting buy-sell provisions of any governing documents. What will the impact be on financing arrangements where lenders restrict or control various aspects of the business, escrow accounts holding shares relating to buy-sell or other transactions, voting Trust arrangements, voting stock issued to nonparticipating heirs, and so on.

The Decedent will be treated as if engaged in a trade or business if any member of the Decedent's family is engaged in such a trade or business. Members of the Decedent's family are defined as spouse, ancestors, lineal descendants of Decedent, lineal descendants of Decedent's spouse, or spouse of any lineal descendants.

If the Decedent's heirs are not family under the above definition, it will not be possible to qualify for this provision.

6. *Principal Place of Business within the United States.* The principal place of the business must be located within the United States.

7. *Restriction on Public Trading.* The business interest will not qualify for this exclusion if the securities involved were traded on a public market within three years of the Decedent's death. This includes stock or debt of the particular business or any controlled group.

8. *Reduction for Passive Investments.* The value of the business interest is reduced by any passive assets, excess cash, or marketable securities in excess of the reasonably expected day-to-day working capital needs of the business. This restriction shall apply to any business if more than 25 percent of its adjusted ordinary gross income for the year of the Decedent's death would qualify as personal holding company income. Working capital needs are determined based on historical averages of business working capital needs in the past.

CAUTION: If the founder of a closely held business is terminally ill, common sense would have it that cash should be conserved and accumulated to plan for the impending disruptions. This rational business step could have the effect of destroying any possibility of qualifying for the very tax benefit intended to help a family business survive such a situation.

Passive assets include assets that produce dividends, interest, rents, royalties, annuities, and certain other types of passive income. This includes interests in a partnership, real estate mortgage investment conduit (REMIC), Trust, and so on. Special rules are provided for real estate under a net lease to a family business.

9. *Ownership of Entities.* Ownership of corporations is determined by the holding of stock possessing the appropriate percentage of the total combined voting power of all classes of stock entitled to vote and the appropriate percentage of the total value of shares of all classes of stock. For partnerships, ownership shall be determined by the appropriate percentage of the capital interests in such partnerships. In the case of tiered partnerships, the ownership of the lower tier interests shall be disregarded in determining the ownership interests in the first tier entity. For lower tier entities the rules shall be applied separately in determining if such entities are QFOBIs.

10. *Material Participation.* Decedent, or a member of Decedent's family, must have materially participated in the business for at least five of eight years preceding the Decedent's death.

11. *Qualified Heirs.* The business interests must pass to qualified heirs and active employees of the business employed by the business for at least 10 years prior to the Decedent's death.

12. *Participation of Heirs.* These qualified heirs must materially participate in the trade or business for at least 5 years of any 8-year period within 10 years following Decedent's death. Material participation is defined to include physical work and participation in management decisions.

13. *Exclusion Can Be Recaptured.* If the qualifications are met, but later failed, recapture rules apply. If within 10 years of the date after Decedent's death any of the following events occur, a portion or all of the tax savings may have to be repaid (recaptured):

- None of the Decedent's heirs materially participate in the business.
- The Decedent's heirs dispose of any portion of their interests in the business to other than a qualified member of the Decedent's family.
- The Decedent's heirs lose their U.S. citizenship (and don't comply with other provisions to assure the IRS that any future tax due will be paid).
- The principal place of the business ceases to be in the United States.

If any of the above recapture events occur, an additional Estate Tax will have to be paid. The amount of the additional Estate Tax is the applicable percentage of the adjusted tax difference attributable to the QFOBI. The applicable percentage is:

Recapture Event Occurs in Following Year	Applicable Percentage for Recapture Calculation
1	100%
2	100%
3	100%
4	100%
5	100%
6	100%
7	80%
8	60%
9	40%
10	20%
After Year 10	None

SPECIAL VALUATION RULES FOR CLOSELY HELD FARMS AND BUSINESSES (CODE SECTION 2032A)

For Estate Tax purposes, assets owned at death are generally valued at their fair market value at the date of death (or six months later at the Alternate Valuation Date). Fair value is the price a willing buyer would pay and a willing seller would accept. It is generally at the highest and best uses value of the asset. For example, if you use land as a parking lot for your business, but a developer could build an office building on the land, the price a developer would pay for the best use of the property, not a price a purchaser would pay for parking lot land, is used. This general valuation rule can create a tremendous hardship for farm or family businesses where assets are used in the business at a lesser value than fair value. The special valuation provisions are intended to mitigate this hardship.

Special use valuation provides an exception from the general rule that property must be valued at its fair market value—highest and best use—for purposes of determining the value includible in a Decedent's Gross Estate. It permits qualifying property to be valued at its current business or farming use. The maximum reduction permitted from using the special valuation rules is a reduction in the Gross Estate of up to $750,000. Thus, the maximum savings is $412,500 at the current maximum 55 percent Estate Tax rate. If the Estate is sufficiently large that the benefits of the Applicable Exclusion Amount are phased out, an effective 60 percent Estate Tax rate will apply and the maximum Estate Tax savings could be $450,000.

An Estate must meet numerous complex requirements to qualify for the benefits of special use valuation. The strict requirements severely limit the usefulness of this provision. The real estate must be used as a farm, in a qualified farming activity, or in a closely held active trade or business other than farming, on the date of the Decedent's death. To qualify, during the 8-year period ending on the date of the Decedent's death, there must have been periods totaling 5 years or more during which the Decedent or his family materially participated in the operation of the farm or business. A qualified farming activity is defined to include cultivating the soil or raising or harvesting any agricultural or horticultural commodity on a farm. The mere passive rental of real estate subject to a net lease where the Decedent is not at risk for loss may not constitute a qualifying closely held trade or business use. If the property is leased to a related party who conducts a qualified farming or closely held trade or business use on the property, this use test can be considered met although the Decedent was not directly involved in the qualified use. The qualified use of the property must have been by the Decedent or a member of his family. The Decedent must be a citizen or resident of the United States. The real property to be valued must be located in the United States. You, as Executor, must elect to have this provision apply to the Decedent's Estate. The election must be made on the Estate Tax return and is irrevocable. Each heir or other person who has an interest in the property must agree in writing to the payment of the Estate Tax saved and the related rules if the qualified use of the property ends, heirs cease the required activities, or any other event triggers recapture. The adjusted value of the real or personal property used by the Decedent or by a member of his family and which was acquired from or passed from the Decedent to a qualified heir, must be at least equal to 50 percent of the adjusted value of the Gross Estate. This is the Gross Estate reduced by mortgages or indebtedness with respect to the property and certain expenses. For purposes of this 50 percent test (and the 25% test to be described) the real and personal property is valued at its fair market value, not at the special use valuation value. The value of the real property used in the farming or closely held business activity must at least equal 25 percent of the adjusted value of the Gross Estate. The qualified real property must pass from the Decedent to a qualified heir. Qualified heir is defined as members of the Decedent's family, including ancestor, spouse, parents, siblings, children, stepchildren, a lineal descendent of the Decedent, a lineal descendant of the Decedent's spouse, a lineal descendant of the Decedent's parents, or a lineal descendant of the Decedent's spouse's parents.

INSTALLMENT PAYMENT OF ESTATE TAX FOR QUALIFIED FAMILY BUSINESS (CODE SECTION 6166)

If certain requirements are met, the Estate Tax attributable to interest in closely held business can be paid in 2 to 10 installments and can be deferred for up to 4 years after the date the tax is due. Thus, the total deferral can be 14 years. To qualify for the deferral, numerous requirements have to be met. This important tax benefit is known as Estate Tax Deferral but is often referred to by the tax Code Section in which it appears, "Code Section 6166."

The following tax benefits can be realized. The tax deferred is the amount of the net Estate Tax that bears the same ratio to the total net

Estate Tax that the closely held business bears to the Adjusted Gross Estate. The statute allows you as the Executor to elect to pay the Estate Tax in up to 10 installments, with the first installment being due not more than 5 years after the date required for the first payment. Interest only needs to be paid for the first 5 years and the date of the last interest payment is the date of the first installment of tax. The interest on the first $1 million of the value of a closely held business may, in some instances, accrue at the favorable 2 percent rate. The time for making the 6166 Election is no later than the time for filing the Estate Tax return or on the last date of the extension of time for filing. A protective election may be made on a timely filed Estate Tax return.

To qualify for the deferral, the threshold requirements must be met. The Decedent must have been a U.S. citizen or resident alien. Only interests in a closely held business may qualify for the deferral of Estate Tax. The interest in the closely held business must exceed 35 percent of the Adjusted Gross Estate. Adjusted Gross Estate is defined as the Gross Estate reduced by debts, administration expenses, and casualty losses. The deductions need not actually be used to offset the Estate Tax. The value of the active business assets are considered for the 35 percent rule. Any closely held business assets that are passive are excluded from the qualifying value of the interest. The value of the interest used in determining whether the 35 percent test is met is the value used for federal Estate Tax purposes. This is the value on the date of death or on the Alternate Valuation Date.

If the closely held business is farming, then, for purposes of the 35 percent test, the interest includes the residential buildings and related improvements that are occupied by the owner or lessee or employees on a regular basis.

Two special elections (choices for your Estate Tax return) can help qualify additional business interests to qualify for Estate Tax Deferral. Both of these Elections require action by you as Executor and will result in a scaleback of the Estate Tax Deferral benefits. You may make an election to have a portion of stock of a holding company that directly or indirectly owns stock in an active trade or business treated as stock in an active company. Partnership interests and stock that is not readily tradable, which is treated as owned by the Decedent at the time of death after applying the family attribution rules (i.e., stock or partnership interests owned by family members is treated as if owned directly by the Decedent) will be included for purposes of the 20 percent test. If you as Executor make either of these elections, the special 2 percent interest rate does not apply. Also, the Estate will not qualify for the 5-year deferral of Estate Tax. What is left is a 10-year payout of the Estate Tax with interest at regular rates.

The Estate can aggregate interest in two or more closely held businesses, if with respect to each, 20 percent or more of the total value of each business is included in the Gross Estate. To determine the 20 percent rule, your Estate can aggregate interest of the Decedent's spouse, and, within the limitation described earlier, the Decedent's family. The Estate Tax, deferred under this provision will become due immediately if any of the following three events occur:

1. The qualifying business is disposed of or liquidated, and the disposition or liquidation exceeds 50 percent of the value of the interest.

2. Interest or installment payments are not made within six months of the due date.

3. If there is undistributed net income, then the acceleration may occur to the extent of such income. Other changes are also excluded from the acceleration of deferred Estate Tax. Certain prescribed reorganizations of the business entities will not cause an acceleration of the deferred Estate Taxes. There is no acceleration if there is a transfer of property due to the death of the Decedent (i.e., under Will, Intestacy, or pursuant to the terms of a Trust).

PLANNING FOR CERTAIN LAND SUBJECT TO CONSERVATION EASEMENTS

A charitable contribution deduction is allowed for both gift and Estate Tax purposes if the Decedent donated a qualified interest in real estate to a charity organized exclusively for conservation purposes. As Executor, you may exclude up to an applicable percentage (the maximum being 40 percent) of the value of any land that is subjected to a qualified conservation easement from the Estate. The value of the property for purposes of this calculation is determined after the qualified conservation easement (restriction) is placed on the property. If the Estate retained any rights to develop the property, the value of these retained rights must be excluded in determining the value of the property that qualifies for the exclusion. The applicable percentage is determined by subtracting from 40 percent (the maximum percentage) 2 percent for each percent or partial percent interest by which the value of the conservation easement involved is less than 30 percent of the value of the land involved (after reduction for the value of the conservation easement).

The exclusion is limited to a maximum exclusion, as shown in Table 18.1.

Granting a conservation easement will not constitute a disposition of the property involved for purposes of the special Estate Tax valuation provisions under Code Section 2032A.

Table 18.1 Phase-In of Maximum Conservation Exclusions

Year	Maximum Conservation Property Exclusion
1998	$100,000
1999	$200,000
2000	$300,000
2001	$400,000
2002 and later years	$500,000

To qualify for this exclusion, the following requirements must be met:

- You must make an irrevocable election to have this exclusion apply on the Estate Tax return.
- The Decedent, or his or her family, owned the land for three years or more ending on the date of death.
- A conservation easement or contribution had been granted by the Decedent, or his or her family.
- The property is located within 25 miles of a national park, metropolitan area, national forest or wilderness area, or within 10 miles of an urban national forest.
- Mortgaged property is only qualified for this exclusion to the extent of the equity (value less debt) in the property.
- The easement must be a qualified conservation easement. This means that the easement must be exclusively for conservation purposes.

DISCLAIMERS

A Disclaimer (also called Renunciation) is a valuable estate and tax-planning technique. A Disclaimer is used when a Beneficiary declines to accept certain assets given to him. Why would anyone turn down money? To protect the assets or save taxes. The following discussion describes these benefits and explains how to accomplish a Disclaimer.

Using a Disclaimer to Protect the Applicable Exclusion Amount When the Will Does Not Include a Bypass Trust

Every Decedent is entitled to use the Applicable Exclusion Amount ($650,000 in 1999) to offset Estate Tax. The most common approach to securing this benefit while providing for a surviving spouse is to fund a Bypass Trust on the death of the first spouse with $650,000 in assets. These assets are available to the surviving spouse but are not taxed in her Estate. However, if the Decedent's Will was simplistic and left everything to the surviving spouse (i.e., it did not even include a Bypass Trust), the benefit of the $650,000 exclusion will be lost. A Disclaimer may be able to resolve this problem.

EXAMPLE: Assume that the Decedent's Will simply bequeathed all assets outright to the surviving spouse. The surviving spouse could then Disclaim up to $650,000 (increasing to $1 million by 2006) of assets. The assets the surviving spouse Disclaimed would pass as provided for in the Will, as if the surviving spouse had died prior to the Decedent. Thus, the Beneficiary contemplating exercising a Disclaimer must carefully review the Will before proceeding. In a typical simple Will for a family, the children usually inherit on the death of the last spouse/parent. Thus, if the surviving spouse were to Disclaim, the assets so disclaimed would pass directly to the children and bypass her Estate entirely. If the Estate were large enough, this would save potentially hundreds of thousands of dollars of federal Estate Taxes on the wife's later death.

Disclaimers and Joint Assets

If all of the Decedent's assets pass outside Probate as a result of Beneficiary designations or joint ownership, insufficient assets may be available to fund the Bypass Trust, even if the Decedent's Will includes the provisions, and the tax benefits may be lost. Also, joint assets and accounts set up years earlier may not reflect the Decedent's current intent. Disclaimers may, depending on state law and other factors, be the method of solving these problems.

EXAMPLE: Assume that Dan Decedent, when he was single, opened several sizable bank accounts that were established in the joint name of Dan Decedent and his sister, Suzy Sister. Since he was single, he named his sister, his only family member, as joint owner to inherit his accounts. Later, Dan Decedent married Wendy Wife and signed a Will including a Bypass Trust to benefit his wife. It is clear that Dan's intent was to have these accounts transferred to the Bypass Trust under his Will to benefit Wendy Wife. Dan Decedent died prior to correcting the title on any of the old accounts from joint title with Suzy Sister to his name alone. As a result, the accounts will pass automatically (by operation of law) to Suzy Sister. Suzy Sister is honorable and wants to respect her brother Dan Decedent's wishes. Therefore, she is willing to give the accounts to Wendy (now Wendy Widow). The difficulty is identifying the mechanism to accomplish this goal. If Suzy Sister simply gave the accounts to Wendy after she received the money, two problems would result. First, Suzy Sister would be making a gift to Wendy Widow that could require Suzy Sister to pay a gift tax cost. Also, if Suzy Sister gave the assets to Wendy Widow, Wendy's Estate would be increased and could face an Estate Tax on Wendy Widow's later death. Thus, tax could be paid twice on the same assets. Good for Uncle Sam, not great for the taxpayers. If instead, Suzy Sister Disclaims the joint accounts on Dan Decedent's death and the Disclaimers are effective, a far better result will occur. To accomplish this, Suzy Sister would file a Disclaimer in Surrogate's Court renouncing any rights or interests in the accounts that she is listed on as a joint owner. The result would then be, assuming that the Disclaimer of the joint accounts was effective, that the account balances would pass on Dan Decedent's death as if Suzy Sister had died prior to Dan Decedent. As a result, the accounts would pass to Dan Decedent's Estate and from his Estate into the Bypass Trust for the benefit of Wendy Widow. Wendy would have considerable access to these funds, but they would not be taxable in her Estate.

If someone seeking to Disclaim receives the assets or any benefit from the assets to be disclaimed, the Disclaimer will not be effective. Therefore, if Suzy Sister took possession of any of the funds in her own capacity, a Disclaimer would not succeed. This rule is extremely strict. If Suzy Sister received one month of interest on the accounts (a nominal amount of money), she would still be prohibited from Disclaiming the entire account.

Requirements for a Disclaimer

Disclaimers to be effective must meet the requirements of a state law (typically, the state where the Will is being probated). If the Disclaimer is held to be defective under state law, it would not be valid for federal Estate Tax purposes.

You should also investigate the account application documents for the accounts to be disclaimed to determine whether any additional issues need to be addressed. Consult with each bank concerning any requirements or penalties before attempting the Disclaimer. If the asset to be Disclaimed is not a bank or brokerage account, have the Estate attorney review the legal documents governing the asset involved.

Most importantly, for a Disclaimer to be effective it must comply with the requirements of the federal Estate Tax laws under Code Section 2518:

- It must be irrevocable (the Beneficiary disclaiming cannot change his mind later).
- It must be in writing.
- it must be unqualified. The Beneficiary cannot place any conditions on the Disclaimer.
- The Beneficiary cannot have accepted the property to be Disclaimed or obtained any benefit from it.
- Once Disclaimed, the property must pass to the next Beneficiary without any directions from the Beneficiary Disclaiming or any benefit to him. The only exception to this latter requirement is made for a surviving spouse. Thus, a surviving spouse could Disclaim a direct bequest and the Disclaimer would qualify even if the result would be for the Disclaimed assets to be transferred to a Trust (such as a Bypass Trust) of which the Disclaiming spouse is a Beneficiary.
- The Disclaimer must be completed within nine months of the Decedent's death, or within nine months of the Disclaiming Beneficiary's attaining age 21.

Tips to Make the Disclaimer Succeed

Personally take a set of signed, witnessed, and notarized documents to each of the banks, brokerage firms, or other persons intended to be bound by the Disclaimer well in advance of the deadline for filing the Disclaimer to assure that all papers are completed and signed to effect the Disclaimer. You should take an original Letters Testamentary and Death Certificate in the event they are requested. Frequently, institutions require compliance with their own forms or administrative procedures.

Arrange to file the Disclaimer and related documents with the Surrogate's Court prior to the deadline for filing. If the Surrogate's Court finds one or more forms inadequate or deficient, you want to be certain to have adequate time to make corrections. The following sample forms illustrate required procedures.

SAMPLE DISCLAIMER COVER LETTER

SUZY SISTER
1000 HONORABLE WAY
GOODTOWN, USA

January 3, 2000

VIA CERTIFIED MAIL RETURN RECEIPT
Ms. Mary Manager
Big Bank Corp.
1000 Financial Way
Anytown, USA

Re: *Renunciation/Disclaimer of All Accounts of Dan Decedent.*

Dear Sirs:

I am the sister of the late Dan Decedent who died on June 2, 1999. I wish to renounce my interests in all accounts of Dan Decedent with your bank in which I was named joint owner and/or beneficiary. To the best of my knowledge, the following accounts were involved (though I would wish to disclaim an interest in any other accounts as well):

a. Savings Account Number 555-3333-333

b. Certificate of Deposit Number 111-3333-22

Please be advised that no distributions from such account have been received by me as the undersigned individual renouncing her rights. Further, I acknowledge that the Big Bank Corp. has made no representations to me concerning the tax effect of the renunciation/disclaimer.

I agree to hold the Bank harmless for any tax or other consequences of the renunciation/disclaimer.

The result of the Disclaimer is intended to be that the assets in the above accounts shall be distributed to Dan Decedent's estate and thus under his will to the Dan Decedent Bypass Trust U/W/D March 3, 1999 ("Bypass Trust"), as provided in Article Third, § 3 of his will. A list of the full legal name, address, and Social Security Number of each Beneficiary of the Bypass Trust, as successor Beneficiaries to me, is attached. The full legal name, address, and Social Security Number of the Trustees of the Bypass Trust as well as the Taxpayer Identification Number of the Bypass Trust, is attached.

In this regard the following documents are enclosed:

1. A formal written renunciation/Disclaimer statement by Suzy Sister, the Sister of Dan Decedent, and a contingent beneficiary under his will.

2. Certificate of Death for Dan Decedent, DOD June 2, 1999.

3. Letters Testamentary dated July 5, 1999, appointing Wendy Widow as Executrix of the estate of Dan Decedent and Wendy Widow and Tammy Trustee as co-trustees of the Bypass Trust.

4. A copy of the will of Dan Decedent, which is Twenty-One pages in length and dated March 3, 1999. The Second Article of said will is the residuary clause which provides that the estate of Dan Decedent should pass to his issue.

5. A copy of the statement for each of the above accounts.

6. A chart with the names, addresses, and Social Security Numbers of each child or other person, constituting all successor beneficiaries.

Sincerely,

Estate of Dan Decedent   Witness:

By: _____   _____
    Wendy Widow, Executrix

_____   _____
Suzy Sister, Surviving Joint Tenant

enc.

[Notary forms omitted].

SAMPLE DISCLAIMER

RENUNCIATION AND DISCLAIMER

STATE OF SOMESTATE
SURROGATE'S COURT: COUNTY OF ANYCOUNTY

In the Matter of the the Estate of Dan Decedent	DISCLAIMER OF INTEREST IN ESTATE PURSUANT TO Law § 3B:9-2
	File No. _____
Deceased	Will Probate Date: August 5, 1999

TO WENDY WIDOW, EXECUTRIX OF THE ESTATE OF DAN DECEDENT AND TO THE SURROGATE'S COURT OF THE COUNTY OF ANYCOUNTY:

KNOW ALL MEN BY THESE PRESENTS:

WHEREAS, Suzy Sister is named joint tenant under certain bank accounts of Dan Decedent.

WHEREAS, the undersigned desires to disclaim and release to the extent provided herein, all of her rights and interests in such assets passing outside the will of Dan Decedent set forth below ("Renounced Assets").

NOW THEREFORE, the undersigned does hereby forever irrevocably and for no consideration disclaim, relinquish, surrender and release, her rights and interests in said Renounced Assets.

I, the undersigned Suzy Sister, domiciled at 1000 Honorable Way, Goodtown, USA, pursuant to Section 3B:9–2 of the Anystate Statutes Annotated, irrevocably and without qualification renounce wholly all of my right, title, interest in and to any portion of the Renounced Assets of Dan Decedent for which I was named joint tenant, being the following assets, located at: Big Bank Corp.,1000 Financial Way, Anytown, USA:

1) Savings Account Number 555-3333-333
2) Certificate of Deposit Number 111-3333-22

The undersigned has not: (i) accepted or exercised any control as beneficial owner over any of the property disclaimed hereunder; (ii) voluntarily transferred, encumbered or contracted to transfer any interest in the property disclaimed hereunder; (iii) executed this Disclaimer in an attempt to defraud any creditors; (iv) made any direction as to how the property subject to this Disclaimer shall pass; (v) received, and is not to receive, any consideration in money or money's worth for this renunciation/Disclaimer from any person or persons whose interest is to be accelerated or increased, or from any other person or persons.

This Disclaimer is executed and filed with the Executrix of the Estate within the required Nine (9) month time period required under Internal Revenue Code Section 2518.

IN WITNESS WHEREOF, the undersigned has set hereunto her hand and seal as of the date set forth below:

Estate of Dan Decedent   Witness:

By: _____   _____
    Wendy Widow, Executrix

_____   _____
Suzy Sister, Disclaimant

[Notary forms omitted].

SAMPLE NOTICE OF DISCLAIMER

DISCLAIMER
STATE OF SOMESTATE
SURROGATE'S COURT: COUNTY OF ANYCOUNTY

In the Matter of the Estate of Dan Decedent Deceased.	NOTICE OF DISCLAIMED INTEREST IN CERTAIN PROPERTY: § 3B:9-2 File No. _____ Will Probate Date: August 5,1999

To: Wendy Widow, Executrix
111 Main Avenue
Anytown, USA

   PLEASE TAKE NOTICE, that Suzy Sister, joint tenant under certain bank and investment accounts (including accounts at Big Bank Corp.) ("Investment Accounts"), has renounced such Investment Accounts and interests to which she is entitled under § 3B:9–2 by the annexed instrument, signed and executed on the dates set forth therein, served upon the Executor of the Estate of Dan Decedent, and filed in the Surrogate's Court of the County of Anycounty.

Dated: September 3, 1999.

_____

Amy Attorney, Esq.
123 Main Street
Big City, Anytown

[Notary form omitted].

CONCLUSION

This chapter has provided an overview of many of the Estate and other tax planning techniques that may be available to the Decedent's Estate. Many of these techniques are technical in nature and must be implemented precisely to succeed. The best approach is to assemble rough balance sheet data on the Estate as quickly as possible and review possible planning opportunities with the attorney and accountant for the Estate. Early identification of planning opportunities is vital to retaining the option to implement them at a later date. Once possible planning opportunities are identified that require the cooperation of other persons (Beneficiaries for Disclaimers, business partners for qualification for special use valuation and other business benefits, etc.), consult with them to determine their level of interest and cooperation.

Part Seven

DISTRIBUTIONS AND WINDING UP THE ESTATE

19 DISTRIBUTION OF ESTATE ASSETS

You have completed the Probate of the Will and the required Court proceedings, collected assets, paid expenses and claims, and addressed the available tax planning options. At this stage of the Probate, you should be prepared to make preliminary distributions or even distributions of significant assets, subject to holding back funds to cover anticipated expenses remaining, tax audits, and so on. If the Estate is small and leaves the Residuary Estate outright (i.e., without any Trust) to the surviving spouse or child, this task may be simple. Just distribute assets to that sole Beneficiary. In many Estates, the situation is much more complex. This chapter provides a discussion of many issues that can affect the distribution of assets to the Beneficiaries. In all cases, your starting point for guidance should be a thorough review of the Decedent's Will. Next, consideration should be given to state law, tax consequences, and the circumstances of the various Beneficiaries. Any issues that are unclear, or distributions that raise problems, should be cleared with the Estate attorney.

PREPAID INHERITANCE

Uncle Joe always wanted to help out his hard-working cousin Cal. So, Uncle Joe put in his will that Cal is to get $25,000. However, two months before Uncle Joe died, cousin Cal came for a visit. Uncle Joe was so touched by Cal's concern and comfort that he gave Cal a check for $25,000. Following Uncle Joe's death, you face an issue. Was the $25,000 Uncle Joe gave Cal shortly before Uncle Joe's death a gift, or was it a prepayment of the Bequest in Uncle Joe's Will, called an Advancement? The answer really depends on inferring what Uncle Joe had intended two months previously. In such a situation, if the amount involved is modest relative to the Estate you might choose to have all Beneficiaries sign off an agreement that the Beneficiary should still receive the amount under the Will. If the amount involved in this example was $2,000 instead of $25,000, it might be far more economical and easier for the Beneficiaries to agree to a quick $2,000 payment so the rest of the Estate could be addressed. However, for

$25,000, they might not be willing. Thus, for larger, contentious, or other distributions that cause you concern because of a possible Advancement, consult with the Estate attorney and consider securing a Court approval of the appropriate interpretation.

WHAT IF THE ESTATE IS TOO SMALL TO MEET THE BEQUESTS IN THE WILL?

Uncle Joe is an avid investor. He is riding high at a market peak and prepares a new Will leaving $100,000 to each of his eight siblings, and the remainder of his estate, the residuary (what is left after the $800,000 distributions), which he estimates at $500,000, to his longtime partner. The stock market roller coaster gets a bit bumpy, and on death Uncle Joe's Estate is worth $750,000. Who gets what? The specific bequests, which are listed first in the Will, exceed the total Estate. Worse, the residuary Beneficiary, who was Uncle Joe's major concern and primary Beneficiary gets nothing. The legal term for this mess is "Abate." The bequests must Abate because the Estate has inadequate assets to fund them. The state may have a law directing how Abatement of bequests should be handled if the Will itself does not address the problem. Discuss with the Estate attorney whether Court confirmation of the distribution plan should be sought.

WHAT HAPPENS IF THE PROPERTY BEQUEATHED IS NOT IN THE ESTATE?

Uncle Joe's Will bequeaths his gold pocket watch to his favorite nephew, Neil. Unfortunately, on Joe's death there is no watch. Joe may have given the watch to someone else or lost it in a poker game, or it may have been stolen. What happens? You cannot distribute what does not exist. The bequest lapses for impossibility. The legal expression for this is to state that the property has Adeemed.

HOW DO YOU TRANSFER OWNERSHIP OF ESTATE ASSETS TO THE APPROPRIATE BENEFICIARY?

When assets have to be actually transferred to the Beneficiary designated under the Will, whether an individual, charity, or Trust for either, you must transfer legal title to the assets involved. If the asset to be transferred is cash, the simplest approach is to write an Estate check to the appropriate Beneficiary. When the Beneficiary deposits or cashes the check, the transfer is completed. For securities, the simplest way is to have the broker or financial consultant at the firm where the Estate brokerage account is maintained consummate an institution-to-institution transfer to the bank or brokerage account of the Beneficiary. You would complete the stock power or other transfer of ownership forms provided by the Estate's broker or banker.

When interests in closely held businesses must be transferred, the actual documents required will vary depending on the legal structure of the business involved. For a corporation, stock powers for transferring stock in the corporation will be signed. A new stock certificate would be completed in the name of the Beneficiary and physically sent via certified mail to that Beneficiary. The corporation may also sign minutes confirming the transfer, a revised shareholder agreement signed by the new shareholder, and the stock ledger that records the stock transactions for the corporation would be amended. For a partnership, an assignment of partnership interest form might be signed, an amendment to the state partnership certificate might be required, and a revised partnership agreement reflecting the Beneficiary/partner would be signed. For a limited liability company, the procedures are similar.

TAX ALLOCATION CLAUSE IN WILL OR STATE LAW AFFECTS DISTRIBUTIONS

For larger Estates, the largest single Beneficiary might be Uncle Sam. How the IRS is to be paid can have a huge impact on what each Beneficiary is to receive.

Every Will should contain a provision governing how any estate or other taxes should be apportioned against the various Beneficiaries and Estate assets. If the Estate has any right to receive reimbursement of Estate Taxes from Beneficiaries who receive assets outside the Probate Estate (e.g., a joint bank account to the Decedent's sister that triggers Estate Tax) collection will be difficult because the joint owner already has control of the money. If the Will or state law permit a set-off against other bequests, or the joint account collection may be possible. In contrast, Beneficiaries of a life insurance policy are generally required to contribute a pro rata portion of the Estate Taxes to the Estate. Similarly, where a client held a General Power of Appointment over particular property, the ultimate Beneficiaries of that property may be required to make a pro rata contribution toward taxes. If the tax allocation clause in the Will requires that these Beneficiaries pay their allocable share of Estate Taxes, more assets will be left in the Estate for distribution to the Beneficiaries listed in the Will. If the Tax Allocation clause is drafted in a precise enough manner to override the statutory presumptions that the Beneficiary of an insurance policy must pay the Estate Tax attributable to that policy, then the Beneficiaries under the Will would receive less. This is why you must carefully review the tax allocation clause for any taxable Estate with the Estate attorney prior to making any distributions.

Most Decedents don't want to burden nominal or token cash legacies (e.g., $500 to my buddy Joe) with a tax burden. However, since the Beneficiary of a cash legacy will have cash to pay the tax, no hardship is created.

EXAMPLE: Dan Decedent's Will states that each of his three sisters is to receive $10,000. Dan's Estate is large and is in a 50 percent tax bracket. If the specific dollar bequests to the sisters are stated to be net of tax (i.e., the sisters are not to bear their proportionate share of Estate Taxes), then you can quickly distribute a $10,000 check to each sister as soon as funds are available, subject to your obtaining a Receipt and Release (see Chapter 20). However, if the Will instead said that every Beneficiary must bear a fair or pro rata share of Estate Taxes, you could not distribute anything to the three sisters until you were confident that you knew the exact final federal Estate Tax liability. For simplicity, if 40 percent of the Estate were, on average, paid in estate and other taxes, each sister should only receive $6,000. Thus, the Tax Allocation clause not only can dramatically affect what a Beneficiary receives but when you can make the distribution, and the complexity of the process.

Most Decedents do not want to burden the Beneficiaries of Personal Property bequests with the tax cost attributable to those bequests. Further, if tax is allocated to such bequests, a true hardship can be created because those Beneficiaries may not have adequate cash with which to pay the tax. Finally, if very valuable Personal Property is involved, special considerations may have to be made. The large Personal Property bequests could be required to bear their proportionate share of tax, and cash bequests or other arrangements made. Consideration must be given to whether the existence and valuation of such property can reasonably be known. If taxes are allocated to such property, can it be collected?

TIP: Review the Will tax allocation clauses with the Estate attorney and understand in advance how the clause works and specifically how it affects each Beneficiary. Consider having the attorney prepare a letter to the Beneficiaries (or separately for each Beneficiary if it is more appropriate) explaining how and why the Estate Tax has affected their distribution. You can be sure that if the concepts are complicated for you and you are meeting with the attorney and accountant for the Estate, the concepts will be impossible for the other Beneficiaries to understand. Further, if 30 percent to 40 percent of the bequest the Beneficiary sees in the Will is not received because of Estate Taxes, you can be sure that the Beneficiary will want an explanation.

BUSINESS AND OTHER AGREEMENTS AFFECT DISTRIBUTIONS

If the Decedent owned stock in a closely held corporation, for example, the provisions of the shareholder agreement for that corporation could have an important effect on the distribution of stock to the Beneficiaries named in the Will. The stock, for example, may become nonvoting on the Decedent's death. The Beneficiary should understand this. Even if the shareholder (or other) agreement did not contain a buyout provision (i.e., requiring the sale of the stock to the corporation or the other shareholders) does not mean that there are not important provisions in the shareholders' agreement that significantly affect your responsibility or the rights of the Beneficiary. There may be notification requirements as prerequisites to the transfer of stock. The Estate may be required to pay the corporation's legal costs for consummating the transfer of stock from the Decedent to the Estate and ultimately to the Beneficiary. Be certain to address any applicable requirements with a corporate attorney.

DISTRIBUTIONS TO CHARITIES

Distributions to charities can raise many issues. If the Will includes charitable bequests, confirm with the Estate attorney whether a formal notice must be given to the state's Attorney General. The purpose of this is to put the state on notice as to a charitable bequest because of the state's interest in making certain that charitable bequests are made.

Does the charity qualify for the Estate Tax charitable contribution deduction? Often, people list a contribution to an organization that they assume is a qualified charity when in fact it is not. This happens when Testators name a foreign charity instead of a United States feeder charity that qualifies for the deduction while accomplishing the same charitable purpose. Some Wills contain savings clauses providing that if the organization is not qualified for the Estate Tax charitable contribution deduction, the bequest lapses.

Some Testators provide conditions, sometimes complex, for how the named charity should use the bequest. These conditions are sometimes so excessive that they are impractical, or the charity will not accept the bequest under the conditions indicated.

Many charities have offices in various cities and states and different related charitable organizations with similar names. If a bequest to a charity is written in terms that are too vague or general, you will first have to confirm precisely what organization you can give the bequest to. You might have the Court interpret the provision and advise you as to which charity should be treated as the Beneficiary. If the charitable bequest was unclear the Court would apply the legal doctrine called Cy Pres to prevent the bequest to the charities from lapsing. This doctrine has the Court interpret the Will in a manner to assure that a charitable bequest is paid to a charity which as close as possible meets the intent in the Will.

A host of charitable type trusts can be formed under a Will, each creating its own issues, distribution standards, and so on. These can include charitable remainder trusts (CRT) and charitable lead trusts (CLT).

NOTE: For detailed discussions of charitable trusts, see Martin M. Shenkman, *The Complete Book of Trusts* (2nd ed.) (New York: John Wiley & Sons, 1997).

CIRCUMSTANCES AFFECT HOW DISTRIBUTIONS SHOULD BE MADE

Once you have determined that a distribution can be made, how much and what property will be distributed, and who the Beneficiary is, all of the issues are not necessarily resolved. The next question is, how will the funds be distributed? The simple and general answer is that the distributions will be handled as provided under the Will. If the Will says that the distribution to cousin Cindy will be "outright and free of trust," and Cindy is an adult, you might simply write out a check for her share and mail it to her.

The conclusions in many situations are not that simple. Many Wills call for the payment of distributions to Trusts for the benefit of the Beneficiaries. The Trustees of those Trusts must carefully review and understand the Trust provisions in the Will so that they will understand how to administer the Trust.

What if there is no requirement for a Trust, just a simple distribution to Cindy Cousin? Simple. But, what if Cindy has developed a severe emotional problem and cannot manage her own affairs, should you simply send her a check to squander? What can be done?

If the designated Beneficiary of a bequest is a minor, you cannot transfer assets to the minor's name. Other issues must be addressed. The remainder of this chapter provides some direction concerning these distribution concerns.

DISTRIBUTIONS IN TRUST

When a distribution is made to a Trust, the Trustee must generally approve the property contributed to the Trust. Once the property is to be accepted, a Receipt and Release (and possibly a Refunding Bond) would be signed by the Trustee. The Trustee will then administer the trust assets as provided for in the Trust terms. When the trust is formed under the Decedent's Will, the provisions of the Trust are included in the Will. The Trustee should invest the assets in accordance with the directions in the Will for that particular Trust. For example, a QTIP Trust must pay income at least annually to the surviving spouse. If the assets are invested in a manner that precludes the realization of any income, the Estate Tax deferral of the marital deduction which is the intent behind the QTIP Trust would be lost. Thus, a QTIP Trust must be invested in a manner that generates reasonable income. A Bypass Trust, in contrast, may, depending on the circumstances of the family, be invested intentionally for long-term growth and in a manner that minimizes current taxable income. This is because any growth in the Bypass Trust assets will not be subject to tax in the surviving spouse's Estate, and no requirement to generate income exists (unless the Will requires it). Distributions would be made from the Trusts involved in the manner that the Will provisions forming the particular Trust provide. And so on. The Will serves as the guidebook for the Trustee of each Trust. If the Will is silent, or the provisions vague, legal advice must be sought. Once each of the Trusts provided for in the Will is funded, each will be a separate tax-paying entity requiring its own tax identification number, tax returns, bank accounts, and so on.

Before making any distributions to any Trust formed under the Will, carefully review with the Estate attorney the calculation of the exact amounts to transfer. Several technical issues could affect the amount of assets to distribute to each Trust and the tax consequences of the distributions. For example, a typical Estate plan for a married couple is to fund the maximum amount in a Bypass Trust that will not trigger Estate Taxes ($650,000 in 1999) and distribute the balance to a marital, or QTIP, Trust. Two approaches can be used to fund these Trusts: a pecuniary bequest, or a bequest of a fractional share of the Estate. Each approach can have different income tax consequences. A fractional share bequest can share proportionately in the appreciation or deprecation of the Estate during the period of Estate administration. A pecuniary bequest does not. Remember all assets owned by the Decedent at death receive a step-up, or increase, in Tax Basis to the fair value at the date of death. Thus, if any asset were immediately sold, no gain or loss would be recognized. However, if an Estate remains open the nine months until the federal Estate Tax return is due, any appreciation or decline in value of the assets would affect the value of assets that can be used to fund these Trusts and the income tax consequences. For example, if the Bypass Trust is funded by reference to the specific dollar amount permitted to be funded to use the maximum available Applicable Exclusion Amount, any appreciated assets used to fund this Trust will trigger taxable gain. Thus, if stock valued at $500,000 at death is worth $625,000 when used to fund the Bypass Trust, a $125,000 taxable gain would be realized. If the Bypass is funded as the pecuniary or dollar amount, then the balance of the estate, the fractional share of the Estate, is used to fund the QTIP Trust. Thus, the appreciation of the Estate's assets during the period of Estate administration would be allocable to the QTIP Trust.

SAMPLE PROVISIONS:

Fractional Share: The bequest in Article IV is intended to be a bequest of a fractional share of my estate and shall share in any appreciation or depreciation during the period of administration.

Pecuniary: The bequest in Article X is intended to be a bequest of a pecuniary amount of my estate and shall not share in any appreciation or depreciation during the period of administration.

Another important matter must be addressed before funding the Bypass Trust. Many people erroneously assume that if the maximum amount of the Applicable Exclusion is $650,000 that $650,000 can be distributed to the Bypass Trust to fund it. This is rarely correct and could trigger an unexpected and avoidable Estate Tax cost. First, any distributions made to persons other than a surviving spouse or charity will use up a portion of the Applicable Exclusion Amount. Thus, if the Will distributed $10,000 to each of Decedent's three sisters, and a painting valued at $25,000 to Decedent's buddy, a total of $55,000 has been given. The maximum Bypass Trust which can be funded is $595,000 [$650,000 – {($10,000 × 3) + $25,000}]. Also, if the Election discussed in Chapter 18 is made to deduct Estate administration expenses on the Estate's income tax return instead of the Estate's Estate Tax return, some of these expenses will reduce the amount that can be funded into the Bypass Trust. If the special deduction for qualified family owned business interests is claimed the Bypass amount could be larger.

DISTRIBUTIONS TO CUSTODIAN (UGMA/UTMA) ACCOUNTS

If the Will provides for a distribution to a person who is a minor, the distributions will have to be made to a custodian under the state's Uniform Gifts to Minors' Act (UGMA) or Uniform Transfers to Minors' Act (UTMA) since title cannot be passed to a minor. The property is the minor's and the custodian can only use the property as permitted by state law, for the benefit of the minor Beneficiary. The custodian for the account may have the power to collect, hold, manage, invest, and reinvest the custodial property; pay to or expend it for the benefit of the minor in an amount reasonably advisable for the support, maintenance, education, and benefit of the minor. A minor owning assets in an UGMA or UTMA account can, after reaching age 14, petition the court to have an accounting of the money, stock, or other assets in the account. The minor, after reaching age 14, can petition the court to require the custodian to make payments for his support, maintenance, or education.

DISTRIBUTIONS TO A BENEFICIARY UNDER A DISABILITY

If a Beneficiary is under a disability due to emotional, physical, or drug-related problems, significant cash or asset distributions may only serve to exacerbate the problems. If the Will includes language permitting the Executor or Trustee to withhold distributions otherwise due to a Beneficiary under a disability, the withholding of funds may provide a temporary solution if the problem resolves itself. Consider the following Will clause:

SAMPLE PROVISION: Whenever pursuant to the provisions of this Will, any donee property shall become distributable to a person under a disability, title thereto shall vest in such person but the payment thereof may be deferred until such disability ceases and, if so deferred, such donee property shall be held by the Fiduciary, who shall apply the principal and income thereof, or so much of such principal and income as the Fiduciary may determine, for the health, education, support and maintenance of such person under a disability, and when such disability ceases, the Fiduciary shall deliver to such person formerly under a disability the then remaining donee property, together with the accumulations, if any, of income therefrom, or if such person should die, the Fiduciary shall deliver the donee property and any accumulations of income to the legal representatives of the estate of such person.

If the situation affecting the Beneficiary does not resolve itself, consult with the Estate attorney concerning the advisability of someone instituting a proceeding for a Court to appoint a Guardian for the disabled Beneficiary (see Chapters 3 and 6).

CONCLUSION

This chapter has highlighted several issues that may arise when you are making the actual distributions of Estate assets to the Beneficiaries involved. First, be certain to understand the Will's provisions. Next, if there is an issue, consult with the Estate attorney concerning your options and the appropriate steps to protect your interests. If necessary, obtain a written agreement of your decision from the Beneficiaries. If the risks are significant, or the issue unresolvable, or if required, obtain Court approval for your intended distribution.

20 OTHER DISTRIBUTION AND WINDING-UP ISSUES

Once all the steps described in the preceding chapters have been addressed, taxes paid, audits resolved, and so on, you can make the final distributions from the Estate and complete the winding up and closing of the Estate. For most Estates, this is not a complex or expensive process because the Estate is distributed to family and close friends, and/or Trusts for the same people. There are usually no contentious issues or suspicions to address. In this typical Probate scenario, you might simply prepare reasonable summary records of the Estate's finances, attach them to simple Receipts and Releases, have the Beneficiaries sign them, and wrap up the Estate. In the more unusual situation, there may be disagreements or concerns between the Beneficiaries, significant problems with the Will, unrelated parties involved, a Court-appointed Guardian for a disabled or minor Beneficiary and other issues that suggest a formal and comprehensive approach will be preferable. This chapter elaborates on these procedures, and offers sample documents and tips on proceeding.

INTERIM VERSUS FINAL DISTRIBUTIONS

If the Estate administration continues for a long period of time (for example, litigation must be settled) you may make several partial distributions to the Beneficiaries. Eventually, when all the issues involved are closed, a final distribution is made and the Estate concluded. Be careful how much you distribute during the earlier distributions to avoid depleting the funds needed later.

RECEIPTS AND RELEASES

When a distribution is made to a Beneficiary you should first have the recipient sign a document called a Receipt and Release. The Receipt is an acknowledgment of the assets or funds received. The Release is a legal document in which the person signing it states that you as Executor, and the Estate, owe him nothing more. The sample form on page 227 is a written acknowledgment that the Beneficiary has no other claims. When you obtain a Receipt and Release, it can provide you with some measure of protection if a claim is later asserted. Asking for the Release will also encourage any Beneficiary with a claim to make it before signing.

CAUTION: Be certain to consult with a lawyer before sending a Release to a Beneficiary to sign. Depending on the nature of the Beneficiary's bequest under the Will, the relationship of the Beneficiary to the Decedent, the assets distributed, and other factors, it may be advisable to modify the form of Release used and in fact use a formal Settlement Agreement (see later in this chapter), which may even be filed formally with the Court. If the bequest is for a percentage of the Estate, an accounting of Estate Assets may be appropriate to attach to the Receipt and Release. Perhaps a formal Accounting may be necessary.

SAMPLE RECEIPT AND RELEASE

STATE OF SOMESTATE
SURROGATE'S COURT, ANYCOUNTY

In the matter of the Accounting
of the Executors of the
Estate of   RECEIPT AND RELEASE

Dan Decedent

Deceased.

STATE OF SOMESTATE   )
                                        ss.:
COUNTY OF ANYCOUNTY   )

KNOW ALL MEN BY THESE PRESENTS that the undersigned, Betty Beneficiary being of full age, does hereby acknowledge receipt from Elliott Executor, as Executor of the Estate of Dan Decedent, deceased (the "Executor" and the "Decedent") of the property listed in Schedule A to this Receipt and Release (the "Property") in full payment and satisfaction of the bequest to the undersigned by part (a) of Article XII of the Last Will and Testament of the Decedent (the "Bequest"), and, in consideration thereof, the undersigned does hereby:

FIRST: Remise, release, and forever discharge the Executor, individually and as such Executor, of and from any and every claim, demand, action, and cause of action, account, reckoning, and liability of every kind and nature for and on account of any and every matter and thing whatever arising from or in any manner relating to, or connected with, the distribution of the Property to the undersigned in full payment and satisfaction of the Bequest.

SECOND: Certify that the undersigned has made no sale, mortgage, pledge, assignment, gift, or other transfer of the right, title, and interest in and to the Property herein distributed to the undersigned in full payment and satisfaction of the Bequest.

THIRD: Agree that the undersigned does hereby indemnify and save harmless the Executor, individually and as such Executor, of and from any and all liabilities, damages, losses, charges, fees, costs, and expenses of whatever kind or nature (including reasonable counsel fees) which the Executor shall at any time sustain or incur by reason of any objection, demand, or claim of whatever kind or nature for, upon, or by reason of, the distribution of the Property to the undersigned in full payment and satisfaction of the Bequest.

FOURTH: Agree that this Receipt and Release shall be binding upon the heirs, distributees, executors, administrators, legal representatives, and assigns of the undersigned, and shall inure to the benefit of heirs, distributees, executors, administrators, legal representatives, and assigns of the Executor.

IN WITNESS WHEREOF, this Receipt and Release has been signed and sealed by the undersigned this March 3, 2001.

_____

Betty Beneficiary

[Notary form omitted].

ACCOUNTING

Once all expenses, including any federal, state, or other taxes, have been paid, and all assets of the Estate have been marshaled, the wind-up phase could include the preparation of a final Accounting by you as Executor. The Accounting should then be submitted to all of the Beneficiaries for their approval. Generally, you should require the Beneficiaries to approve the Accounting in writing and sign a Release to the Estate and you absolving you both of any further liability. Once you have received the Releases and acceptance of the final Accounting, any assets remaining can then be distributed to the Beneficiaries. A final income tax return should then be filed for the Estate. The Estate attorney can advise you as to whether there are any other local requirements. For example, in some states, and for some Estates, an inventory or Accounting may have to be filed with the Court. If the Court requires an Accounting, it may have to be a formal Accounting that has to be done in a specified manner. The Accounting illustrated here is a less expensive and informal version that may suffice in some situations.

Formal versus Informal Accounting

The terminology and requirements for an Accounting vary from Court to Court and depending on the facts in the particular Probate. In some Courts, an informal Accounting is possible. This avoids the costly and detailed formal accounting, the requirements of which may be set forth in great detail by the Court. In an informal accounting, you may provide a sworn statement to the Court stating that you have sent an informal Accounting to all Beneficiaries, the required notice to Creditors has been published, and so on. After the passage of a statutory time period, the Estate is closed. Once the requirements are complied with, you may be discharged as Executor.

In a formal Accounting or closing of the Estate, a more comprehensive approach is required, which again varies from Court to Court. It may require a comprehensive formal Accounting be filed with the Court and that all persons interested in the Estate be given a formal notice of the intent to close the Estate. Once the requirements are complied with, you can be discharged as Executor.

TEMPLATES FOR AN EXECUTOR TO ACCOUNT TO THE BENEFICIARIES

The Account of Elliott Executor, Executor under the Last Will and Testament of Dan Decedent, deceased, covering the period of administration from June 3, 1999, the date of death, to January 21, 2000, shows as follows:

Assets Received by Executor:

Principal Received, per Schedule A	$
Net gain on sale or transfer of assets, per Schedule B	$
Income received, per Schedule C	$
Total Receipts	$_____

Charges:

Funeral, administration expenses, and debts of decedent, per Schedule D	$
Estate taxes paid, per Schedule E	$
Commission paid, per Schedule F	$
Distributions made, per Schedule G	$_____
Total charges	$
Cash on hand, per Schedule H	$_____
Proposed distributions, per Schedule I	$_____

_____   _____
Date   Elliott Executor, Executor

Schedule A—Principle Received

Description/Source	Unit Amount	Total Value
Balance to be brought forward		

Schedule B—Gain (Loss) on Sale of Assets

Name of Stock or Other Asset	No. Shares/Description	Date	Estate Tax Basis	Value	Gain (Loss)
Balance to be brought forward					

Schedule C—Income Received

Asset/Source of Income	Time Period	Amount
Balance to be brought forward		

Schedule D—Funeral and Administration Expenses and Debts of Decedent Paid

Date	Name	Amount
Balance to be brought forward		

Schedule E—Estate Taxes Paid

Date	Jurisdiction	Amount	Comment
Balance to be brought forward			

Schedule F—Commissions Paid

Date	Executor	Amount	Value
Balance to be brought forward			

Schedule G-1—Distributions Made:
Total Distribution to Betty Beneficiary

Date	Description	Value
	Total	

Schedule G-2—Distributions Made:
Total Distribution to Bobby Beneficiary

Date	Description	Value
	Total	

Schedule G-3—Aggregate Distributions Made:
Total Distribution of Estate of Dan Decedent

Date	Beneficiary	Description	In Payment of	Value
Balance to be brought forward				

Schedule H—Cash on Hand as of Date of Accounting

Date	Account/Description	Amount	Comment
Balance to be brought forward			

Schedule I—Proposed Distributions

Payee	Purpose/Description	Amount
Larry Lawyer	Balance of attorney fees	
Amy Accountant	Balance of accounting fees	
Betty Beneficiary		
Bobby Beneficiary		
Balance to be brought forward		

SAMPLE AGREEMENT TO SETTLE ACCOUNT

STATE OF ONESTATE
SURROGATE'S COURT
COUNTY OF ANYCOUNTY

Accounting of Elliott Executor
as Executor of the Last Will and

Testament of   AGREEMENT SETTLING ACCOUNT

    Dan Decedent   File No. _____
               Deceased.

AGREEMENT made as of the 21st day of January 2000, by and between Elliott Executor, as Executor of the Last Will and Testament of Dan Decedent, deceased (in such capacity, the "Executor"), parties of the first part, and said Betty Beneficiary individually and Bobby Beneficiary (collectively, the "Beneficiaries"), parties of the second part.

WITNESSETH:

WHEREAS:

a. Dan Decedent (the "Decedent") died on June 3, 1999, a resident of and domiciled in the County of Anycounty, State of Onestate.

b. Letters Testamentary were issued to the Executor by the Surrogate's Court, County of Anycounty, State of Onestate.

c. The Executor wishes to render an account of their acts and proceedings as such Executors for the period from June 3, 1999, the date of the Decedent's death, to January 21, 2000 (the "Accounting Period"); to make final disposition of the Decedent's estate (the "Estate") in the manner hereinafter provided; and to be discharged by the Beneficiaries of and from any and all liability for the Executor's actions with respect to the Estate during the Accounting Period and in making such final distribution.

d. The Beneficiaries wish to avoid the expense that would attend the preparation of schedules of account in form that would permit their judicial settlement and the expense that would attend the judicial settlement of such an account, and have requested the Executor to submit to them an account (the "Account") of the Executor's acts and proceedings for the Accounting Period in the form annexed hereto and to accept, in lieu of a judicial settlement of the Account, the releases and indemnities hereinafter provided.

e. The Executor submitted the Account to each of the Beneficiaries, and each of the Beneficiaries has examined the Account and is satisfied that the Account contains in all respects a full, complete, and true statement of all of the acts and proceedings of the Executors in connection with the administration of the Estate during the Accounting Period, and that there is no error or omission in the Account to the prejudice of any of the Beneficiaries.

f. All of the parties hereto are full age and sound mind and are fully advised of their rights in the premises.

NOW, THEREFORE, in consideration of the foregoing premises and of the mutual covenants and agreements herein contained, and of the agreement by the Executors, at the request of the Beneficiaries, to render the account in the form annexed hereto without requiring the preparation of an account in form that would permit it to be judicially settled and without requiring a judicial settlement of the Account at this time, and of other good and valuable consideration, receipt of which is hereby acknowledged:

FIRST: Each of the Beneficiaries does hereby acknowledge and agree that the Account is in all respects just, true, proper, and correct and that it contains a full disclosure of all of the acts and proceedings of the Executor in connection with the administration of the Estate during the Accounting Period, and each of the Beneficiaries does hereby ratify, approve, and confirm the Account and each and every one of the acts, proceedings, collections, and disbursements set forth therein, and waive the right to enforce the judicial settlement of the Account, or of any account of the Executors for the Accounting Period, in any Court whatever.

SECOND: Each of the parties hereto does hereby agree that the Executor shall pay over and distribute the property of the Estate remaining in his hands, as shown in Schedule H of the Account, and the income, if any, received therefrom subsequent to the Accounting Period, as follows:

(1)   To Larry Lawyer, the balance of the attorney fees $.

(2)   To Amy Accountant, the balance of the accountant's fees $*.

(3)   To Betty Beneficiary, the sum of $*, plus one-half of the income earned subsequent to the Accounting Period, if any.

(4)   To Bobby Beneficiary, the sum of $*, plus one-half of the income earned subsequent to the Accounting Period, if any.

THIRD: Each of the Beneficiaries does hereby remise, release, and forever discharges the Executor, individually and as such Executor, of and from any and all, and all manner of, action and actions, cause and causes of action, suits, debts, dues, sums of money, accounts, reckonings, bonds, bills, specialties, covenants, contracts, controversies, agreements, promises, variances, trespasses, damages, judgments, incidents, executions, claims and demands whatever, whether in law or in equity, which she or he ever had, now has or shall or may have for, on, or by reason of any act, omission, collection, disbursement, cause, matter, or thing whatsoever, recited, contained, appearing, or set forth in the account or in this Agreement Settling Account, or reasonably to be inferred from anything therein or herein contained, or for, upon, or by reason of anything done or omitted to be done by the Executors in the administration of, or otherwise in connection with the Estate, or in making final distribution of the property of the Estate remaining in the Executor's hand and of the income, if any, received therefrom subsequent to the Accounting Period in the manner provided in Article SECOND hereof.

FOURTH: Each of the Beneficiaries agrees to, and does hereby, indemnify and save harmless the Executor, individually and as such Executor, of and from any and all liabilities, damages, losses, charges, fees, costs, and expenses of whatever kind or nature (including reasonable counsel fees) which the Executors shall at any time sustain or incur by reason of any objection, demand, or claim of whatever kind or nature made or asserted against the Executor by anyone for, upon, or by reason of any action, omission, collection, disbursement, cause, matter, or thing whatsoever recited, contained, appearing, or set forth in the Account or in this Agreement Settling Account, or reasonably to be inferred from anything therein or herein contained, or for, upon, or by reason of anything done or omitted to be done by the Executor in the administration of, or otherwise in connection with, the Estate, or in making final distribution of the property of the Estate remaining in the Executor's hand and of the income, if any, received therefrom subsequent to the Accounting period in the manner provided in Article SECOND hereof.

FIFTH: The parties hereto agree that the Executor may at any time, if the Executor in the sole and absolute discretion shall deem it advisable to do so, and without notice to any party hereto, either (a) record or file this Agreement Settling Account and/or the Account in accordance with the provisions of any statute, law or rule of court of the State of One State or of any other State as an instrument settling the account of the Executor for the Accounting Period or (b) institute or conduct legal proceedings to obtain a judicial settlement of the Account.

SIXTH: Each of the Beneficiaries shall, and does hereby, certify that she or he has heretofore made no sale, mortgage, pledge, assignment, gift, or other transfer of her or his right, title, and interest in and to the Estate and that she or he shall hereafter make no such sale, mortgage, pledge, assignment, gift, or other transfer.

SEVENTH: The parties hereto agree that the provisions of this Agreement Settling Account shall be binding upon and shall inure to the benefit of the respective heirs, legatees, legal representatives, successors, and assigns of the parties hereto.

EIGHTH: The parties hereto agree that this Agreement Settling Account constitutes the entire understanding among the parties, may be executed in one or more counterparts, cannot be changed orally and shall be construed in accordance with the Law of the State of Onestate.

IN WITNESS WHEREOF, each of the parties hereto has executed this Agreement Settling Account and affixed his or her seal, all as of the day and year first above written.

_____

Elliott Executor, Executor

_____

Betty Beneficiary, Beneficiary

_____

Bobby Beneficiary, Beneficiary

[Notary form omitted].

TERMINATION OF A TRUST

A Trust formed under the Decedent's Will may be accelerated or terminated in a limited number of circumstances, which may include the following:

No Trust Purpose Remaining

If the only purpose of the Trust that remains unfulfilled is to confer on successive Beneficiaries their respective interests, consenting adult Beneficiaries should be permitted to consent to the termination of the Trust since this alone is not a sufficient Trust purpose. Where it does not appear that the settlor had any purpose in creating a Trust other than to enable the Beneficiaries successively to enjoy the Trust property, the Beneficiaries can compel termination of the Trust. Where all the objects of the Trust have been accomplished and where all parties beneficially interested in the Trust desire to have the Trust terminated, and where all interests have vested, the court may order the termination of the Trust.

The court will not permit an acceleration where it would defeat the intent of the donor of the Estate. If the Trust is not a spendthrift Trust, the Beneficiary may destroy it by making a conveyance or surrender to the Trustee, or by giving the Trustee a release provided the Beneficiary was fully competent to act and was not under any disability.

The general rule is that the parties seeking to terminate a Trust must prove that they constitute the entire class of Beneficiaries. But who are "all persons beneficially interested"? At least one Court has said that it is not necessary to include all contingent Beneficiaries.

What if the Beneficiaries are alive, but are minor children, or are disabled and thus unable to make legal decisions for themselves? The consent of these children or disabled Beneficiaries is required, but they themselves cannot provide the consent. If a Court will accept the decision of a Guardian of these individuals, then the trust can be revoked or amended.

A Trust can be terminated in accordance with the terms of the Trust agreement.

Operation of Law

A Trust can be terminated or modified by operation of law. There are several possibilities when state law may require the termination of a Trust, for example, violation of the rule against perpetuities.

Disclaimer

Where a Disclaimer is exercised, the Trust Estate passes to those entitled to the next succeeding Estate. In one case, where the income Beneficiary Disclaimed his right to income, the income went to the persons entitled to the next Estate.

CONCLUSION

Once your duties as Executor are fulfilled, you should make final distributions to all Beneficiaries, obtain Receipts acknowledging all distributions and Releases from the Beneficiaries from any further claims accompanied by an informal Accounting of the Estate. If required by the Court, or if recommended by the Estate attorney, a formal Accounting, Settlement Agreement, and Closing may be warranted. Diligence during this final stage of the Probate process remains important for you to avoid personal liability.

GLOSSARY

Abatement: If there are insufficient assets in the Estate to pay all of the distributions the Will provides for, the distributions must be reduced. Such a reduced bequest is said to have abated.

Accounting: See **Formal Accounting** and **Informal Accounting**.

Accrued Interest: Interest income earned on a bank account which was earned but unpaid at death is Accrued Income and must be reported as an asset on the Estate Tax return and when received as income on the Estate's income tax return.

Adeemed: If the Will provides for the distribution of a particular asset, say a painting, and the painting did not exist when the Decedent died, the bequest of the painting must lapse. Such a bequest is said to have adeemed.

Adjusted Gross Estate: The value of all assets owned by the Decedent reduced by certain debts and expenses.

Administrator: If the Decedent died without a Will (Intestate), the Court will appoint a person or Administrator to handle the Estate, whose functions are similar to those of an Executor.

Advancement: If the Decedent paid an amount or distributed property to an intended Beneficiary before his death with the intent that it be an advance payment of the intended inheritance, it is called an advancement. An advancement should replace the bequest under the Will.

Affidavit: Statement made, often signed under the penalties of perjury, for a specific purpose. For example, the Witnesses to a Will may sign an Affidavit stating the facts that occurred when the Will was signed.

Alternate Valuation: While an Estate is usually valued as of the date of the Decedent's death, it can alternatively be valued at the date 6 months following death if the value is lower.

Ancillary Probate: A Probate proceeding in a state other than where the Decedent was Domiciled.

Annual Exclusion: Every person is permitted to give away up to $10,000 per year (indexed) to any other person without incurring any gift tax. There is no limit on the number of people the Decedent could have made these gifts to in a year. To qualify for this exclusion, the gifts must be a gift of a present interest, meaning that the recipient can enjoy the gift immediately. This can present problems when you make gifts to Trusts. This exclusion can be doubled to $20,000 per person (indexed) per year, if the Decedent was married and his spouse consented to join in making the gift. See **Gift Splitting**.

Applicable Exclusion Amount: The amount that each person can give away, in aggregate, during lifetime or at death (i.e., under a Will) without incurring federal Estate tax. This amount is $650,000 in 1999 and is scheduled to increase to $1 million in 2006. This amount is often, but not always, bequeathed under the Decedent's Will to a Bypass Trust.

Applicable Exclusion Trust: See **Bypass Trust.**

Attestation Clause: The last portion of a Will that includes one or more lines for the Testator, required number of Witnesses, and for the Notary to sign. The format can vary from state to state.

Basis: The cost of an asset increased by the cost of any improvements and reduced by depreciation or amortization deductions. This is used to calculate gain or loss on sale. On death, the Decedent's Basis in most assets are increased to the value of those assets as reported on the Decedent's Estate tax return. See **Step-Up in Basis.**

Beneficiary: A person who receives the benefits of a Trust or of transfers under the Will.

Bequest: A distribution of cash or an asset other than real estate under a Will.

Bond: A legal arrangement whereby a third-party financial institution guarantees the performance of a Fiduciary.

Burden of Proof: The requirement of one side to a lawsuit to prove certain aspects of their case for the matter to proceed. If the party to the lawsuit does not meet its burden of proof, the other side will prevail. When a Will contest occurs, the challenger must meet certain Burdens of Proof for the case to proceed.

Buy-Sell Agreements: Contractual arrangements governing the transfer of ownership interests (stock or partnership interests) in a closely held business. These often rely on insurance to provide the necessary funds.

Bypass Trust: A Trust formed typically under Decedent's Will to receive, hold, and invest assets up to the Decedent's Applicable Exclusion Amount. The purpose of a Bypass Trust is to hold assets for the benefit of the Decedent's surviving spouse (and possibly other heirs) without those assets being taxed in the surviving spouse's Estate.

Charitable Remainder Trust: The Decedent could have donated property or money to a charity, reserving the right to use the property, or to receive income from it for a specified time (a number of years, the duration of your life, or the duration of the Decedent's life and the life of a second person such as his spouse). When the agreed period is over, the property belongs to the charitable organization. The Trust can be an annuity trust (pays a fixed amount each year) or a unitrust (pays an amount to you based on a percentage of asset values held by the charity).

Code Section 303: This provision of the tax laws permits certain sales of stock to be treated as redemptions. This provides favorable capital gains treatment.

Code Section 754 Election: An election made to have the tax Basis in a partnership or limited liability company interest increased to reflect the value of the entity's underlying assets.

Code Section 2032A: This provision of the tax laws provides a favorable method of valuing interests in closely held business or real estate assets at the value being used, not the best or highest value.

Code Section 2057: This provision of the tax laws provides a deduction for certain qualifying family-owned business interests.

Code Section 2518: This provision of the tax laws provides the rules for disclaiming assets.

Code Section 6166: This provision of the tax laws provides for the deferral of the payment of estate taxes for up to 14 years on closely held business interests.

Co-Executor: Two or more persons serving as Executors.

Community Property: Some state's laws provide that where a couple acquires any asset during marriage, the husband and wife will be considered to have a one-half interest in the property.

Co-Trustee: Two or more persons serving as Trustees.

Consanguinity: The degree of closeness of a particular relative.

Consent: A written agreement to abide by a particular decision or arrangement.

Conservator: A court-appointed person in charge of the affairs of a disabled or minor Beneficiary. See **Guardianship.**

Committee: See **Conservator.**

Complaint: A formal legal document filed in Court in order to commence a legal proceeding, such as one to have a photocopy of a lost Will admitted as the original.

Cost Basis: See **Tax Basis.**

Court: The institution which handles and supervises Probate and related matters. See **Surrogate's Court, Probate Court,** or **Orphan's Court.**

Credit Shelter Trust: See **Bypass Trust.**

Cy Pres: A legal doctrine that Courts use to prevent a charitable bequest under a Will from lapsing.

Death Certificate: A formal document issued by the appropriate governmental agency confirming the name, address, and date of death of the Decedent. Any original Death Certificates must be used to obtain release of many assets, be attached to a federal Estate tax return, and so on.

Decedent: The person who died.

Deferral of Estate Tax: Where a sufficient portion of the Decedent's Estate is comprised of assets in a closely held and active business, his estate may qualify to pay the estate tax attributable to these assets over a 14-year period instead of within 9 months of death.

Designated Beneficiary: A person indicated to be the recipient of a pension or retirement plan where such designation is made with the necessary formalities.

Devise: The bequest of real property under a Will.

Disclaimer: Filing of formal documents in the Court stating that the intended Beneficiary of a Bequest or Devise does not wish to accept it. This results in the asset passing to another Beneficiary. This is often done to save taxes. For the disclaimer to be effective, it must be executed as required under state law. It often must be completed within 9 months of death. Also referred to as *Renunciation.*

Domicile: The permanent home of the Decedent that becomes the location in which Probate proceedings are commenced.

Donee: A person who receives a gift.

Donor: A person who makes a gift.

Durable Power of Attorney: A document in which the Decedent granted certain people the authority to handle financial matters. Where a Power of Attorney is durable, it will remain valid even if the Decedent becomes disabled, but it always terminates on death.

Election: A decision or choice to be made between alternative tax treatments. Elections must generally be made by checking an appropriate box or attaching a statement to a tax return. To be effective, the specific requirements of the election being made must be complied with and the return must be filed on a timely basis.

Elective Share: The portion of a Decedent's assets which the surviving spouse can claim under the Spousal Right of Election laws in the state where the Probate occurs. See **Spousal Right of Election.**

Estate: Assets owned by the Decedent at death. Be careful not to confuse Taxable Estate with Probate Estate; they can differ substantially.

Estate Tax: The tax assessed on the value of the Decedent's assets as reduced by certain expenses and liabilities.

Estate Tax Deferral: A portion of the Estate tax attributable to interests in certain business assets can be deferred for up to 14 years. See **Code Section 6166.**

Estate Tax Return: If the Decedent's assets exceed the Applicable Exclusion Amount, a tax filing must be made to report the Estate's assets, less expenses and liabilities to the IRS.

Executor: The person charged with administering and managing the Decedent's estate. An Executor (male) or Executrix (female) is appointed under a Will. Many states refer to this person as the Personal Administrator. The Executor is a Fiduciary for the estate.

Executor Fees: The compensation which the person serving as Executor is entitled. State law usually restricts the amount that can be paid.

Fiduciary: A person serving in a position of trust. It is typically used as a generic term to encompass Executors, Trustees, and Guardians.

Filing: The procedure of mailing or delivering documents or tax returns to the Court or IRS.

Final Tax Return: After death, a last income tax return must be filed for the Decedent.

Formal Accounting: An analysis of all assets received by the Estate, the gains or losses, income and expenses realized by the Estate, and distributions to Beneficiaries, which is made in a detailed manner conforming to specific statutory and Court requirements.

General Power of Appointment: The right given to a person, the power holder, to direct where certain assets can be distributed. This right must include the right to designate the Decedent, his creditors, his Estate, or the Creditors of his

Estate as recipients. This specific inclusion will assure that the assets subject to this General Power of Appointment will be included in the Decedent's Estate for tax purposes. This is generally done to avoid imposition of a Generation Skipping Transfer (GST) tax.

Generation Skipping Transfer (GST) Tax: A transfer tax imposed in addition to a gift or Estate tax on transfers to skip persons such as grandchildren.

Gift: Where the Decedent transferred property without receiving something of equal value in return, the federal government will assess a transfer tax where the value of the gift exceeds the annual exclusion and the Decedent's Applicable Exclusion Amount is exhausted.

Gift Splitting: If the Decedent and his spouse join in giving an Annual Exclusion.

Gross Estate: The value of all assets owned by the Decedent at death. Some important tax benefits are based on certain assets meeting specified percentages of the Gross Estate.

Guardian: The person responsible for the person and/or property of a minor. Generally, the Guardian is appointed under the Decedent's Will. If not, a court will appoint one.

Guardian Ad Litem: A person appointed by the court to protect the interests of a minor.

Guardianship: The arrangement or relationship of a Court-appointed person designated with the responsibility of managing the assets and/or affairs of a specified disabled or minor beneficiary, and that person.

Heir: Relative or other person to receive a distribution or bequest under a Decedent's Will.

Holographic Will: A handwritten Will prepared by the Testator. It may, or may not, be valid depending on the circumstances involved and applicable state law requirements.

Income in Respect of a Decedent: Income earned, such as interest accrued on a bond that is included in the Decedent's federal Estate tax calculation as an asset, and which is also reported on the Decedent's final income tax return. A credit for the Estate tax paid may be claimed.

Informal Accounting: An analysis of all assets received by the Estate, the gains or loss, income and expenses realized by the Estate, and distributions to Beneficiaries, which is made in a manner that the Beneficiaries agree to, but which does not conform to the specific statutory and detailed Court requirements. An Informal Accounting is used to minimize the substantial costs and time requirements of completing a Formal Accounting.

Inheritance Tax: A number of states assess a tax based on the value of property that Beneficiaries inherit.

Installment Sale: A sale where taxable gain is recognized over a number of years as the payment for the property sold is received.

Insurance Trust: A trust established to own the Decedent's life insurance policies and thereby prevent them from being included in the Decedent's Estate if the transfer was complete. The Decedent did not die within three years of making the transfer.

Intangible Asset: Ownership interests in copyright, royalty, and other similar assets.

Inter-Vivos Trust: A trust created during the Decedent's lifetime. Also called a **living trust.**

Intestacy: If the Decedent did not sign a Will, he or she will have died Intestate. Since there is no Will to direct what should happen, the laws of the state where the Decedent resided will determine who should serve as Executor (sometimes called Administrator), who will receive property, and so on.

Inventory: A formal listing of the Decedent's assets, sometimes required to be filed with the Court.

IRD: See **Income in Respect of a Decedent.**

Irrevocable: Where a trust cannot be changed after the Decedent established it, the trust is irrevocable. This is an essential characteristic to have the assets you give to the trust removed from the Decedent's Estate.

Joint Tenancy: Where the Decedent and his spouse, or another person, own assets as joint tenants, when one of them dies the property automatically passes to the surviving joint tenant.

Lapse: When a distribution or bequest under a Will cannot be made, it is said to lapse.

Last Will and Testament: See **Will.**

Legacy: Property transferred by Decedent's Will. The person receiving it is called the Legatee.

Letter of Instruction: A nonbinding letter from the Decedent providing information on personal matters relevant to the Estate.

Letters Administration: A formal document given to you by the Court after the Intestacy Proceeding has been completed confirming your authority to act as Administrator.

Letters Testamentary: A formal document given to you by the Court after the Will has been admitted to Probate confirming your authority to act as Executor.

Letters Trusteeship: A formal document given to you by the Court after a Will, which includes one or more Trusts (e.g., a Bypass Trust or QTIP Trust) has been admitted to Probate confirming your authority to act as Trustee.

Limited Power of Appointment: The right given to a person, the power holder, to direct where certain assets can be distributed. However, it cannot include the right to designate the Decedent, his Estate, or the Creditors of his Estate as recipients. This restriction will generally prevent the assets subject to a Limited Power of Appointment from being included in the Decedent's Estate for tax purposes.

Living Trust: See **Revocable Living Trust.**

Living Will: A document addressing medical and related matters concerning the Decedent. May include data on organ donations, and so on.

Marital Deduction: Assets bequeathed to the Decedent's surviving spouse or to certain qualifying Trusts for the benefit of the Decedent's surviving spouse (see **QTIP** and **QDOT**) qualify for an unlimited estate tax deduction.

Marshalling Assets: The process by which you as the Executor collect all the assets of the Estate and apply them to pay expenses and eventually distribute them to the heirs.

Notary: A person who has complied with a particular state's requirements to witness documents and place a seal or stamp on them indicating that the document has been signed with a specified degree of formality. Requirements and procedures differ by state.

Notice of Probate: Formal indication to a Beneficiary or other person that a Probate of the Decedent's Will has or shall occur.

Orphan's Court: See **Surrogate's Court.**

Pecuniary Bequests: Specific dollar distributions provided under a Will.

Personal Administrator: See **Executor.**

Personal Property: Furniture, equipment, artwork, and other movable property as contrasted to land and buildings which are **Real Property.**

Personal Representative: See **Executor.**

Per Stirpes: Distribution by representation. If child A has 3 children and child B has 2, and each child was intended to receive 50 percent of the Estate, if both child A and child B die, child A's 3 children each receive ⅓ of 50 percent and child B's 2 children each receive ½ of 50%. State laws vary.

POD Account: An account, such as a bank account, which specifies that on the death of the primary account holder the account will be paid to the next named person. "John Doe, P.O.D., Jane Smith" means that the account is Paid On Death of John, to Jane. This is a non-Probate asset.

Pour Over Will: A Will that distributes assets into a Revocable Living Trust for ultimate distribution.

Power of Appointment: The right given to a person, the power holder, to direct where certain assets can be distributed. For example, the Decedent's mother may have left the Decedent the right under her Will for the Decedent to designate under his Will, how and when his children should inherit assets from a Trust formed under his mother's Will.

Preliminary Letters: If Letters Testamentary cannot be obtained quickly enough, it may be possible to have the Court issue temporary or preliminary Letters Testamentary that provide you with limited rights to act on behalf of the Estate until final or full Letters Testamentary are issued.

Present Interest: A gift must be a gift of a present interest (the Beneficiary can enjoy the property given immediately) for it to qualify for the annual $10,000 (indexed) gift tax exclusion.

Probate: The process of having a Will admitted to Court and receiving Letters Testamentary authorizing the Executor to act on behalf of the Estate. The term Probate is generally used to include not merely the Court proceeding, but the entire process of settling an Estate. This process includes identifying and obtaining control over assets, reviewing and applying the Will, paying all debts and taxes, and distributing assets as required under the Will.

Probate Asset: An asset that passes through the Estate. This is an asset that is governed by the Will and the probate process. A jointly owned asset that passes directly to the joint owner on death would not be a probate asset. Nor would an IRA account that is paid directly to the named beneficiary.

Probate Court: See **Surrogate's Court.**

Probate Estate: All Probate Assets comprise the Probate Estate. Compare this to the Taxable Estate. The difference is important and often misunderstood.

Probate Petition: The main or initial filing with the Court for commencing the Probate proceeding.

Qualified Domestic Trust (QDOT): A Trust that will qualify for the unlimited Estate tax marital deduction when the surviving spouse is not a U.S. citizen.

Qualified Terminable Interest Property Trust (QTIP): This is a Qualified Terminable Interest Property Trust under the Will designed to qualify for the unlimited estate tax marital deduction. It is not available to a noncitizen surviving spouse.

Real Property: Land and buildings, as contrasted to **Personal Property.**

Receipt and Release: A document signed by a Beneficiary acknowledging that he or she has received what the Will or Trust provides for, and that there are no further claims.

Refunding Bond: An agreement or arrangement whereby a Beneficiary of an Estate agrees to return or refund any or all of a distribution received if necessary.

Remainder Beneficiary: The person, Beneficiary, intended to receive assets or income from a Trust or Estate only after a prior person's interest ends or is satisfied.

Renunciation: See **Disclaimer.**

Required Beginning Date (RBD): Distributions from qualified plans and IRAs must usually begin by the required beginning date. This is April 1 of the year following the year in which the Decedent reached age 70½.

Residuary Estate: The Probate assets remaining after the payment of debts, taxes, expenses, specific bequests, and so forth.

Reversionary Interest: Where Decedent gave property away but there is some possibility that the property will return to him, this is said to be a Reversionary Interest. A sufficient Reversionary Interest can cause the asset to be taxable in the Decedent's Estate.

Revocable Living Trust: A legal arrangement whereby assets are typically transferred before death to a Trust to avoid the need for those assets to be subject to Probate.

Right of Election: See **Spousal Right of Election.**

Rule Against Perpetuities: Most states have a requirement that a Trust must terminate not later than some specified time.

Self-Canceling Installment Note (SCIN): Some loans are arranged to include this provision that cancels the note on the death of the lender.

Self-Proving Affidavit: A formal statement at the end of a Will that meets certain required formalities so that the Witnesses may not have to appear in Court to prove the Will.

Self-Proving Will: If a Will is signed with certain required formalities, the Witnesses may not have to appear in Court.

Settlement Agreement: A written arrangement wherein parties, such as adverse beneficiaries, agree to a resolution of a dispute.

Simultaneous Death Provision: This is a clause in the Will, or if none, it is an issue that state law will govern. If a bequest is to be made to a beneficiary who died in a car accident with the Decedent, for example, who is deemed to have died first? This can have important implications concerning who inherits what assets. If the named beneficiary is deemed to survive, his or her Estate will receive the bequest and distribute the property according to his or her will. If the named beneficiary is considered to have died first, then the Decedent's Will for which you are responsible will determine who gets the property.

Small Estate Probate: Special simplified, less costly, proceedings may be available for smaller Estates.

Spousal Right of Election: A surviving spouse is protected under the laws of most Estates. These laws provide generally that if the Decedent left an inadequate proportion of his assets to his spouse, she can sue the Estate and claim a minimum statutory share.

Step-Up in Basis: On death, assets held by the Decedent receive a Tax basis, in most but not all circumstances, equal to the fair market value of those assets at death.

Successor: An Executor or Trustee designated to serve in the event that the person listed previously in the Will or Trust cannot serve.

Summary Probate: An expedited Probate available to certain smaller Estates.

Surety: A company which offers, for a fee, a Bond which a Fiduciary may have to post to guarantee performance.

Surrogate's Court: The Court where proceedings relating to filing and proving Wills and related matters are handled. May be referred to as Probate Court, Orphan's Court, or other names, depending on the state involved.

Taxable Estate: The assets that are subject to inclusion in the Decedent's Estate for tax purposes (e.g., filing a federal Estate tax return). Many assets that are not included in the Probate Estate are included in the taxable Estate. The fact that an insurance policy is paid directly to the Decedent's sister on death as the named beneficiary doesn't mean that the proceeds are not included in the Decedent's taxable Estate.

Tax Allocation Clause: The provisions of a Will that direct which bequests and assets should be used to pay taxes.

Tax Basis: The cost, plus improvements, less depreciation, and subject to certain other adjustments, of an asset. Tax basis is used to calculate the capital or other taxable gain when an asset is sold. On death, assets held by the Decedent generally have their tax basis stepped-up to fair value.

Tenancy by the Entirety: Where husband and wife are joint tenants.

Testamentary Capacity: In order for a person to sign a Will that will be respected as the means of distributing that person's assets on death, a number of conditions must be met. One of these is that the person had to have Testamentary Capacity to sign the Will. This means the person had to have sufficient knowledge to understand what he or she was doing, the assets involved, and the natural objects of his or her bounty (e.g., children).

Testator: The person (male) who signed a Will. The female is referred to as Testatrix.

Trust: A legal arrangement where a person, called the grantor or testator, transfers assets to a person called a Trustee who will manage those assets for the benefit of the Beneficiary.

Trustee: The person (fiduciary) who manages and administers a Trust.

Undue Influence: When a person or circumstance had a significant and inappropriate impact on the Testator's decision as to what to include, or exclude, from his Will, this situation is called Undue Influence and may be a reason for a Will challenge.

Uniform Gifts (Transfers) to Minors Act (UGMA or UTMA): A method to hold property for the benefit of a minor person, such as the Decedent's child, which is similar to a Trust, but which is governed by state law. It is simpler and much cheaper to establish and administer, but is far less flexible.

Venue: The Court that has the right to handle a particular Probate matter.

Virtual Representation: A legal principle whereby a Remainder Beneficiary (e.g., a grandchild who will inherit if the child dies) can be represented in a legal proceeding without formal service by virtue of the person under whom they would claim.

Waiver: A formal written statement whereby the signer gives up certain rights.

Will: A document in which a person, called the Testator, sets forth his or her wishes as to who should manage his or her estate, how assets should be distributed, and so forth.

Will Challenge: When a person, sometimes but not always a Beneficiary named in a Will, commences a legal proceeding to question the validity of the Will.

Will Substitute: Techniques used to transfer assets on death without the Probate process. For example, owning assets in joint name results in the surviving joint owner taking title on the death of the other joint owner.

INDEX